COST-JUSTIFYING USABILITY

COST-JUSTIFYING
USABILITY

EDITED BY

RANDOLPH G. BIAS
IBM Corporation
Austin, Texas

DEBORAH J. MAYHEW
Deborah J. Mayhew & Associates
West Tisbury, Massachusetts

ACADEMIC PRESS
Harcourt Brace & Company, Publishers

Boston   San Diego New York
London   Sydney   Tokyo   Toronto

This book is printed on acid-free paper ∞

ACADEMIC PRESS, INC.
525 B Street, Suite 1900, 92101-4495

United Kingdom Edition published by
ACADEMIC PRESS LIMITED
24–28 Oval Road, London NW1 7DX

Library of Congress Cataloging-in-Publication Data
Cost-justifying usability / [edited by] Randolph G. Bias, Deborah J.
  Mayhew.
     p.   cm.
   Includes bibliographical references and index.
   ISBN 0-12-095810-4 (alk. paper)
   1. User interfaces (Computer systems)   2. Value analysis (Cost
control)   I. Bias, Randolph G.   II. Mayhew, Deborah J.
QA76.9.U83C67   1994
004'.01'9–dc20   93-38583
                                                      CIP

Printed in the United States of America
94 95 96 97 BC 9 8 7 6 5 4 3 2 1

To Cheryl, Travis, and Drew,
a very father-friendly family

and

To Katie Ann,
a very special daughter

With love, justifiably

Contents

Preface

"Prove it!"

All your life you've been confronted by this imperative.

"I can jump over that fence."

"Prove it."

"I know enough about history to pass that test."

"Prove it."

"I would be an asset to this company."

"Prove it."

"It would be smart for us to invest in quality."

"Prove it."

So now you're a usability engineer. Or you aspire to be one. Or you want to hire one or fund one out of your budget. Or you are simply taking it upon yourself to help create the most user-friendly product you possibly can. One way or another, you are interested in being a champion of the cause of usability. But first you must convince your management (or yourself) to invest money, time, and/or other resources in usability efforts. And so you, using all your education and talent and accumulated wisdom, go to your manager (or whisper in your own ear) and say, "It will most certainly pay off to expend some resource on usability." Why should you be surprised when you hear . . . "Prove it"?

All your hard-won and diligently maintained knowledge about experimental design and statistics does you no good now. Your manager isn't interested in some general discussion of hypothesis testing and confidence intervals and between- versus within-subjects designs. All your technical expertise in usability techniques and academic knowledge of human cognition, all your inspiration and passion for usability and even your firm (but unsubstantiated) belief that usability really does pay off, will not help you now. Because neither is your manager interested in (at this point) your knowledge and skill in the arena of usability. This is not science, nor is it religion. It is engineering—but more, it is business. And the cognitive scientist/usability engineer—the usability champion of any ilk—in the mid-1990s and beyond must be prepared to cost-justify any proposed usability engineering efforts. Further, those cost justifications must be well-communicated, convincing, and demonstrably reliable.

Trouble is, there's no reason to expect us to have any idea how to do this. None of the usual backgrounds of the people who most commonly serve as usability champions—human factors, cognitive psychology, computer science, technical communications—have traditionally included such business-oriented topics as cost justification in their curricula. Thus, few usability champions have any idea of how or where to begin to build a solid business case for their proposals in the language of business, the "bottom line." Frankly, rather than learning how to cost-justify our efforts, as a field we have tended to whine about not being appreciated and wonder why more resources aren't earmarked for usability. That is a poor strategy; it's their (the product managers') ball (of resources), and we need to play by their rules. And those rules include the rules of finance, of cost-benefit analyses, and of profitability.

In gathering the contributions to this book, our goal was to empower usability champions of any background with the awareness, the tools, the methods, and the language to compete for those development resources—to compete based not on the intangible benefits and the inherent rightness of usability, or the insightfulness or whim of those who hold the purse-strings, but on equal ground with the other areas vying for resources, areas that have a solid history and tradition of demonstrating their dollar value.

In the final chapter of this volume, we assert that usability support isn't "just barely worth it," rather its benefits usually easily outweigh its costs. We believe that the collection of chapters in this book contains the information necessary for the usability champion to support this assertion in his or her own environment and to demonstrate objectively and explicitly the value of usability.

We would like to acknowledge the professionalism of all the contributors to this volume, all of them expert usability engineers. Each has contributed a unique and important piece to the whole. We would be eager to work with all of them again. We acknowledge also the talented help we received from these people at Academic Press: Chuck Arthur, Chuck Glaser, Cindy Kogut, Kathleen Tibbetts, and Mary Treseler.

I (RGB) would like to thank three friends who selflessly advanced my understanding of economics and business finance: Sue Weaver, Donde Ashmos, and Kandace Tornquist. Irene Hernandez graciously provided support, material and otherwise, at IBM. Clayton Lewis and Cheryl Bias each provided valuable substantive comments and encouragement. And last, I would like to acknowledge the contributions—general and specific, historical and ongoing—of a great friend and great scientist, Doug Gillan—everyone should have such a colleague.

I (DJM) would like to thank Marilyn Mantei for the first article I encountered on the topic of cost-justifying usability, which she published in 1986 ("Techniques for incorporating human factors in the software life-cycle," *Proceedings of STA-III Conference: Structured Techniques in the Eighties: Practice and Prospect*; Chicago, June 1986). This was a real eye-opener for me, published just about the same time I began my consulting practice and had to start marketing my skills and services in a more formal way. All the work I have subsequently done with and on the topic of cost-justifying usability traces back ultimately to Marilyn's framework, first offered in that original article.

Randolph G. Bias
Austin, Texas

Deborah J. Mayhew
Martha's Vineyard, Massachusetts

Contributors

Numbers in parentheses indicate the pages on which the authors' contributions begin.

Nuray Aykin (177), AT&T Bell Laboratories, 101 Crawfords Corner Road, PO Box 3030, Holmdel, New Jersey 07733-3030

Randolph G. Bias (3, 287, 319), IBM Corporation, 11400 Burnet Road, Austin, Texas 78758

Louis G. Blatt (203), AT&T Global Information Solutions, Human Interface Technology Center, Technology & Development Division, 500 Tech Parkway, Atlanta, Georgia 30313

Ruven Brooks (273), Schlumberger Laboratory for Computer Science, PO Box 200015, Austin, Texas 78720-0015

Mary E. Cox (145), IBM Corporation, Research Triangle Park Programming Laboratory, Research Triangle Park, North Carolina 27709

Susan M. Dray (111), Dray & Associates, 2115 Kenwood Parkway, Minneapolis, Minnesota 55405

Kate Ehrlich (73), Lotus Development Corporation, 1 Rogers Street, Cambridge, Massachusetts 02142

Mary C. Harrison (203), AT&T Global Information Solutions, Human Interface Technology Center, Technology & Development Division, 500 Tech Parkway, Atlanta, Georgia 30313

Richard L. Henneman (203), AT&T Global Information Solutions, Corporate Cognitive Engineering Group, Technology & Development Division, 500 Tech Parkway, Atlanta, Georgia 30313

Clare-Marie Karat (45, 111), IBM TJ Watson Research Center, 30 Saw Mill River Road, Hawthorne, New York 10532

Marilyn Mantei (9), University of Toronto, Department of Computer Science and Faculty of Information Studies, 10 Kings College Road, Toronto, Ontario, Canada M5S 1A4

Charles L. Mauro (123), Mauro & Mauro Design, 524 Broadway, Fourth Floor, New York, New York 10012

Deborah J. Mayhew (9, 159, 287, 319), Deborah J. Mayhew & Associates, Panhandle Road, PO Box 248, West Tisbury, Massachusetts 02575

Jakob Nielsen (245), SunSoft, MTV19, 2550 Garcia Avenue, Mountain View, California 94043

Paige O'Neal (145), IBM Corporation, Research Triangle Park Programming Laboratory, Research Triangle Park, North Carolina 27709

Wayne L. Pendley (145), IBM Corporation, 11400 Burnet Road, Austin, Texas 78758

Janice Anne Rohn (73), SunSoft Inc., Usability Engineering Center, 2550 Garcia Avenue, Mountain View, California 94043-1100

Part I

A Framework

Chapter 1

Wherefore Cost Justification of Usability: Pay Me Now or Pay Me Later—But How Much?[1]

Randolph G. Bias

IBM Corporation
Austin, Texas

Ease of use doesn't happen by accident. Hardware and software product managers, who must decide where to place development resources, have various factions clamoring for their attention (and for those concomitant resources). Designers and programmers want tools, testers want hardware, managers want more people, and everyone wants more time. With perhaps only one counterexample, all of these players are able to quantify, more or less accurately, the benefit that will accrue to the product manager if they are awarded the desired resources: so many lines of code in the plan, a certain number of person-days, and this many additional test machines will fetch the product manager X tested components with Y fewer defects and Z supporting publications by the end of the fiscal year.

Into this product development fray we, the usability engineers, march. We are the aforementioned possible counterexample. Our predecessors were ill-armed. They would argue strongly and boldly for more resources spent on the usability of the product, more lines of code set aside for usability improvements, more time devoted to iteratively testing the prod-

---

[1]Adapted with permission from *Proceedings of the Human Factors Society 34th Annual Meeting,* 1990. Copyright 1990 by the Human Factors and Ergonomics Society, Inc. All rights reserved.

uct's usability and then to implementing usability enhancements. But what happened when the product manager asked those professionals, "What if I don't make these improvements?" Or, "what will my net delta be if I implement only enhancement number 12?" Most likely, our intrepid forebears offered a short soliloquy on generalization from sampled data to an entire population, and perhaps mumbled something about alpha errors as they skulked out the door.

Especially in these competitive and economically constrained times, all contributors to any sort of development effort must be able to justify their contributions or be prepared to suffer the budgeting axe. This is particularly true for human factors professionals, whose ultimate product, usability, has a history of being considered a luxury. A budding organization called the Usability Testing Professional Users Group (now the Usability Professionals Association) surveyed its membership and found that "cost/benefit analysis" was the number one concern.

Good usability of computer products is not a luxury; customers are unequivocal in their call for more usable products. Most executives are aware of this. Still, the usability engineer labors in an area where all the related disciplines have long-established metrics for quantifying their costs and benefits. Lines of code, person-months, problem-tracking reports, bugs per thousand lines of code, and system test scenarios are just a handful of the many quantitative tools that measure effort and quality—tools that engineers and computer scientists deal with so facilely. It is this milieu that the usability engineer enters, admonishing that the product must be made "more usable."

And this works fine as long as development time and money are not tight and the product manager acknowledges the value of usability engineering. But if time is tight, money is constrained, the product manager is not sold on the value of usability engineering, or even if this product manager is simply being economical, the usability engineer is likely to hear one of the following questions in response:

How *much* more usable must the product be?
How will we know if our product is more usable?
What will qualify as "usable enough"?
How much will it cost me to make it more usable?
How much additional revenue will this added usability yield?

This book is intended to arm the usability engineer with the tools required to answer these questions meaningfully.

Today's usability engineers can be better schooled in the ways of quantifying the value of their support and can offer cost justifications of their proposed contributions. In this book, we provide concrete sugges-

tions for those human factors practitioners who are vying
ment (or grant or contract) resources and are interested in b(
of quantifying and justifying their support of a product
project or related endeavor.

A Few Definitions

In this book, we use the terms "human factors professional," "human factors practitioner," and "usability engineer" interchangeably. We are focusing on the professional, regardless of educational training or job description, who is responsible for designing good usability into a product or process, testing the usability of a product or process, or purchasing or adopting the most usable product or process.

So far we have been intentionally vague in our reference to "software or hardware product" and "product development manager." We intend to present cost-justification methods that will apply in a wide variety of settings. We will focus our attention frequently on the development of computer products, as this is the most common environment in which human factors professionals practice. However, we believe that the framework and methods that the contributing authors present in the following chapters are equally applicable to supporting the development of ergonomically sound hammers or the design of a cafeteria with a smooth traffic flow or indeed the design and development of any product or process. Also, we will address some situations other than new product development, such as human factors support of internal (to the company) computing services and hardware buying decisions.

Objectives

In offering some answers to the question, "How can we better cost-justify usability?", we have three objectives:

1. To sensitize the reader to the need to cost-justify usability.
2. To present the usability engineer with a framework for considering cost-benefit analyses.
3. To present the usability engineer with explicit examples of successful, generalizable methods of justifying usability, in enough detail to allow replication of their use.

We recognize that specific products and processes and development or data processing environments have idiosyncrasies that will make them more or less receptive to the application of the methods presented in the ensuing chapters. We have tried, through guidelines agreed on by the contributing authors and through editorial consistency, to present the cost-justification methods in ways that will maximize their generalized applicability.

Audience

Our primary audience is expected to be human factors practitioners. This audience includes members of a human factors department, individual human factors practitioners integrated into development departments, or independent human factors consultants (from within the company or from without). People who are interested in designing the most usable product, or in testing products for usability before the customers do, or in providing the most usable in-house workflow, or in buying the most usable cache of computer products will find this book useful. These professionals believe that such products and processes are best developed, maintained, or acquired when someone with training and/or expertise in usability is involved as the users' advocate.

We expect that the human factors researcher, in a private research lab or in a government or university lab, may well be interested in the following cost-justification methods too.

Finally, we trust that the human factors educator will want to include these methods as part of a human factors curriculum.

Overview

Following this introductory chapter are two more chapters rounding out Part I, "A Framework." After reading these three chapters, the reader should not only have an increased awareness of why one would want to cost-justify usability, but also be familiar with the language of cost-benefit analyses and with one specific but broadly applicable model for cost justification.

In Chapter 2, Deborah J. Mayhew, owner and principal consultant of a small usability consulting firm, and Marilyn M. Mantei, an academician with varied industry experience, present a broad overview of cost-benefit analysis for any collection of human factors tasks or activities associated with a development project. Their chapter covers the general assumptions and methods of cost-benefit analyses, offering and supporting detailed estimates of costs and benefits. Their chapter also characterizes important differences between vendor companies that produce products to sell and information systems departments that serve internal users. They further establish the relationship between cost justification of human factors support and the greater arena of software economics, demonstrating how to plan a usability program.

In Chapter 3, Clare-Marie Karat, a human factors psychologist for IBM who teaches workshops on the topic of usability cost-benefit analyses, offers a way to approach cost justification by using a business case model. She addresses metrics for cost-benefit analyses that will be referred to throughout the rest of this volume.

Part II is titled "Approaches to Cost-Justifying Usability," and provides three more parochial, but comprehensive perspectives on the issue. In Chapter 4, Kate Ehrlich and Janice Rohn, usability professionals at SunSoft, Inc. (Ehrlich has since moved to Lotus Development Corporation), offer "A Vendor's Perspective." Exploring the stages of acceptance of user-centered design among the development community, they examine usability engineering methods that are best designed to influence developers at the various stages of acceptance. After specifying the initial and sustaining costs of such usability engineering, they highlight the benefits that serve as motivators for vendor companies. Next, in Chapter 5, Susan Dray, formerly of IDS Financial Services and now principal of Dray & Associates, and Clare-Marie Karat team up to offer the Internal Development Project perspective. Using a specific, extended example as a vehicle, they highlight the different costs and benefits in an internal development effort and illustrate Karat's business case approach from Chapter 3. Completing Part II, Chapter 6 by Charles Mauro, president of Mauro & Mauro Design and Mauro/HFE, provides the unique view of the human factors contractor. Noting that cost justification is the "life blood" of the successful usability contractor, Mauro offers principles for determining what cost justification methods fit the clients' needs.

Part III consists of four varied case studies. In Chapter 7, Paige O'Neal, Mary Cox, and Wayne Pendley, all human factors professionals with IBM, present "UPAR Process: Dollar Measurement of a Usability Indicator for Software Products." They provide a way to interpret "user errors" and translate them into a cost language that everyone is familiar with: dollars. In Chapter 8, Deborah J. Mayhew illustrates a cost-benefit analysis in the context of upgrading computer hardware—a common concern in these days of rampaging technology. AT & T Bell Laboratories' Nuray Aykin outlines in Chapter 9 a model for estimating software development costs and offers a case study illustrating software reuse. Completing the case studies in Chapter 10, Mary Harrison, Richard Henneman, and Louis Blatt of NCR Corporation describe a design for a cost-justification tool that would take into account varied user-centered design costs plus the various benefits to end users, the users' organization, and the development organization.

Part IV of this book consists of four chapters of special issues. In Chapter 11, SunSoft's Jakob Nielsen offers the intriguing and practical "Guerrilla HCI: Using Discount Usability Engineering to Penetrate the Intimidation Barrier." He extends his earlier work on discount usability engineering, first offering, then validating, abbreviated usability engineering programs. Then, striking a resonant chord with Ehrlich's and Rohn's stages of acceptance, he offers a series of steps in the increased use of usability engineering in software development. Ruven Brooks offers Chapter 12, which is part approach (as in Part II) and part case study (as in Part III), but goes still further. He discusses, in "Justifying Prepaid Human Factors for User Interfaces," his experience with inherently complex applications for highly trained, high-status, high-salary users and addresses some intangible benefits of usability engineering strategies. The editors of this volume consider, in Chapter 13, "Organizational Inhibitors and Facilitators." We identify myths, beliefs, and attitudes, plus organizational incentives, practices, and structures that help and hinder the application of usability engineering to a development project. The chapter is intended to help human factors professionals know how best to identify their situations and choose their projects and approaches to maximize their success factors. We conclude with a chapter of summary and synthesis, where we consider, among other things, the dining room table, football teams, and Thomas Jefferson.

So, how can we cost-justify usability?

Chapter 2

A Basic Framework for Cost-Justifying Usability Engineering

Deborah J. Mayhew

Deborah J. Mayhew & Associates
West Tisbury, Massachusetts

Marilyn Mantei

Department of Computer Science
Faculty of Information Studies
University of Toronto
Toronto, Ontario
Canada

Introduction

Initially, usability engineering may seem to the uninitiated software developer to be a wide assortment of disparate techniques, all of which are advertised to improve the software interface and which, if not used, will lead to ruin. Indeed, many techniques have been developed since the mid-1970s when the field of computer–human interaction first emerged, but what has also been established is an accepted structure for integrating usability engineering into the overall software development life cycle. And, enough studies have been run in the laboratory and in the field to understand the benefits and expected costs associated with different techniques of usability engineering.

9

This chapter presents a framework for cost-justifying usability engineering by examining the various techniques of usability engineering, discussing their place in the software development life cycle, and describing methods for calculating their costs and estimating their benefits. We begin by presenting an overall plan for incorporating usability engineering techniques into the software development life cycle. We refer to this as the *usability engineering program.*

The Usability Engineering Program

Any discussion of the costs of usability engineering must start with some consideration of what usability tasks will be conducted and what their costs will be. Methodological approaches to usability engineering have been evolving since the 1970s. Contributions by a number of authors are summarized in the following sections.

Gould and Lewis

One of the early references to a usability engineering methodology was offered by Gould and Lewis (1985). Gould and Lewis described a very general approach to usability engineering involving three global strategies:

1. *Early focus on users and tasks:* This strategy involves applying such tasks as user profiling, task analysis, prototyping, and user walkthroughs.
2. *Empirical measurement:* Such tasks and techniques as questionnaire administration, laboratory and field usability studies, and usage studies represent some of those available for collecting objective, quantitative performance and satisfaction data.
3. *Iterative design:* Systems built using a user interface management system (UIMS) allow radical changes to the interface (as opposed to the application code itself) to be made quickly and easily in response to empirical data. This makes iterative testing and redesign feasible.

Gould and Lewis were vague in specifying how these global usability strategies could be integrated into an overall software development life cycle and which techniques should be applied. Nevertheless, their ideas were quite revolutionary at the time. They offered a case study in which they applied their approaches, but it involved a small project team heavily populated with usability expertise and a fairly simple product. They also cited many obstacles present in larger, more complex development projects and project team organizations that make incorporating their usability approaches difficult.

Mantei and Teorey

Mantei and Teorey (1988) offered a more detailed and specific set of usability tasks and specified how they might be integrated into a typical development life cycle. Their integrated life cycle is summarized in the accompanying table, with the vertical dimension representing a timeline:

Development Phases	Usability Tasks
	Market analysis
Feasibility study	
Requirements definition	
	Product acceptance analysis
	Task analysis
Global design	
Prototype construction	
	User testing and evaluation
System implementation	
Product testing	
	User testing
Update and maintenance	
	Product survey

Nielsen

Nielsen (1992) has specified ten different usability tasks and techniques that represent a more detailed expansion of Gould's and Lewis's three major usability principles. He relates these only very loosely to existing software development life cycles by dividing them into predesign, design, and postdesign phases. The usability tasks and techniques that he specifies include:

Predesign
1. Know the user (includes user profiling and task analysis)
2. Competitive analysis
3. Setting usability goals

Design
4. Participatory design
5. Coordinated design of the total interface (including standards)

6. Guidelines and heuristic analysis
7. Prototyping
8. Empirical testing
9. Iterative design

Postdesign
10. Collect feedback from field use

Nielsen notes that these usability techniques should not be applied merely in a simple linear methodology, as might seem implied, but in fact represent techniques that can be applied throughout the development life cycle. He also notes the importance of getting these techniques incorporated into the overall project plan.

Nielsen also reports the results of a survey of 13 usability engineers, in which they were asked to rate the impact that these tasks and techniques had on the usability of products designed with them. Those rated highest for impact included (roughly in order of highest to lower impact):

Iterative design
Know the user (in particular, task analysis)
Empirical testing
Participatory design
Collect feedback from field use

Shneiderman

Shneiderman (1992) offers a "lifecycle for interactive-systems development," which he emphasizes can be "adapted to meet the widely varying needs of specific projects," and which he presents as a series of stages, including specific tasks and techniques. His stages, and some of the tasks included in them, are summarized as follows:

1. Collect information
      Interview users
      Submit questionnaires to users
      Plan and schedule usability tasks
      Perform task analyses
      Plan testing strategy
2. Define requirements and semantics
      Define high-level goals and middle-level requirements
      Create task objects and actions
      Create guidelines, document, and process for enforcement

3. Design syntax and support facilities
    Design feedback for each action
    Develop error messages and error handling
    Carry out pencil-and-paper pilot tests
4. Specify physical devices
    Consider color, screen size, and resolution
    Specify pointing devices
    Consider noise level, lighting, and table space
5. Develop software
    Produce top-down modular designs
    Enable monitoring of user and system performance
6. Integrate system and disseminate to users
    Ensure user involvement at every stage
    Conduct acceptance tests
    Provide adequate training
7. Nurture the user community
    Provide on-site, telephone, and on-line consultants
    Conduct interviews with users
    Monitor usage frequencies
    Respond to user suggestions for improvements
8. Prepare evolutionary plan
    Measure user performance regularly
    Schedule revisions regularly

Like Nielsen, Shneiderman also emphasizes the iterative nature of these stages and tasks.

Mayhew

Mayhew (1992) offers a comprehensive, detailed methodology for usability engineering set in the context of a particular but typical software development life cycle. Her methodology includes specific management, information gathering, design, and testing tasks, most of which have been cited by the other authors referred to previously. Her methodology differs from that used by others in that it is more detailed in specifying how to integrate usability techniques into an already existing software development life cycle. The methodology consists of a set of usability tasks applied in a particular order at specified points in an overall system development life cycle.

The usability tasks, listed in the proper order of their application during development life cycle phases, are listed below.

Phase I: Scoping

1. Project plan
2. User profile
3. Hardware/software definition

Phase II: Functional Specification

4. Task analysis
5. User interface (UI) goal setting
6. Training and documentation definition

Phase III: Design

7. User interface mock-up
8. Style guide
9. Detailed user interface design
10. User interface prototype
11. User interface prototype test plan
12. User interface prototype testing

Phase IV: Development

13. Develop training and documentation
14. User interface test plan

Phase V: Testing/Implementation

15. User interface testing
16. User interface evaluation

These usability *tasks* in turn are based on general usability *techniques*, including interviews, questionnaire administration, observation, mockups, walk-throughs, prototyping, among others.

Mayhew emphasizes, as do the other authors cited, the iterative nature of this usability engineering program. Many tasks overlap or can be carried out in parallel. For example, functional specification, carried out by the application project team, and task analysis, conducted by the user interface engineers, are highly interrelated tasks that can be carried out more or less in parallel with close communication between groups. On the other hand, user interface goal setting cannot proceed until task analysis is complete. And, there is no point in testing if there is no intention of going back and redesigning in response to feedback. One can never assume that the solution implemented for one problem hasn't introduced new ones. It is important to retest as well. Thus, all cited authors agree, usability engineering, just as any other aspect of software design and development, is an iterative process with feedback loops between tasks and phases.

Every development organization has a different development methodology, a different life cycle consisting of unique phases and tasks carried out in unique sequence. The life cycle that is the basis for Mayhew's usability methodology is just one possible life cycle. Mayhew emphasizes, as does Shneiderman, that the usability tasks included in this life cycle, and the more generic techniques upon which they are based, can be integrated into any existing software development life cycle. They represent a collection of usability tasks and techniques that can be drawn upon and tailored to integrate with any development methodology. As such, they represent the potential cost categories in a cost-benefit analysis of usability engineering.

The following sections address how the costs and benefits of these individual tasks and techniques can be estimated in a quantitative form.

Estimating Costs

Calculating the cost of adding a usability engineering program to a software development project is fairly straightforward. First, one must plan which usability tasks will be applied.

Many of the usability engineering tasks cited by the aforementioned authors, such as user profiling, task analysis, and empirical measurement, can be carried out by drawing upon a small set of general usability techniques, including:

1. *User interviews:* These are structured or free-form one-on-one discussions with users.
2. *User questionnaires:* Structured questionnaires are given to users who are asked to complete and return them.
3. *Usage studies:* These studies tally statistics describing different aspects of actual use of systems, manual or automated. When conducting usage studies of automated systems, software monitors may be installed to gather usage statistics. Usage statistics may also be gathered by structured observation.
4. *Task walk-throughs:* This is a simulation of actually carrying out a specific task, on a manual or automated system, to write a description of a task or to evaluate the efficiency of the task under the current or planned system.
5. *Field observation:* Users are unobtrusively observed carrying out tasks in their natural habitat on either manual or automated systems.

6. *Usability testing:* A variety of laboratory techniques are used for collecting performance data (e.g., time and errors) from a representative sample of end users performing a representative set of tasks on a simulation, prototype, or system.

For example, a user profile might be developed primarily through a user questionnaire, supplemented with some user interviews, and a task analysis might be carried out through a program of field observation, usage studies, and several iterations each of user interviews and task walkthroughs. Each individual technique can be costed out, and then a plan for carrying out a task can be formulated and its cost calculated by simple addition of the costs of individual techniques.

Other more specific techniques that might also need to be costed out include:

1. *Style guide development:* A set of user interface standards and conventions that will apply to a single system or to some set of related systems is developed.
2. *Prototype construction:* building user interface prototypes use prototyping tools.
3. *Prototype changes:* The user interface prototype is edited in response to test results during iterative testing and redesign.

Additional one-time costs that may have to be factored into an analysis include:

1. *Usability lab setup:* Testing and observation rooms separated by one-way glass, and work stations, furniture, video equipment, analysis software, are among these costs.
2. *Purchase of prototyping tool:* This is software specialized for mocking up user interfaces efficiently for the purpose of usability testing.

First an overall plan for a usability engineering program is laid out, and then the costs can be calculated by breaking the tasks down into techniques, breaking the techniques down into steps, and breaking the steps down into personnel hours and equipment costs.

Let us consider a hypothetical plan for a program of usability engineering for a software development project and then see how we would estimate the costs. Table 2.1 presents a sample plan for such a program, based on Mayhew's usability engineering methodology discussed previously. The first column (Life Cycle Stage) lists the phases in the overall software development life cycle in which each planned usability task listed in the second column (UI Task/Technique) will take place. Usa-

Table 2.1 Planned usability engineering program and estimated costs

Life Cycle Stage	UI TASK/Technique	Cost/ Technique	Number/ Technique	Total Cost ($)
—	HF lab setup	20,000	1	20,000
Scoping	USER PROFILE			
	User interviews	2,425	2	4,850
Functional specification	TASK ANALYSIS			
	User interviews	2,425	4	9,700
	User questionnaire	6,000	1	6,000
	Usage study	6,220	1	6,220
Design	Style guide	16,800	1	16,800
	Simulation test	6,220	3	18,660
	Purchase of UIMS	15,600	1	15,600
	Prototype construction	5,600	1	5,600
	PROTOTYPE TESTING			
	Prototype test	6,220	3	18,660
	Prototype change	280	20	5,600
Testing/ implementation	SYSTEM UI TESTING			
	Prototype test	6,220	3	18,660
	Prototype change	280	20	5,600
	UI EVALUATION			
	User survey	6,000	1	6,000
	User interview	2,425	3	7,275
	Usage study	6,220	1	6,220
Total cost				**$132,185**

bility *tasks* are listed in capital letters, and planned *techniques* for carrying out tasks are listed below them. The fourth column (Number/ Technique) indicates how many times each technique will be carried out to accomplish a task.

The third column (Cost/Technique) presents the cost of carrying out the corresponding technique once. These costs are derived below. The fifth column (Total Cost) is derived by multiplying the unit cost of a technique by the number of times it will be carried out to accomplish a task. The sum of all the costs in this column represents the total cost of the planned usability engineering program for this development project. Note that this total cost represents the cost of *adding* usability engineering tasks to the overall development project budget. It does *not* represent the total *project* budget which includes all other software development costs. Thus, in this example, we would be proposing to *add* $132,185 to the overall project budget, whatever that might be.

Note also that the cost of constructing a usability lab and purchasing a UIMS have been charged entirely to this one application development project when, in fact, both can be reused for many projects. Thus, one could have amortized the costs of these items across several or maybe even many projects, which would reduce the costs attributed to this project. Charging these costs entirely to one project is therefore a very conservative way to conduct the cost-benefit analysis.

The cost of each technique listed in Table 2.1 was estimated by breaking the technique down into small steps, estimating the number of hours required for each step by different types of personnel, and multiplying these hours by the known fully loaded hourly wage of each type of in-house personnel (if outside consultants or contractors are used, their simple hourly rate plus travel expenses would apply). Fully loaded hourly wages are calculated by adding together the cost of salary, benefits, office space, equipment, and other facilities for a type of personnel and dividing this by the number of hours worked each year by that personnel type. The figures used to generate the following examples are arbitrary, and one would have to substitute the actual fully loaded hourly rates of personnel in one's own organization in an actual analysis. Additional costs, such as equipment and supplies, were also estimated and added in to the total cost of each technique. Cost estimates for each usability engineering technique included in the preceding usability engineering program are calculated as follows. In these calculations, usability engineers and developers are figured in at $35 per hour and users at $25 per hour. Other types of personnel are figured as indicated.

Usability Lab Setup

Lab design and equipment selection: 160 hours @ $35/hour	$5,600
Carpenters and electricians: 80 hours @ $25/hour	2,000
Video cameras, VCRs, one-way mirror	12,400
Total	**$20,000**

User Interviews

10 interviewees for 1 hour @ $25/hour	$250
Interviewer @ $35/hour:	
16 hours designing interview	
10 hours conducting interview	
28 hours analyzing results	1,890
3 support staff @ 5 hours each @ $15/hour	225
Videotapes	60
Total	**$2,425**

User Surveys/Questionnaires

Development of survey: 40 hours @ $35/hour	$1,400
Pilot testing: 40 hours @ $35/hour	1,400
Distribution and collection: 20 hours @ $15/hour	300
Responding: 80 users for 1/2 hour @ $25/hour	1,000
Coding and entering data: 20 hours @ $15/hour	300
Analyzing results: 40 hours @ $35/hour	1,400
Computer time	100
Supplies and duplicating costs	100
Total	**$6,000**

Usage Study, Simulation Test, or Prototype Test

Development of test: 40 hours @ $35/hour	$1,400
Pilot testing and revisions: 40 hours @ $35/hour	1,400
Running test: 40 hours @ $35/hour	1,400
Subjects: 10 @ 2 hours @ $25/hour	500
Analyzing results: 40 hours @ $35/hour	1,400
Videotapes:	120
Total	**$6,220**

Style Guide

Author: 240 hours @ $35/hour	$8,400
Committee: 4 @ 60 hours @ $35/hour	8,400
Total	**$16,800**

Purchase of UIMS

Reviewing packages: 160 hours @ $35/hour	$5,600
Cost of average package:	10,000
Total	**$15,600**

Prototype Construction (does not include design)

Screen layouts: 80 hours @ $35/hour	$2,800
Screen transitions: 80 hours @ $35/hour	2,800
Total	**$5,600**

Prototype Change in Response to Testing

Screen layouts: 4 hours @ $35/hour	$140
Screen transitions: 4 hours @ $35/hour	140
Total	**$280**

The number of hours estimated for each step in each technique are based on the authors' experience. Different usability engineers have different approaches to conducting these techniques and may take more or less time to carry them out. In conducting one's own cost-benefit analysis, time estimates for these techniques should be based on one's own experience. However, the basic formulas are generic, so that time estimates and cost factors may simply be plugged in.

Estimating Benefits

Calculating the costs of a usability engineering program is relatively straightforward, as described previously. Estimating the benefits is a little trickier, but is not too difficult if one has experience as a usability engineer and follows the guidelines set forth in this chapter and throughout the book.

First one needs to decide the relevant audience for the analysis and then what the relevant categories of benefits are for that audience, because not all potential benefits are relevant to all audiences. Just to take two examples (these and others are addressed in Part II), consider the different benefit categories relevant to an internal development organization developing software for internal company use, and a vendor company selling software on the open market. The relevant benefits to these two types of organizations might include:

Internal Development Organization

1. Increased user productivity
2. Decreased user errors
3. Decreased training costs
4. Savings gained from making changes earlier in design life cycle
5. Decreased user support

Vendor Company

1. Increased sales
2. Decreased customer support
3. Savings gained from making changes earlier in the design life cycle
4. Reduced cost of providing training (if training is offered through the vendor company)

Note that while the primary benefit relevant to the internal development organization might be increased user productivity, this is not usually of direct concern to a vendor company (even though it should be). The vendor company is more concerned with selling more products and decreasing their product support costs. Thus, in a cost-benefit analysis, one wants to focus attention on the potential benefits that are of most interest to the audience for the analysis.

Note that these benefits represent just a sample of those that might be relevant in these two types of organizations. Others might be included as appropriate, given the business goals of the organization and the primary concerns of the audience, and could be calculated in a similar fashion as follows.

Once the best set of potential benefits to focus on has been selected, these benefits must be estimated. The goal is to estimate the magnitude of each benefit that would be realized *if* the planned usability engineering program (with its associated costs) were implemented, compared with if it were not. Thus, for example, one would estimate how much *more* productive users would be on a system that was engineered for usability compared with on a system that was not.

To estimate each benefit, choose a unit of measurement for the benefit, such as throughput time per screen or per task in the case of productivity, or number of major errors per year, in the case of errors. Then—and this is the tricky part—make an assumption concerning the magnitude of the benefit for each unit of measurement: for example, a one-second savings per screen, or a reduction of four errors per year (the procedure for making this assumption is discussed in the next section). Finally, multiply the estimated benefit per unit of measurement by the number of units. Benefits can be expressed in units of time and then converted to dollars, given the value of time.

For example, let's first consider the benefits relevant to an internal development organization. Imagine a typical data entry system being developed for 250 intended users. Assume there will be two to four primary screens on this system representing the main entry screens where users will spend most of their time, and that users on the average will process about 60 of these screens per day. Now suppose that these users work 230 days a year, at a fully loaded hourly wage of $25. Now make the assumption that if a usability engineering program were included during development, the result would be screens allowing users to process them one second faster than screens that were developed without the benefit of usability engineering techniques. Assuming a benefit of one second per screen, 60 screens per day, 230 days per user, and 250 users, the total productivity benefit in a year adds up as follows:

Increased Productivity

250 users
60 screens per day
230 days per year
Processing time per screen reduced by 1 second
Hourly rate of $25

250 users * 60 screens * 230 days * 1/3600 hours * $25 = $23,958/year
Total   **$23,958**

Thus, usability engineering techniques that resulted in a benefit of one second per screen in this case would produce a benefit worth $23,958 in the course of a year. Note that if the system was in production over several years, as most are, this benefit is realized each year. It is not a one-time benefit, even though the costs of achieving the benefit are one-time costs incurred only in the first year during development.

Now consider another category of benefits: decreased cost of training users. In fact, many organizations spend huge amounts of money training users on new software systems. Suppose that the typical training program for software developed by a particular development organization was one week. Now make the benefit assumption that applying usability engineering techniques would result in an interface that was easier to learn, and therefore easier to teach, and in fact would result in a 10% reduction in the typical required training time. Suppose again that there were 250 intended users. If they each spent four hours less in training, and their fully loaded hourly wage was $25, then the benefit may be estimated as follows:

Decreased Training

Typical one-week training course reduced by 10% or four hours
250 users
Hourly rate of $25

250 employees * 4 hours * $25 = $25,000 in first year
Total   **$25,000**

Unlike productivity, this would be a one-time benefit, realized when the system was first introduced, but not again in later years. That is, users only need to be trained once. However, if there were significant turnover in the organization, this benefit figure might be higher, as new employees must be trained as well.

Also note that the same usability engineering program would likely produce both productivity and training benefits. That is, these benefits are different results of the same techniques and thus add together for a total benefit.

Still another category of benefits that would also likely be additive with productivity and training benefits is decreased user errors. Consider a particular type of error not uncommon on poorly designed user interfaces: errors that result in significant lost time and that are not eliminated through training, practice, or experience. For example, one well-known word processor had the same function key close a document in one context and cancel an edit in another. Not surprisingly, users commonly forgot which context they were in and canceled an edit when they meant to simply close their document. Users reported that they continued to make this error even after years of experience on the system, and that the edit they lost was often a lengthy one, such as several pages of inserted text. The time they lost in recovery each time that they made the error ranged from a few minutes to as much as 15 minutes.

Considering this type of error, suppose that usability engineering techniques would reveal some of the errors and allow elimination of them during development, thus eliminating an average of 0.2 errors per user per day (one error per week), each saving a recovery time of two minutes. These are the benefits assumptions. Now again consider the 250 users working 230 days a year at $25 per hour, and the benefit is calculated as follows:

Decreased Errors

250 users
0.2 errors eliminated per user per day
2 minutes in recovery time per error
230 work days per year
Hourly rate of $25

250 user * 0.2 errors * 230 days * $0.833/error = $9,580 per year
Total   **$9,580**

Decreased errors of this sort would be realized each year that the system was in production and can be added to the benefits of productivity and training, as they are different benefits resulting from the same usability engineering program.

Let us consider as an example one more type of benefit relevant to the internal development organization: savings gained from making changes earlier in the design life cycle or decreased late design changes. If usability testing is done early in the development life cycle, changes may be made to eliminate problems and achieve benefits much more cheaply, because code has not been written, manuals have not been published, and users have not been trained. Changes made late in development or after production may require rewriting code, republishing manuals, and retraining users all of which are very expensive. Thus, catching and fixing usability problems early in the development life cycle can substantially reduce costs down the line. The value of catching and solving usability problems early can be estimated by making the conservative assumption that changes made early cost only one-fourth of what the same changes made late would cost (Mantei and Teorey, 1988). Supposing that about 20 changes would be made in the course of early iterative testing and redesign and that each change would take about a day of developer time at a fully loaded hourly wage of $35, the benefit of early detection and resolution of usability problems could thus be calculated as follows:

Decreased Late Design Changes

Changes made early cost 1/4 of changes made after implementation
20 changes made early
1 day per change
Hourly rate of $35

Early change cost = 20 changes * 8 hours * $35 = $5,600
Late change cost = 4 * early change cost = $22,400
Savings = Late change cost − early change cost = $16,800 in first year
Total   **$16,800**

This is again a benefit of the same usability engineering program that produced the other benefits described earlier, and thus can be added to them. It is a one-time benefit, rather than a yearly benefit during the production lifetime of the system.

Now we can add up the estimated benefits of the usability engineering program in our example and compare them to the costs. Let us assume a production lifetime of five years for our system.

Benefit Category	Benefit per Year	Number/Years	Total
Increased productivity	$23,958	5	$119,790
Decreased training	25,500	1	25,500
Decreased errors	9,580	5	47,900
Early design changes	16,800	1	16,800
Total			**$209,490**

Comparing this total benefit of $209,490 with the one-time cost of the usability program of $132,185 shows an overall benefit of $77,305. Even the benefits in the first two years, which add up to $150,676, outweigh the costs by $18,491. Clearly, the proposed usability engineering program will more than pay for itself, as long as the benefits assumptions are actually realized. And this is the key: *How do we know what benefits assumptions are realistic?* How do we come up with them? The next section will address these questions.

But first, let's run through a similar example, this time in the case of a vendor company, where the set of benefits categories will be slightly different. In the case of the vendor company, the primary benefit of interest is not productivity, but sales.

A wide variety of trade magazines and product review companies purchase and/or receive free the new software releases that are sent to market. Approximately 15% (Nielsen, 1993) of reviews in microcomputer computer trade journals is devoted to analyzing the *user friendliness* or *usability* of new software products. *The New York Times*, the *Financial Times*, and the *Wall Street Journal* have weekly columns that evaluate software. Potential customers read these columns and make purchase decisions based on the evaluations, including the user interface portion. The review columns evaluate the usability of both the user manuals and the user interface. *Consumer Reports* has been including evaluations of the user interfaces to consumer products, as well as investigating their reliability and safety. Trade journals for products in the industry perform similar services for the customer.

In addition to publications, software products often undergo reviews from user groups and companies whose sole purpose is to review major expensive software products. The trend has been to include a review of the user interface as well as the functionality of the software. Later adopters call companies who have installed the product earlier. In today's competitive market with multiple companies competing for market share, the quality of the user interface has begun to have an impact on sales.

The same impact on sales holds for version numbers of products. These are reviewed just as carefully by the above stakeholders not only to determine the quality of the user interface but also to determine if prior problems have been fixed. In addition to ascertaining what new features a product has added, reviewers also look at how much effort a user has to make to adapt to the new version.

While it is difficult to predict exactly what impact usability engineering programs will have on product sales, it should be pretty clear to everyone that usability is now an aspect of competitive edge. Making some conservative estimate of increased sales in one's cost-benefit analysis is likely to be accepted by the relevant audience, especially if they are reminded of the facts just described.

To estimate increased sales benefits, consider relevant market forces such as current market share, trends of the market, and strengths and weaknesses of the competition, and choose some conservative and realistic assumption concerning the number of new sales that could be attributed to increased usability alone. Then, simply multiply this number by the known profit margin of the product. For example, suppose that a vendor primarily sells hardware, but includes software, and the usability of the software is what helps sell the hardware. Profit margins on hardware products can be high. Thus, one might make the following estimate of increased sales of hardware due to enhanced usability of software:

Increased Sales

25 more systems sold due to enhanced usability
Profit margin per product = $2,500

25 systems * $2,500 = $62,500
Total   **$62,500**

This, of course, is a one-time benefit. Next consider another benefit category of interest to vendor companies: decreased customer support costs.

Today's customer service operation is an extensive business. One major software vendor has so many callers on its customer hotline that the company has hired its own disk jockey to play music and give software advertisements while the customers are on hold. An interface that is understandable and easy to learn from either the manual or an on-line tutorial will generate fewer customer requests for help and significantly lower the number of people needed to handle the customer hotline. This reduction in personnel costs can be estimated as a potential benefit of applying usability engineering techniques during development.

For example, suppose that a vendor has 2000 customers and that there are many end users at each customer site who may call the customer support line. Suppose that many of these calls arise from confusion over the user interface or poorly designed manuals and that the average length of a call is 10 minutes. Now assume that better user interfaces and better manuals could reduce customer calls by four per year per customer. Finally, suppose that the fully loaded hourly wage of the customer support engineers is $35. The benefit would then be calculated as follows:

Decreased Customer Support

2000 customers
Eliminate 4 calls per year per customer
10 minutes per call
Customer support engineer fully loaded hourly wage = $35

2000 customers * 4 calls * 1/6 hours * $35 = $46,667
Total   **$46,667**

This is a yearly benefit, as long as the product is in use. The conservative estimate of reducing four calls per year per customer site takes into account that there may be more calls the first year, but fewer calls in later years as the users become more experienced.

The next benefit of interest to vendors is decreased cost of providing training. Whether the vendor bundles the cost of training in with the product or sells the training as a separate product, it is crucial to keep the cost down in order to compete in the marketplace. Again suppose the vendor has 2000 customer sites and must provide an average of one training course per site (some sites might not require any, and some might require more than one, depending on the number of users that need to be trained). Assume that a better-designed product could reduce the typical two-day training program by four hours. And suppose that the fully loaded hourly wage of trainers is $30. Thus, the training benefit can be calculated as follows:

Decreased Training Costs

2000 customers
1 training class per customer
4 hours less per training class
Trainer fully loaded hourly wage = $30

2000 customers * 1 course * 4 hours * $35 = $280,000
Total   **$280,000**

This again is a one-time benefit. Finally, the same benefit of early design changes that was described in the case of the internal development organization will apply to the vendor, as follows:

Decreased Late Design Changes

Changes made early cost 1/4 of changes made after implementation
20 changes made early
1 day per change
Hourly rate of $35

Early change cost = 20 changes * 8 hours * $35 = $5,600
Late change cost = 4 * early change cost = $22,400
Savings = Late change cost − early change cost = $16,800 in first year
Total   **$16,800**

Now we can again add up the estimated benefits of the usability engineering program in our example for the vendor company, and compare them to the costs. Let us again assume a product lifetime of five years.

Benefit Category	Benefit per Year	Number/Years	Total
Increased sales	$62,500	1	$62,500
Decreased support	46,667	5	233,335
Decreased training	280,000	1	280,000
Early design changes	16,800	1	16,800
Total			**$592,635**

Comparing this total benefit of $592,635 with the one-time cost of the usability program of $132,185 shows an overall benefit of $460,450. Even the first year benefits, which add up to $405,967, outweigh the costs by $273,782. Again, the proposed usability engineering program will more than pay for itself, as long as the benefits assumptions are actually realized. Now, let us turn to the problem of how to generate realistic, convincing benefits assumptions.

Justifying the Assumptions Made for Benefits

The basic assumption of a cost-benefit analysis of usability engineering is that the improved user interfaces that are achieved through usability engineering techniques will result in such tangible, measurable benefits as those described in the previous section (e.g., one second per screen, 10 hours per course, 1.5 errors per day at 2 minutes each, 25 more products sold).

The audience for the analysis is asked to accept these assumptions of certain estimated, quantified benefits as *reasonable and likely minimum benefits*, rather than as precise, proven, specific benefits. Proof simply does not exist for each specific application and its users that an optimal user interface will provide some specific, reliable performance advantage over some unspecified but suboptimal user interface which would result in the absence of a usability engineering program.

How can we generate—and convince our audience to accept—the inherent assumptions in the benefits that we claim in a given cost-benefit analysis? First, it should be pointed out that *any* cost-benefit analysis for *any* purpose must make certain assumptions that are really only predictions of the likely outcome of investments of various sorts. The whole point of a cost-benefit analysis is to try to evaluate in advance, in a situation in which there is some element of uncertainty, the likelihood that an investment will pay off. The trick is basing the predictions of uncertainties on a firm foundation of known facts. In the case of a cost-benefit analysis of usability engineering, there are several foundations upon which to build predictions of benefits.

First, there is ample published research that shows measurable and significant performance advantages of specific user interface design alternatives under certain circumstances. Examples of design alternatives for which performance data exist include:

Use of color
Choice of input devices
Use of windowing
Use of direct manipulation
Screen design
Menu structure

Benefit assumptions can thus be defended by referring to studies of such design alternatives. Available studies that explore the benefits of design alternatives typically vary one narrow aspect of design, such as fill-in form design, use of windows, use of color, or response time, keeping all other design variables constant, and measure human performance on some simple, well-defined task.

From these studies, a representative sample of which is summarized later in this section, we can extrapolate to make some reasonable predictions about the order of magnitude of differences we might expect to see in optimized user interfaces.

Note that these studies reveal productivity improvements that can be realized through only one design alternative when all others are held constant. That is, they compare two interfaces that vary in only one way, such as use of color or windows.

For example, Bly and Rosenberg (1986) (see Table 2.2) found that for a relatively complex task involving many files, screens, and interactions, overlapping windowing allowed certain types of users to perform 150 seconds faster as compared with simple, tiled windows. Other studies (see Christ, 1975, Table 2.2) show that, on the average, adding color effectively to a screen allows users to perform certain simple search tasks two to four seconds faster as compared with monochrome screens.

We can imagine a typical application and complex task involving, say, three screens, each of which must be searched for information. We could argue that, in principle, certain types of users ought to be able to perform a complex task 150–162 seconds faster on an interface with effective use of color and overlapping windows than on one without overlapping windows and with no or ineffective use of color. That is, appropriate use of color will allow the user to search a screen two seconds faster, and there are three screens. Being able to display the three screens as overlapped versus tiled windows will allow other aspects of the task (such as compare, edit, verify, etc.) to be performed 150 seconds faster.

More to the point is the *general* finding that different design alternatives *such as* use of color and use of windows can make a difference of as much as 2½ minutes on a complex task. Unfortunately, we cannot use

Table 2.2   Design alternatives constrained by hardware

Task Type	Study	Design Alternatives	User Task	Performance Difference (in seconds)
Simple search/select	Savage *et al.*, 1982	Fill-in field: broken underline vs. dot column separators vs. reverse video	Estimate field length, find cursor	1
	Christ, 1975	Color vs. other visual cues such as high intensity	Search for items by visual cue	2–4
	Card *et al.*, 1978	Input device: mouse vs. cursor keys	Point and select target on screen	1
	Albert, 1982	Input device: touch screen vs. cursor keys	Point and select target on screen	11
Simple task	Roberts and Moran, 1982	Direct manip-ulation vs. command language	Simple editing task (e.g., move a paragraph)	30
Complex task	Cohill and Williges, 1982	On-line help vs. manual	Complex editing (e.g., make many different edits to a document	386
	Magers, 1983	Standard help system vs. modified help system (requires more memory, faster response time)	Complex file manipulation including file retrieval, copy, read, delete, send, create	1416
	Davies *et al.*, 1985	Windowing vs. nonwindowing	Complex file manipulation including retrieval, read compare, edit	25

Continued

Table 2.2 *Continued*

Task Type	Study	Design Alternatives	User Task	Performance Difference (in seconds)
	Bly and Rosenberg, 1986	Overlapping vs. tiled windows	Complex file manipulation including retrieval, read, compare, edit	150
	Barber and Lucas, 1983	Response time (4–24 seconds)	Complex transactions in database environment including add, change, verify, inquire, send, report	168

data from these studies directly to make simple specific interface design decisions because such techniques as color and windows have many different possible implementations, and the optimal ones will always depend on the specifics of the users and tasks of a particular application and their interaction with all other aspects of user interface design. Thus, usability engineering during the development of specific products is always necessary to develop optimal interfaces. The research does not provide simple generic answers to design questions. However, what the research does provide are *general ideas* of the *magnitude of performance differences that can occur between optimal and suboptimal interface design alternatives.*

The basic benefit assumptions made in any cost-benefit analysis can thus be generated and defended by referring to the wide body of published research data that exists. A sample of the research data that can provide part of the basis for benefit assumptions in a cost-benefit analysis is included in this section to give the reader a basic sense of the order of magnitude in performance differences that can result from variations in user interface design. There is not enough detail in this summary to explain the method and results of each study completely, but this is not the purpose. Rather, the reader should gain from this summary a sense that, for instance, it is reasonable and realistic to assume that an opti-

Table 2.3   Design alternatives *not* constrained by hardware

Task Type	Study	Design Alternatives	User Task	Performance Difference (in seconds)
Simple search/select	McDonald *et al.*, 1983	Ordering of menu item: random vs. categorical	Find and select a target menu choice	4
	Perlman, 1984	Menu selection codes: mnemonic vs. nonmnemonic letters	Find and select a target menu choice	1
	Teitelbaum and Granda, 1983	Screen design consistency: consistent vs. inconsistent item location across screens	Find item on screen	1
Simple task	Miller, 1981	Depth vs. breadth in a menu hierarchy	Find and select target menu choice at lowest level of hierarchy	3
	Barnard *et al.*, 1982	Specific vs. general command names in command language	Find and select target menu choice at lowest level of hierarchy	60–180
Complex task	Ledgard *et al.*, 1980	Command language syntax: notational vs. English-like	Complex editing (e.g., make many different edits to a document)	60–360

mized user interface design would allow users to perform complex tasks 2 1/2 minutes faster than they could on a suboptimal user interface.

Tables 2.2 and 2.3 briefly summarize the results of 16 published research studies. These studies are divided into groups. The first grouping divides the studies into those studying design alternatives that are *constrained by hardware* (Table 2.2) and those studying design alternatives that are *not constrained by hardware* (Table 2.3).

For instance, Christ (1975) (Table 2.2) looks at the effects of color. This is a software design alternative constrained by hardware. McDonald *et al.* (1983) (Table 2.3), on the other hand, look at the effects on search performance on menu screens of different ways of ordering menu choices. Menu choices can be ordered in different ways regardless of hardware capabilities.

Studies are further divided within each of these two groups according to the type of task that users are asked to perform. It is important to understand this in order to extrapolate from these findings when making specific benefits estimates for a particular cost-benefit analysis.

Some studies look at *simple search/select* tasks, where the user is shown one screen and asked to find something on it, count things on it, and possibly select something with an input device. The main thing these studies have in common is that the type of interaction on which performance measures are based involves only a single screen and only one simple operation.

A second group of studies look at *simple tasks*. These may involve more than one screen and more than one operation. Examples are moving a paragraph of text from one screen to another or navigating through a menu hierarchy to find a target menu choice.

A third group of studies is based on *complex tasks*. These are comparable to meaningful pieces of work that users might do and usually involve multiple screens and many different operations. Examples are making many different kinds of edits to a whole document, preparing a report based on information found in other files, and problem solving using information in a database.

In general, complex tasks are simply more involved than simple tasks, i.e., they require more screens and operations, and both simple and complex tasks are based partly on multiple simple search/select tasks. When studies compare design alternatives, performance differences tend to be greatest for complex tasks and greater for simple tasks than for simple search/select tasks. This suggests that, when users perform complex tasks, they do indeed take advantage of small, per-screen decreases in processing time to become more productive overall.

Each study is referred to by authors and year (see references for full citations) and described in terms of the design alternatives it compared and the user task on which performance is measured. A performance difference (in seconds) is given for each, which summarizes the advantage of one design alternative over the other in terms of task performance time. For instance, Savage *et al.* (1982) (Table 2.2) compared broken underline versus dot column separators versus reverse video as a way to display input fields on a screen. Users were asked to estimate the number of character positions in fields and find the cursor on a screen with many fields. The field type that resulted in the best performance on these tasks allowed users to perform the tasks approximately one second faster than the alternative field types.

The main conclusion for our purposes, to be drawn from these sample studies is that individual design alternatives, such as those varied in these studies, potentially can improve performance on simple search/select tasks (i.e., for single operations on single screens) by a few seconds, on simple tasks by as much as one or two minutes, and on complex tasks by anywhere from one or two minutes to as much as one-half hour, depending on the complexity of the task. Note that, in these studies, everything but the specific design alternative being compared was held constant, so that these improvements are due entirely to these alternatives and not to other design differences or differences in product functionality.

Again, keep in mind that what we are inferring from these studies is not specifically how to optimize a user interface (although there is indeed something to be learned about designing interfaces from these studies). We are more interested here in getting a general feel for the magnitude of performance differences that can be achieved in an optimized interface due to the use of usability engineering techniques, as compared with the suboptimal interface that would result in the absence of a usability engineering program.

In a cost-benefit analysis, we want to err on the side of conservative estimates of benefits. Thus, it seems entirely reasonable to assume that design alternatives that optimize, for example, choice of input device, use of color, use of windows and screen design will allow simple search/select tasks (involving a single operation on a single screen) to be performed one second faster on the average (the figure we assumed in our sample estimate of benefits), as compared with suboptimal alternatives.

We could also assume that optimal design alternatives will decrease the time for users to perform *simple tasks* by as much as five seconds, and *complex tasks* by as much as 15 seconds as compared with a suboptimal design alternatives These are extremely conservative assumptions, given the data summarized here and, as such, seem reasonable for the purpose of carrying out a convincing cost/benefit analysis.

Part of the reason for being so conservative in making benefits assumptions is that any cost-benefit analysis has an intended audience who must be convinced that benefits outweigh costs. Assumptions that are very conservative are less likely to be challenged by the relevant audience, thus increasing the likelihood of acceptance of the cost/benefit conclusions. In addition, conservative benefits assumptions help to manage expectations. It is always better to achieve a greater benefit than was predicted in the cost-benefit analysis than to achieve less benefit, even if it still outweighs the costs. Having underestimated benefits will make future cost-benefit analyses more credible and more readily accepted.

This discussion has focused on providing a rationale for assuming *increased productivity* benefits. Other categories of benefits, such as *decreased training time* and *decreased user errors*, are also assumed in a cost-benefit analysis. Although complete discussion of research relevant to these benefits is beyond the scope of this chapter, these assumptions can also be based on research results that focus on these measures (i.e., learning time and error rate/time).

One question that might be asked at this point is whether or not the benefits of each design alternative are additive: That is, for example, if color can improve performance on a simple search/select tasks by two seconds, and a mouse can improve selection time by one second (see Table 2.2), do a mouse and color combine to improve performance by three seconds? More generally, does each individual improvement to the user interface increase the overall performance advantage in a simple additive fashion? Studies tend to isolate one variable at a time, rather than directly investigate the additive effects of design alternatives, so we do not generally have specific research on this question. However, it seems likely that there is some additive effect, although it may not be a simple one, since the cognitive processes that different design variables facilitate may overlap somewhat.

Again, the conservative approach when estimating potential benefits is probably to assume something less than a simple sum of the estimated benefits for each design variable, but something more than simply the largest benefit among the individual benefits. For example, instead of assuming that optimizing ordering of menu choices, menu selection technique, and menu design consistency will result in a total benefit of six seconds on a simple search/select task (see Table 2.3), one might decide to estimate a benefit of five seconds—smaller than the sum of the benefits of the three design variables, but larger than the single largest benefit among these three design variables.

Besides citing relevant research literature, there are other ways to arrive at and defend one's benefit assumptions in a cost-benefit analysis. Actual case histories of the benefits achieved as a result of applying usability engineering techniques are very useful in helping to defend the benefits assumptions of a particular cost-benefit analysis. A few published case histories exist (e.g. Karat, 1989, and others in this volume), but even anecdotes are useful.

In addition, experienced usability engineers can draw upon their own general experience evaluating and testing software user interfaces and their specific experience with a particular development organization. Familiarity with typical interface designs from a development organization allows the usability engineer to decide how much improvement to expect from applying usability engineering techniques in that organization. If the designers are generally untrained and inexperienced in interface design and typically design poor interfaces, the usability engineer would feel comfortable and justified defending more aggressive benefits claims. On the other hand, if the usability engineer knows the development organization to be quite experienced and effective in interface design, then more conservative estimates of benefits would be appropriate, on the assumption that usability engineering techniques will result in fine tuning of the interface, but not radical improvements. The usability engineer can assess typical interfaces from a given development organization against well-known and accepted design principles, usability test results, and research literature to help defend the assumptions made when estimating benefits.

Using Cost-Benefit Analysis to Plan a Usability Engineering Program

We have now established a basic framework for the cost-benefit analysis of any usability engineering program by describing how to estimate both costs and benefits. Karat's Chapter 3 takes the basic calculations described in this chapter to the next step by showing how the basic costs and benefits are translated into *return on investment (ROI)* figures so that the value of adding usability engineering can be compared to other projects under consideration. Karat also illustrates basic accounting practices for calculating the *net present value (NPV)* of money that is invested in usability now and produces a return in sales later. Incorporating these accounting principles puts the usability plan in a form that can be evaluated more readily by individuals concerned about the company's cash flow, capital investment, and long-term viability.

One useful application of the basic cost-benefit analysis is to help plan out a sensible, cost-effective usability engineering program for a given development project. One could calculate the *minimum* likely benefits from even the most bare-bones usability engineering program, and then use this figure as the maximum budget for the project, and decide what and how many usability tasks and techniques to include in the program to get the most out of this budget.

Certain parameters in the cost-benefit analysis have a major impact on the magnitude of potential benefits. For example, when considering productivity—of primary interest to the internal development organization—the critical parameters are the number of users and the volume of transactions. When there are a large number of users and a high volume of transactions, even very small performance advantages in an optimized interface add up quickly to significant overall benefits. On the other hand, where there are a small number of potential users and a low volume of transactions, benefits may not add up to much even when the potential per transaction performance advantage seems significant.

For example, consider the following two scenarios. First, imagine a case where there are 5,000 users and 120 transactions per day per user. Even a half-second advantage in this case adds up:

5000 users * 120 transactions * 230 days * 1/2 second = 19,167 hours

If the users' hourly rate is $15, the savings are:

19,167 hours * $15 = $287,505

This is a pretty dramatic benefit for a tiny improvement on a per transaction basis! On the other hand, if there were only 25 users and they were infrequent users, with only 12 transactions per day, even if a per transaction benefit of one minute could be realized, the overall benefit would only be:

25 users * 12 transactions * 230 days * 1 minute = 1,150 hours

At $15 per hour, the overall productivity benefit is only:

1,150 hours * $15 = $17,250

Thus, in the case of productivity benefits, costs associated with optimizing the user interface are more likely to pay off when there are more users and more transactions.

In the case of the sales benefit for a vendor, the critical parameter is profit margin. If the profit margin per product is low, then a very large number of additional sales would have to be achieved due to usability alone for the usability costs to pay off. On the other hand, if the profit margin per product is high, as in the preceding example, then only a small number of increased sales due to usability would be necessary to pay for the usability program. Thus, these critical parameters are going to determine directly how much can be invested in usability and still pay off.

To plan the budget for a usability engineering program then, start out by calculating the costs of the most aggressive usability engineering program that one would like to implement, including, for example, user profiling, task analysis, style guide development, lab construction, and iterative testing and redesign until goals are met. Then estimate benefits, using *very conservative* benefits assumptions. If benefits still outweigh costs dramatically, as they usually will when critical parameters are favorable, then one can easily make a good argument for even the most aggressive usability engineering program, because only the most conservative claims concerning potential benefits have been made, and as such can be defended easily. In fact, one can then go back and redo the benefits calculations using more aggressive, yet still realistic, benefits assumptions, and show that in all likelihood an even more dramatic overall benefit will be realized, even from a significant investment.

If, however, benefits and costs in the initial calculation seem to match up fairly closely, then one might want to consider scaling back the planned usability engineering program, maybe even to just a bare-bones plan (see Chapter 11 for guidelines.) One is still likely to realize the very conservative assumptions made concerning benefits with just these minimal usability techniques, and thus one could predict with confidence a healthy return on investment from a more conservative approach to usability engineering. This is probably wiser in the long run than making overly optimistic claims concerning potential benefits, spending a lot to achieve them, and then perhaps not achieving them and losing credibility.

To illustrate this planning strategy, consider the following two scenarios. First, revisit the first example in the section called "Estimating Benefits," which involved the internal development organization building a system for 250 high-frequency users. Fairly conservative assumptions were made concerning benefits: screen time reduced by one second, training time reduced by four hours, 0.2 errors eliminated per day per user at two minutes saved per error. Even with these fairly conservative assumptions, the full usability engineering program, including lab construction, was predicted to be paid off in the second year of production, with net benefits continuing to accrue after that. In fact, if one had made the more aggressive and yet still realistic benefits assumptions of training time reduced by 10 hours and 1.5 errors eliminated per day, the benefit would have summed to $175,104 in the first year alone, outweighing the costs of $132,185 by $42,919, and to $558,320 over five years, outweighing the costs by $426,135. Thus, one could argue, even the most conservative assumptions predict a fairly dramatic payoff of a comprehensive usability engineering program, but the likelihood is that the payoff will be higher still.

In contrast, suppose one again started out by costing out a comprehensive usability engineering program at $132,185. In this case, however, suppose that there are only 150 intended users performing 60 transactions per user per day. Now let's see how the benefits sum up:

Increased Productivity

150 users
60 screens per day
230 days per year
Processing time per screen reduced by 1 second
Hourly rate of $25

150 users * 60 screens * 230 days * 1/3600 hours * $25 = $14,375/yr
Total   **$14,375**

Decreased Training

Typical 1 week training course reduced by 10% or 4 hours
150 users
Hourly rate of $25

150 employees * 4 hours * $25 = $15,000 in first year
Total   **$15,000**

Decreased Errors

150 users
0.2 errors eliminated per user per day
230 work days per year
2 minutes in recovery time per error
Hourly rate of $25

150 user * 0.2 errors * 230 days * $0.833/error = $5,748 per year
Total   **$5,748**

Decreased Late Design Changes

Changes made early cost 1/4 of changes made after implementation
20 changes made early

1 day per change
Hourly rate of $35

Early change cost = 20 changes * 8 hours * $35 = $5,600
Late change cost = 4 * early change cost = $22,400
Savings = Late change cost − early change cost = $16,800 in first year
Total   **$16,800**

Totaling up the benefits over a five-year production lifetime, we get a very different predicted benefit in this case:

Benefit Category	Benefit per Year	Number/Years	Total
Increased productivity	$14,375	5	$71,875
Decreased training	15,000	1	15,000
Decreased errors	5,748	5	28,740
Early design changes	16,800	1	16,800
Total			**$132,415**

In fact, comparing this total benefit of $132,415 to the one-time cost of the usability program of $132,185 shows an overall benefit of only $230 over a five-year period. Even though the benefits assumptions were conservative and the planned usability program to achieve those benefits was aggressive, it still seems risky to make an investment that, based on conservative assumptions, really doesn't show a payoff even over the course of five years. In this case, one would want to scale back the planned usability engineering program and its associated costs. Because the benefits assumptions made were so conservative, it is likely that they will be achieved even with a minimal usability effort.

Perhaps in this scenario we should plan to do only a simple user profile, a very quick and dirty task analysis consisting of just three rounds of interviews and then three iterations of usability testing to catch major flaws and be sure that we have achieved the predicted benefits. The costs of this scaled-back usability engineering program are shown in Table 2.4. The costs of $41,985 compare favorably even to the first-year benefits of $51,923 and certainly to the five-year benefits of $132,415. And, it is likely that even this minimal program will produce these very conservatively estimated benefits.

Thus, one can use the general framework for cost-justifying usability engineering laid out in this chapter (and elaborated on in Chapter 3) to plan a sensible usability engineering program likely to pay off as predicted. Remember that when an organization is first experimenting with usability engineering techniques and is still skeptical about their value, it is wise to make very conservative cost-benefit arguments and then to

Table 2.4   Costs of scaled-back usability engineering analysis

Lifecycle Stage	UI TASK/Technique	Technique	Number/ Technique	Total Cost
Scoping	USER PROFILE			
	User interviews	2,425	2	4,850
Functional specification	TASK ANALYSIS: User interviews	2,425	3	7,275
Design	Prototype construction	5,600	1	5,600
	PROTOTYPE TESTING:			
	Prototype test	6,220	3	18,660
	Prototype change	280	20	5,600
Testing/ implementation				
Total cost				**$41,985**

show after the fact that much larger benefits were in fact realized. Once an organization has several positive experiences investing in usability, it will be more receptive to more aggressive proposals for usability engineering programs and to more optimistic benefits assumptions in the cost-benefit analyses.

Where Do We Go from Here?

This chapter and the next, which elaborates on this framework, are intended to provide a foundation for the rest of the book, which includes more specific approaches to cost justification laid out in Chapters 4–6, the rich variety of case studies offered in Chapters 7–10, and the special issues addressed in Chapters 11–13. The basic framework is quite simple. Costs incurred need to be compared to benefits predicted. Since usability is such an important issue in today's software, costs will rarely exceed expected benefits. The purpose of this book is to give the software development manager information on how to make the business case for bringing in much-needed usability engineering. The chapter by Karat that follows further elaborates on the business case analysis.

References

Albert, A. E. (1982). The effect of graphic input devices on performance in a cursor positioning task. *Proceedings of the Human Factors Society 26th Annual Meeting,* 79–82.

Barber, R. E. and Lucas, H. C. Jr. (1983). System response time, operator productivity, and job satisfaction. *Communications of the ACM* **26,** 972–986.

Barnard, P., Hammond, N., MacLean, A., and Morton, J. (1982). Learning and remembering interactive commands. *Proceedings, Human Factors in Computer Systems* (March), 2–7.

Bly, S. A., and Rosenberg, J. K. (1986). A comparison of tiled and overlapping windows. *CHI '86 Proceedings,* 101–106.

Card, S. K., English, W. K., and Burr, B. J. (1978). Evaluation of mouse, rate-controlled isometric joystick, step keys, and text keys for text selection on a CRT. *Ergonomics* **21,** 601–613.

Christ, R. E. (1975). Review and analysis of color coding research for visual displays. *Human Factors* **17,** 542–570.

Cohill, A. M. and Williges, R. C. (1982). Computer-augmented retrieval of HELP information for novice users. *Proceedings of the Human Factors Society 26th Annual Meeting,* 79–82.

Davies, S. E., Bury, K. F., and Darnell, M. J. (1985). An experimental comparison of a windowed vs. a non-windowed operating system environment. *Proceedings of the Human Factors Society 26th Annual Meeting,* 250–254.

Gould, J. D. and Lewis, C. (1985). Designing for usability: Key principles and what designers think. *Communications of the ACM* **28**(3), 360–411.

Karat, C.-M. (1989). Iterative usability testing of a security application. *Proceedings of the Human Factors Society 33rd Annual Meeting,* 273–277.

Ledgard, H. F., Whiteside, J. A., Singer, A., and Seymour, W. (1980). The natural language of interactive systems. *Communications of the ACM* **23,** 556–563.

Magers, C. C. (1983). An experimental evaluation of on-line HELP for non-programmers. *Proceedings, CHI '83,* 277–281.

Mantei, M. M. and Teorey, Toby T. J. (1988). Cost/benefit for incorporating human factors in the software lifecycle. *ACM Communications* **31**(4), 428–439.

Mayhew, D. (1992). *Principles and Guidelines in Software User Interface Design.* Englewood Cliffs, NJ, Prentice-Hall, Inc.

McDonald, J. E., Stone, J. D., and Liebelt, L. S. (1983). Searching for items in menus: The effects of organization and type of target. *Proceedings of the Human Factors Society 27th Annual Meeting* **2,** 834–837.

Miller, D. P. (1981). The Depth/breadth tradeoff in hierarchical computer menus. *Proceedings of the Human Factors Society 25th Annual Meeting* **2,** 296–300.

Nielsen, J. (1992). The usability engineering lifecycle. *Computer* (March) 12–22.

Nielsen, J. (1993). *Usability Engineering.* Boston, Academic Press.

Perlman, G. (1984). Making the right choices with menus. *Proceedings, Interact '84* **1,** 291–295.

Roberts, T. L. and Moran, T. P. (1982). Evaluation of text editors. *Proceedings, Human Factors in Computer-Systems* (March) 136–141.

Savage, R. E., Habinek, J. K., and Blackstad, N. J. (1982). An experimental evaluation of input field and cursor combinations. *Proceedings of the Human Factors Society 26th Annual Meeting*, 629–633.

Shneiderman, B. (1992). *Designing the User Interface: Strategies for Effective Human–Computer Interaction*, 2nd ed. Reading, MA, Addison Wesley.

Teitelbaum, R. C. and Granda, R. E. (1983). The effects of positional constancy on searching menus for instructions. *CHI '83 Proceedings*, 150–153.

Chapter 3

A Business Case Approach to Usability Cost Justification

Clare-Marie Karat

IBM TJ Watson Research Center
Hawthorne, New York

Introduction

This chapter focuses on the merits of cost-benefit analysis of usability engineering, the financial benefits resulting from usability engineering, the nature of cost-benefit analysis and its relationship to business cases, the different published cost-benefit methodologies, as well as anonymous case study data. Professionals working in usability engineering have recently recognized the need to communicate the cost-benefit and value of this work more effectively. Chapanis (1991) has discussed the human factors profession's need to improve its communication of the content and value of human factors and usability engineering. Curtis (1992) has called on usability engineers to make better business cases to executives about the effect of a product's user interface on the market and to search actively for human factors opportunities that will have visible impacts. I agree with the themes presented by these authors. When I engage in human factors work, I need to be able to communicate the content and value of human factors activities to the people and organizations I support in order to reach out to them successfully. The managers of these organizations must make pragmatic decisions about the allocation of resources. Towards achieving successful integration of human factors considerations in development projects, I have found it important to address project management concerns regarding time, personnel, and financial resources required for human factors work, as well as the resulting economic benefits from its inclusion in projects (Karat, 1990, 1993b).

Cost and revenue accountability are high priorities for organizations in both the public and private sectors. The value of human factors activities in improving the usability of systems and products must be quantified in financial terms to these organizations. This analysis is relevant for products developed by an organization for internal use as well as products developed for external customers. I urge human factors professionals involved with development projects to include their work's cost-benefit analysis as a standard component of communication activities. I propose that these activities become proactive; these analyses can be a part of the initial business cases for proposed projects as well as part of the reviews of projects that are underway or completed.

Why Measure the Cost-Benefit of Human Factors?

Human factors practitioners must become proficient at communicating the idea that successful use of human factors resource is an economic "win-win" situation for the organizations they support, the end users of the usability-engineered products, the customers who buy the products, and the human factors practitioners themselves (Karat, 1991, 1992, 1993b). In the past, human factors practitioners have often relied on descriptions of improvements in end user performance and satisfaction with usability-engineered products to communicate their work's value. Human factors engineers can increase their value to organizations by providing financial data regarding human factors work's impact on organizational areas of concern. These areas of concern might include time and cost reductions for product development, as well as postrelease revenue increases and cost reductions. Providing human factors cost-benefit information to project managers gives them a more complete and accurate basis for decisions, helps human factors successfully compete for resource, and facilitates human factors becoming part of the critical development path. Informing management about human factors work's contribution to fiscal and organizational goals demonstrates an understanding of those goals and illustrates the supporting role that human factors can play in achieving them.

Providing human factors information about products to other groups in an organization such as education, system maintenance, and marketing is an efficient and effective way to support them in achieving their goals and can help these groups reduce the time and monetary resource necessary to complete their product-related work. Education groups can use product usability data to improve the quality of training courses and product documentation. A usability-engineered product can result in significant reductions in required maintenance support, and required changes can then occur on a more aggressive schedule that satisfies customers and end users. Improved education deliverables and reduced system maintenance needs can together produce reductions in costly product information updates. Marketing groups can benefit from human factors data about a product's financial value for customers, such as increased end user productivity, quality of work deliverables, client and end user satisfaction, and reduced end user training and support costs.

Cost-benefit data on human factors can be used by practitioners to improve the efficiency of human factors methods used in particular situations. Human factors engineers can use these data to understand the trade-offs involved in using different usability engineering techniques within project resource constraints and development schedules (Karat, 1990, 1993a; Karat, Campbell, and Fiegel, 1992). Human factors cost-benefit data (preproject estimates and postproject feedback) can guide management decisions regarding the prioritization of human factors resource allocation among a variety of projects, as well as decisions about the number of human factors laboratories and jobs appropriate for an organization. This feedback is also important in documenting unsuccessful use of human factors resource due to factors such as practitioners' impractical decisions or lack of product team commitment to usability. Organizations can use both success and failure data to improve the efficient and effective use of human factors resource.

Usability Engineering in the Software Life Cycle

The scope of opportunity for usability engineering's contribution to the financial status of organizations and development projects can be demonstrated by discussing the software life cycle; an analogous case may be made for human factors work in hardware development. Recent data suggest that the user interface is 47%–60% of the lines of system or application code (MacIntyre, Estep, and Sieburth, 1990). A graphical user interface (GUI) is minimally 29% of the software development budget and increases with available function (Rosenberg, 1989). The user interface has been documented as commanding 40% of the development effort (Wixon and Jones, 1992).

Recent estimates show that 80% of software life cycle costs occur during the postrelease maintenance phase (Pressman, 1992). A review of maintenance work undertaken shows that 80% of necessary maintenance is due to unmet or unforeseen user requirements, and 20% is due to "bugs" or reliability problems (Martin and McClure, 1983). Analysis of these compiled data reveals that usability engineering has the potential to make significant contributions to software quality and projects' financial success, given that a substantial amount of project life cycle effort and resource is devoted to the project's user interface.

What Contributions Can Usability Engineering Demonstrate?

Organizations can reap financial benefits by including human factors work when they develop systems for organizational use and products for external customers. Inclusion of human factors work in software and hardware development can reap both short-term and long-term benefits. Short-term benefits are defined as those that accrue during product development; long-term benefits are those observed after product release. A crucial short-term benefit is the reduction in development cost and time. This key benefit can have a rippling effect throughout the product's life cycle. Pressman (1992) estimates the increasing cost of a change during development as one unit during project definition, 1.5–6 units during project development, and 60–100 units during maintenance after project release. Defining user requirements, testing usability prototypes, and performing usability walkthroughs early in development can significantly reduce the cost of identifying and resolving usability problems and can save time in software development.

In a software development project, the product's usability and quality are interdependent. Just as the product code has defect-free objectives, product usability merits objectives. Design reviews are cost-effective and save development time (Gilb, 1988; Pressman, 1992); similarly, measurable usability objectives, usability testing, and walkthroughs early in development also reduce development time and cost. Scerbo (1991) and Bosert (1991) make the case that usability engineering is a part of quality functional deployment (QFD), a process used for structuring development process through a primary focus on customer requirements.

Through QFD, reducing development time by one-third to one-half is possible.

Long-term financial benefits of usability-engineered internal and external products may include, for example, increases in sales or revenues, user productivity, and user satisfaction, and decreased costs for training and support, service, product documentation personnel, and maintenance, as well as decreased user errors (Karat, 1990, 1992, 1993b). The benefits of offering customers and end users quality products that are highly usable and satisfying may cover other aspects, as particular benefits vary from product to product.

Reducing the development time required to bring a usability-engineered product to market can result in substantial financial returns to the organization beyond the initial savings attributable to the time reduction. Increased sales or revenues is one long-term benefit of usability-engineered products. House and Price (1991) cite data showing that companies generally lose 33% of after-tax profit when they ship products six months late, as compared with losses of 3.5% when they exceed product development budgets by 50%. Conklin (1991) states that speeding up development is a key goal for integrating usability effectively into product development and that a one-quarter delay in bringing a product to market may result in the loss of 50% of the product's profit.

Usability-engineered software can accrue increased revenues from external customers due to the increased marketability of a product with demonstrated usability, increased end user productivity, and lower training costs. Conklin (1991) states that another goal for product development usability is speeding up market introduction and acceptance by using usability data to improve marketing literature, reach market influencers and early adopters, and demonstrate the product's usability and reduced training cost. He says, for example, that speeding up market acceptance may increase revenues 10%, the equivalent of getting the product to market three months earlier. The 10% in revenues might reflect either 10% higher volume in sales or a more valued product that is marketed at a 10% higher price. Wixon and Jones (1991) documented a case study of a usability-engineered product with a revenue increase of 80% over the first release of the product that was built without human factors. The second release achieved revenues 60% over project projections, and customers cited the usability of the product in buying decisions.

The discussion of increased revenues resulting from usability engineered products has focused thus far on products developed for external customers. More and more internal development organizations are now charging other organizations for their services and products, reaping benefits from their "sales" of usability-engineered products to internal customers similar to those described for external products. Finally, usability-engineered products result in fewer returned products.

In some instances, the financial benefits to the organization variables are manifested differently depending on whether the usability engineered product is developed for internal use or is marketed to external customers and end users. For example, for internal development projects (where someone in the organization is the customer for the system developed), increased user productivity and decreased user errors realized from these internal products are direct benefits to the organization and may help the organization lower or stabilize personnel costs. To an organization developing products for external sale, increased user productivity and decreased errors are indirect benefits to the organization in that the productivity and organizational information can be used to market the products' value to customers, realizing higher revenues. The customers using the external products would realize the direct benefits of these improvements. As a rising standard of living depends on improvements in productivity (Roach, 1991), this potential benefit of usability engineering merits attention from internal and external customers.

Usability-engineered internal development projects can result in decreased training, support, service, product documentation, and personnel costs, and increased user satisfaction. End-user training for a usability-engineered internal system can be one hour, as compared with one week for similar systems designed without it (Karat, 1993b). In an anonymous case study, human factors work on a system eliminated the need to reprint and distribute a manual, an estimated savings of $40,000 for one year. In another anonymous case study, the investment in usability engineering allowed an organization to eliminate the development of a ten-hour education course to support the application, resulting in a savings of $140,000. The $140,000 savings amount does not include savings in employee time for those people who would have taken the course (Karat, 1993b).

The financial benefits of some of the variables mentioned may result from a combination of factors. For example, the improved usability of a dedicated system and increased user satisfaction may result in lower employee turnover that represents a large financial savings to the organization. Schlesinger and Heskett (1991) cite data illustrating that the total costs of employee turnover are 1.5 times an employee's annual salary. In a published case study, Schlesinger and Heskitt (1991) state that a 10% reduction in employee turnover in two divisions of a hotel chain was worth more than the combined profits made by the two divisions.

For organizations that develop and market products for external customers, the financial benefits in the service areas mentioned are realized in more indirect ways. For example, organizations may be able to set more competitive service rates for customers while realizing acceptable rates of return on investment. These rates may help the organization gain new customers and retain current ones.

Usability-engineered products may result in financial benefits (direct for internal products; indirect for external products) related to space savings, equipment and consumable cost reductions, and lowered risk and improved work process control. Space savings may result from reduced accommodation areas as well as current and archive filing space (Christian, 1990). Equipment and consumable cost reductions refer to stationery supplies, photocopying, and filing equipment. And improved security and audit trails and safety (lowered risk of human error) may result in decreased costs as well.

Finally, decreased maintenance costs can be a large, direct financial benefit to an organization that produces usability-engineered internal and external products. Usability engineering may never be able to identify and resolve all user requirement issues during product development; however, if half of the issues currently handled during maintenance were instead resolved during development, it would represent a very large cost reduction. Moreover, it would provide the organization's software maintenance employees with an opportunity to complete more rewarding and productive activities. Martin and McClure (1983) found that $20–30 billion was spent worldwide on maintenance. Studying backlogs of maintenance work shows that an "invisible" backlog is 167% the size of the declared backlog. Anonymous case study data show that internal development organizations are spending the majority of their resources on maintenance activities and thus cannot initiate development of strategic new systems.

This overview of usability engineering's financial benefits defines the scope of opportunity available to organizations investing in this resource. Based on the published and anonymous case study data and my ten years of experience in software design and usability work, I believe that an organization either pays relatively little to invest in usability engineering during product development and reaps the associated financial benefits, or the organization pays relatively more before and much more after product release for usability and associated problems left unaddressed in a product. Investment in usability engineering is generally a good business decision. I recommend that human factors cost-benefit data be included as part of a proposed project's business case and as part of the regular management review of a project underway. The remainder of the chapter focuses on methodology for capturing and analyzing the data for a business case approach to cost justifying usability engineering and examples of published and anonymous case study data that use this methodology. (As a note, the anonymous case-study data have been provided to me over the last few years by practitioners in the field. They must remain anonymous due to the sensitivity or confidential nature of the data.)

What Is Cost-Benefit Analysis?

Cost-benefit analysis is a method of analyzing projects for investment purposes, and proceeds as follows (Burrill and Ellsworth, 1980):

1. Identify the financial value of expected project cost and benefit variables.
2. Analyze the relationship between expected costs and benefits using simple or sophisticated selection techniques.
3. Make the investment decision.

How Do Cost-Benefit Analyses Relate to Business Cases?

Business cases are a mechanism for proposing projects, tracking projects, and communicating with the organization at large. A business case includes:

- A project description,
- A market analysis regarding the proposed project,
- An analysis of expected benefits and costs for "business as usual" as compared with "business as proposed,"
- Staffing and equipment requirements for the proposed project,
- A project timetable,
- An analysis of project dependencies, and
- A risk analysis for the project.

Organizations use business cases as a means of making investment decisions. A company or group generally allocates resources to projects that will accomplish organizational goals. These goals may include, for example, financial, social, or legal milestones. Groups are forced to make decisions about the distribution of limited resources among their many organizational goals and related benefits. Business cases provide an objective and explicit basis for these investment decisions. Competing projects are judged against each other, based on standards for return on the investment of resources. Other political factors may influence the decision, but the business case provides a documented statement of the case for investment. In the case of investment in usability engineering, cost-benefit judgments have been made largely in the absence of formal cost-benefit analyses and business cases. In these instances, the data on which the decision is made and the standard being used to judge usability engineering's value are at best unclear. At the project management level, usability engineering has been competing for resources against other groups who *do* have objective cost-benefit data available for management review. Projects with usability resource assigned have been competing for funding against other projects, without a complete and accurate business case. It is critical that usability engineers assume responsibility for collecting and providing data that will benefit our profession as well as the project teams and larger organizations that we support.

Assessing Costs and Benefits of Usability Engineering

In human factors cost-benefit analysis, one general approach is to compare the costs and benefits of a proposed usability-engineered product with those for a product developed as usual (without human factors) by the organization. Alternatively, if there are several competing usability engineering proposals for a product's development, they may be contrasted with each other.

The goal of the analysis is to determine the cash value of the positive difference in a product due to human factors. The first task in cost-benefit analysis of human factors work is to identify and quantify financially each of the expected costs (e.g., human factors and programming personnel, end user, walkthrough and testing) and the benefits (e.g., lower training costs, higher sales, increased productivity) of usability engineering. Estimates of all significant human factors cost and benefit variables in the project's life cycle are required for analyzing the relationship between the two. In identifying and quantifying human factors costs and benefits, consider the following guidelines:

1. The variables that are relevant for the analysis will vary depending on the focus of the product and the context of its use.
2. There will be differences in the key benefit and cost variables for products for internal and external products (e.g., the previ-

ously described difference in the benefit of increased productivity for internal and external products).
3. Initial analyses often overlook benefits and costs, so distribute a draft analysis of the benefit and cost variables to project team members and people with different backgrounds in your organization to gain the wisdom of their different perspectives and expertise.

After the variables have been identified, the second step is to separate the tangible and intangible benefits and costs. Tangible variables are those that can be quantified financially; intangibles such as organizational image are not easily measured (Due, 1989). I recommend that the list of intangible variables be kept and referred to periodically, as methods for quantifying the variables may surface at a later time.

The third step is determining the value of the tangible benefits and costs. The goal is a unit or per-hour cash value of benefits and costs and estimates of the total numbers involved for use in the summary analysis. To define the financial value of the variables, establish contacts in development, maintenance, marketing, personnel, financial analysis, business planning, education, and service groups in your organization. Also contact users and customers for available data regarding cost-benefit calculations. Use past data, estimates from projections, or group decision data (Galegher, Kraut, and Egido, 1990) and document your sources. Regarding personnel data, ensure that your estimates are based on fully burdened rates (i.e., all benefits and overhead included), and account for raise projections and productivity ratios (i.e., the value used by your personnel or business group to reflect that people are not productively engaged 100% of the time at work). Identify savings and costs as initial or ongoing by year. Finally, review and update your cost-benefit data periodically and as significant changes in the project occur.

Benefit Calculations Examples

The following are five brief examples that illustrate how to calculate the the benefit of usability engineering. The examples are a mixture of actual case study data and composite cases.

Increased Sales or Revenues. Based on "buy decision" data from usability tests and surveys, it is estimated that the new usability-engineered system will have sales that are 25% higher in the first year compared with "product development as usual." The system will sell for $200, and estimates are that 5000 usability-engineered systems will be sold the first year. What is the value of the human factors benefits in increased revenues for the first year?

Additional systems sold based on usability = 1000
System cost = $200
Increased revenue = 200 × 1000 = $200,000

Increased Sales or Revenues. Case study data on usability engineering involvement in the copier business in the 1980s demonstrate impressive revenue increases for these products (Brown, 1991; Wasserman, 1991).

- Initial situation: Declining revenues and unnecessary service calls due to perceived unreliability of machines.
- Usability data initially ignored, rejected, or suppressed.
- Economic forces dictated need for change, and new focus on social context of copier use and iterative prototyping led to product redesign.
- Revenue rose immediately when redesigned machines reached the market; a $1 billion increase over three years.
- Cost-benefit of usability engineering very positive; if human factors costs are estimated at $2 million, then cost-benefit ratio = 1:500
- Company awarded Malcolm Baldrige Award for Quality in 1989.

Increased User Productivity. Three iterations of usability testing were completed on a system (Application 1) before it was installed to replace a previous one. Users (22,876) worked with the old system about 12 times a day (Karat, 1990). What were the human-factors-related benefits in increased user productivity for the first three tasks users completed on the day of transfer?

- Reduction in user time to complete a task on Application 1 from initial to final user interface design:
    Total = 4.67 minutes
- Projected benefits in increased user productivity on first three tasks:
    End user population = 22,876
    22,876 × 4.67 minutes = 1,781 hours
    1,781 hours × Productivity ratio × Personnel costs = $41,700
- The computed savings of $41,700 do not include savings in further use of the system, elimination of the training and help desk, reduced user errors, and reduced maintenance.

Increased User Productivity. Three iterative usability prototype tests were conducted on a system (Application 2) that is employed by users to complete 1,308,000 tasks per year (Karat, 1990). The usability work resulted in an average reduction of 9.6 minutes per task. What were the first-year benefits in increased user productivity due to human factors?

- Reduction in time on task for Application 2 from initial design to final user interface design:
    Average savings = 9.6 minutes
- Projected first-year benefits due to increased user productivity:
    Tasks per year = 1,308,000
    1,308,000 × 9.6 minutes = 209,280 hours
    209,280 hours × Productivity ratio × Personnel costs = $6,800,000

Decreased Personnel Costs. As stated earlier, Schlesinger and Heskett's (1991) data show that total costs of employee turnover are 1.5 times the employee's annual salary. A business has 500 employees using a dedicated software system in the performance of their jobs. There is currently a 25% employee turnover rate per year. Average annual employee salary is $20,000. The user interface of the system is improved, based on user requirements, and employee turnover is reduced by 20%. What is the value of the resulting 20% reduction in employee turnover the first year?

    Previous yearly employee turnover = 125
    New yearly employee turnover = 100
    Reduction in employee turnover = 25
    Average annual employee salary = $20,000
    Value of reduction in employee turnover = 25 × 20,000 × 1.5 = $750,000

Usability Engineering Costs

The costs of usability engineering include costs for one or more of the following activities (Karat, 1990, 1991, 1993a; Mantei and Teorey, 1988):

    End user requirements definition
    User profile definition
    Focus groups
    Task analysis
    Benchmark studies
    Usability objectives specification
    Studies of end user work context

Style guide development
Initial design development
Design walkthroughs
Paper-and-pencil simulation testing
Thinking-aloud studies
Heuristic evaluations
Prototype development (high or low fidelity)
Usability tests (laboratory or field)
Prototype redesign
Surveys and questionnaires

This list provides some perspective on the range of activities that may be employed in developing a usability-engineered product. In my experience as a usability engineer, I have not observed more than six of these activities completed for any one project. The usability work on a project is tailored to a project's requirements, time frame, and resources.

When calculating the costs of usability engineering activities, consider these additional cost calculation guidelines:

1. Regarding personnel costs, include costs for all development team support, other support, or contract services, and all participant costs.
2. If a permanent usability laboratory is built, costs may be prorated based on the number of usability tests to be conducted for a given period of time.

The guideline regarding usability laboratory costs applies to the purchase of new equipment as well. As an alternative, the costs of equipment and the laboratory may be included in fully burdened personnel costs as overhead expense.

Cost and Cost-Benefit Calculation Examples

Usability Engineering Costs for Application 1. Usability work for the study described as Application 1 (Karat, 1990) included task analysis, development of a low-technology prototype, three iterations of usability testing (field prototype test, laboratory prototype test, and laboratory system integration test) and redesign. The work was completed across seven months. Usability costs were as follows:

Usability resource (fully burdened salary rate) = $18,800
Participant travel = $700
Test-related development work = $1,200
Total cost for a year = $20,700

Cost-benefit ratio for usability work:

> Projected benefits in increased productivity (first three tasks) =
> $41,700
> Costs of usability activities = $20,700
> Cost-benefit ratio = 1:2

Or stated another way,

> Return factor = 2 (House and Price, 1991)
> Cost-benefit ratio (including elimination of help desk and reduced
> maintenance) = 1:10 or Return factor = 10

Usability Engineering Costs for Application 2. Usability work for the internal product called Application 2 (Karat, 1990) included a benchmark test (field test), development of a high-technology prototype, three iterations of usability prototype testing (all laboratory), and redesign. The work was completed across 21 months. Usability costs were as follows:

> Usability resource = $23,300
> Participant travel = $9,750
> Test-related development work = $34,950
> Total cost for two years = $68,000

Cost-benefit ratio of usability work:

> Projected first-year benefits in increased productivity = $6,800,000
> Costs of usability activities = $68,000
> Cost-benefit ratio = 1:100
> Or return factor = 100

Simple Cost-Benefit Analysis Techniques

The analysis technique used to compare the quantified cost and benefits for a project may be either simple or sophisticated. One simple analysis technique called the *cost-benefit ratio* has been demonstrated in the preceding cost-calculation examples. To calculate a cost-benefit ratio, the benefit amount is divided by the cost amount to determine the ratio of costs to $1 of benefits. In the cost-calculation example for Application 1, $40,700 was divided by $20,700 to achieve a cost-benefit ratio of 1:2. For every $1 spent on usability engineering, $2 were saved. In this example, the cash benefits were the first year of system use. *Return factor* is another way of reporting the same analysis of costs and benefits.

Payback Period

Payback period is an investment evaluation method based on determining the amount of time (e.g., year units) that it will take to generate net cash flows (cash benefits) to recover the initial investment in the project (Burrill and Ellsworth, 1980). The procedure for using the payback period analysis technique is as follows:

- Payback period is the smallest value of k such that $R_1 + R_2 + ... + R_k \geq C$, where R = cash benefits in a year minus the costs in that year and C = initial development cost.
- Projects are selected for investment if the payback period is less than the organization's standard (e.g., four years).
- Competing projects are ranked on the basis of increasing payback periods; those with shorter payback periods are judged as better investments.

Payback Period Example. A project requires an initial outlay of $75,000, and net cash inflows for the project in the first six years are $10,000, $25,000, $20,000, $20,000, $20,000, and $10,000, respectively. The project will be withdrawn or replaced after six years. The organization's standard payback period for projects is four years. Should this project be selected for investment purposes?

Answer: According to the payback method, the answer is yes, as the sum of the net income for the first four years is equal to or greater than the initial investment outlay.

$$10,000 + 25,000 + 20,000 + 20,000 \geq 75,000$$

While the method is widely used, easy to compute, and provides some control over risk exposure, it is not a measure of project profitability (e.g., cash inflows from years 5 and 6 are not included in the analysis in the previous example), and it fails to adjust for the timing of cash inflows. The time value of money is the focus of sophisticated analysis techniques.

Sophisticated Selection Techniques

Background

Cost-benefit techniques that adjust for the timing of cash inflows are interest-based or sophisticated selection techniques. Time-adjusted cash flow selection techniques are based on the idea that money has a time value and that, by calculating the present value of future cash inflows from a project, including an acceptable rate of return, and specifying the time period in which the cash returns are received, better investment decisions can be made (Gordon and Pinches, 1984). The concept focuses on the analysis of present and future costs and benefits for a project in terms of the present-day value of all the monies. The formula is as follows for calculating the present value of one future cash flow:

$$P = F_n \, (1/(1 + i))^n$$

where

P = present value,
F = future cash inflow in time period n,
i = discount rate, the minimum acceptable rate of return for investments, and
n = number of time periods in years.

To simplify the calculation, the expression $(1/(1 + i))^n$ is called the present value interest factor (PVIF). A chart of the computed values of PVIF is found in Table 3.1. To find a value of PVIF, select the value for a particular discount rate (between 12% and 35%) and a period of time (between one and 10 years) on the chart and read the resulting PVIF value.

Present Value of a Future Cash Flow Example. If a project will result in one future cash inflow of $50,000 in the second year and the discount rate is 15%, what is the present value of the future yield?

F = 50,000
PVIF = 0.7561
P = 50,000 (0.7561) = $37,805.

The next step is to be able to calculate the present value of several cash inflows across time. The present value of project benefits (cash inflows) across a number of years is calculated by summing the separate cash flows. The formula for the calculation is as follows:

$$P = F_1 \, (1/(1 + i))^1 + F_2 \, (1/(1 + i))^2 + ...F_n \, (1/(1 + i))^n$$

Table 3.1 PVIF chart (Present value of $1 in period x)

Period	12%	13%	14%	15%	16%	17%	18%	19%
1	.8929	.8850	.8772	.8696	.8521	.8547	.8475	.8403
2	.7972	.7831	.7695	.7561	.7432	.7305	.7182	.7062
3	.7118	.6931	.6750	.6575	.6407	.6244	.6086	.5934
4	.6355	.6133	.5921	.5718	.5523	.5337	.5158	.4987
5	.5674	.5428	.5194	.4972	.4761	.4561	.4371	.4187
6	.5066	.4803	.4556	.4323	.4104	.3898	.3704	.3521
7	.4523	.4251	.3996	.3759	.3538	.3332	.3139	.2959
8	.4039	.3762	.3506	.3269	.3050	.2848	.2660	.2487
9	.3606	.3329	.3075	.2643	.2630	.2434	.2255	.2090
10	.3202	.2946	.2697	.2472	.2267	.2080	.1911	.1756

Period	20%	21%	22%	23%	24%	25%	26%	27%
1	.8333	.8270	.8197	.8130	.8065	.8000	.7937	.7874
2	.6944	.6830	.6719	.6610	.6504	.6400	.6299	.6200
3	.5787	.5645	.5507	.5374	.5245	.5120	.4999	.4882
4	.4823	.4665	.4514	.4369	.4230	.4096	.3968	.3844
5	.4019	.3860	.3700	.3552	.3411	.3277	.3149	.3027
6	.3349	.3186	.3033	.2888	.2751	.2621	.2499	.2383
7	.2791	.2633	.2486	.2348	.2218	.2097	.1983	.1877
8	.2326	.2176	.2038	.1909	.1789	.1678	.1574	.1478
9	.1938	.1799	.1670	.1552	.1443	.1342	.1249	.1164
10	.1615	.1486	.1369	.1262	.1164	.1074	.0992	.0916

Period	28%	29%	30%	32%	34%	35%		
1	.7813	.7752	.7692	.7576	.7463	.7407		
2	.6104	.6009	.5917	.5739	.5569	.5487		
3	.4768	.4658	.4552	.4348	.4156	.4064		
4	.3725	.3611	.3501	.3294	.3102	.3011		
5	.2910	.2799	.2693	.2495	.2315	.2230		
6	.2274	.2170	.2072	.1890	.1727	.1652		
7	.1776	.1682	.1594	.1432	.1289	.1224		
8	.1388	.1304	.1226	.1085	.0962	.0906		
9	.1084	.1011	.0943	.0822	.0718	.0671		
10	.0847	.0784	.0725	.0623	.0536	.0497		

where

P = present value,
F = future cash flow in project years $1 - n$,
i = discount rate, and
n = number of project years.

Present Value of Cash Inflows Example. If the projected cash flows from a project are $50,000, $100,000, and $200,000 for years 1–3, respectively, and the discount rate is 17%, what is the present value of the projected benefits?

F_1 = $50,000
F_2 = $100,000
F_3 = $200,000
i = 17%
n = 3
P = 50,000 (0.8547) + 100,000 (0.7305) + 200,000 (.6244)
  = 42,735 + 73,050 + 124,880 = $240,665

Net Present Value

Net present value (NPV) is a sophisticated selection technique. NPV is the present value of the benefits (inflows) from a project minus the present value of the project cost (outflows). The formula for NPV is as follows:

$$NPV = F_1 \left(1/(1 + i)\right)^1 + F_2 \left(1/(1 + i)\right)^2 + ...F_n \left(1/(1 + i)\right)^n - C$$

where

F = future cash inflows in years $1 - n$,
i = discount rate,
n = number of years the project runs, and
C = present value of project cost (outflows).

The procedure for using NPV to make an organizational investment decision is that a project is selected for investment if and only if the NPV is positive. Competing projects can be ranked in order of decreasing NPV if investment amounts are relatively equal. Otherwise, rank order according to profitability index (see following section).

NPV Investment Decision Example. In the previous example, the present value of the project's projected inflows for the first three years was $240,665. If the present value of the project's cost (outflows) is $200,000, should the project be accepted for investment? *Answer:* yes, because the NPV is positive.

$$NPV = 42,735 + 73,050 + 124,880 - 200,000$$
$$= 240,665 - 200,000 = \$40,665$$

When competing projects are of unequal sizes, compare them by means of a *profitability index*. The profitability index (PI) is simply another way of stating the relationship between the present value of project inflows and outflows. PI is calculated as follows:

PI = Present value of project inflows/ Present value of project outflows

Using data from the previous example,

$$PI = 240,665/200,000 = 1.20$$

Internal Rate of Return

The most popular sophisticated analysis technique is the internal rate of return (IRR). IRR is closely related to NPV. IRR is the actual rate of return that an investment in a project will bring if cash inflows and outflows are as projected. Organizations set a minimum rate of return that investment in the project must achieve in order to be considered acceptable. If the IRR is greater or equal to the minimum return rate, it may be accepted. Otherwise, the investment proposal should be rejected. To calculate IRR, solve for the value of i in the formula for NPV that will make NPV become zero. Solve by successive approximation, graphing, or computing the value of i. Many business calculators have programs for computing the value of i. As an alternative, the next example solves for i by successive approximation.

IRR Calculation Example. In the previous example, NPV = $40,665 when i = 17%. Since NPV is positive, select a higher value for the discount rate to lower NPV towards zero. With i = 27%,

$$NPV = 50,000 \ (0.7874) + 100,000 \ (0.6200) + 200,000 \ (0.4882) \\ - \ 200,000 \\ = 39,370 + 62,000 + 97,640 - 200,000 = -\$990$$

Since the NPV is now on the negative side, lower the discount rate to raise the NPV towards zero. With i = 26%,

$$NPV = 50,000 \ (0.7937) + 100,000 \ (0.6299) + 200,000 \ (0.4999) \\ - \ 200,000 \\ = 39,685 + 62,990 + 99,980 - 200,000 = 2,655$$

Therefore, the IRR is between 26% and 27%.

Further Interest-Based Selection Issues

These interest-based selection methods (e.g., NPV, IRR) can also be adjusted to take into account other factors such as (Gordon and Pinches, 1984):

- Risk: the probability of generating the expected revenues.
- Interaction between projects: the extent to which an organization's products compete for the same customer dollars.
- Unequal project lives: two proposed projects have different expected lifecycles (e.g., three years versus five years).
- Capital rationing: the idea that an organization has a fixed amount of money to invest in projects.
- Abandonment: the point at which a project is halted.
- Inflation: the effects of the expected inflation rate on the calculations.
- Different discount rates: the need for higher rates for different groups of projects.

See Gordon and Pinches (1984) for a detailed discussion of these topics.

There are associations among the measures that should be noted. Cost-benefit ratio and return factor express the same information; profitability index extends these measures by including the time value of money. Net present value and internal rate of return are related and provide information about different parts of the same formula.

Analysis of Changing Project Circumstances

The following exercises illustrate the use of a sophisticated analysis technique in a project with changing circumstances. Questions are presented and answers are provided after each of the four parts.

Exercise, Part 1

In this exercise, we will analyze the consequences of decisions regarding human factors work on a project and determine the overall contribution of human factors to the project's success.

A new product is under development. It will be completed in nine months and will be on the market by the end of year 0. There will be no human factors work on the project during its development. The present value of the investment in the project for its entire life cycle is $230,000. Projected net revenues from the sale of the product are expected to be $100,000, $100,000, and $100,000 for years 1–3, respectively. After three years, the product will be replaced.

Question 1: What is the internal rate of return for this project without human factors?

Answer to Part 1. *Question 1:* What is the internal rate of return (IRR) for this project without human factors?

Solution: To calculate IRR, solve for i in NPV so that NPV = 0.

$$NPV = F_1 (1/(1 + i))^1 + F_2 (1/(1 + i))^2 + ...F_n (1/(1 + i))^n - C$$

For today, work with units of 1000 to simplify cash values and two decimal points of precision in the PVIF values. See the PVIF chart in Table 3.1. In Part 1, the values are:

F_1 = $100,000 or 100 units
F_2 = $100,000 or 100 units
F_3 = $100,000 or 100 units
C = $230,000 or 230 units

Try i = 12%, where PVIF = 0.89, 0.80, and 0.71 for years 1–3.

$$NPV = 100(0.89) + 100(0.80) + 100 (0.71) - 230$$
$$= 89 + 80 + 71 - 230 = 10$$

NPV is positive, so raise i to lower NPV towards zero. Try i = 15%, where PVIF = 0.87, 0.76, and 0.66 for years 1–3.

$$NPV = 100(0.87) + 100(0.76) + 100(0.66) - 230$$
$$= 87 + 76 + 66 - 230 = -1$$

NPV is negative, so lower i to raise NPV towards zero. Try i = 14%, where PVIF = 0.88, 0.77. and 0.68 for years 1–3.

$$NPV = 100(0.88) + 100(0.77) + 100 (0.68) - 230$$
$$= 88 + 77 + 68 - 230 = 3$$

So IRR for the three years of the project is between 14% and 15%.

Exercise, Part 2

Now, a business case is made for including human factors in this project. The project manager will allocate $50,000 for usability engineering activities over the nine-month development period. Usability activities will be included in the project plan being developed now. The project manager would like an overview of the resources and time schedules required for the usability engineering work on the project.

Question 2: What usability activities would you outline for the nine-month development period to achieve the maximum human factors benefit for the $50,000 investment in the project?

Answer to Part 2. *Question 2:* What usability activities would you outline for the nine-month development period to achieve the maximum human factors benefit for the $50,000 investment in the project?

Solution: The human factors activities would be tailored to the specifics of the project and would include a mix of activities to accomplish human factors goals within the resource constraints and project time schedule. Trade-offs regarding resources required for, and benefits to be achieved from, the use of various human factors techniques would be analyzed, and decisions would then be made. As stated above, specific activities chosen would depend on the project circumstances. In general, the human factors work would include activities to identify user issues (e.g., benchmarking, end user requirements definition, usability objectives specification, studies of end user work context) and iterative usability reviews, walkthroughs, and testing of representations of the user interface (e.g., low- and high-technology prototypes, integrated system).

Exercise, Part 3

Based on past project data, it is expected that, by including human factors in project development, the project can be delivered on the same time schedule and at a present value investment cost of $250,000, including $50,000 for human factors. Including human factors in the project is expected to lower development, training, service, and maintenance costs such that the net investment cost for human factors is $20,000 ($230,000 + $50,000 for human factors − $30,000 in human factors–related project life cycle cost reduction = $250,000 total present value of investment cost). Projected net revenues are expected to be $100,000, $200,000, and $100,000 for years 1–3, respectively.

Question 3: What is the internal rate of return for the project that includes usability engineering in development?

Question 4: What is the internal rate of return on the investment in human factors on this project?

Answer to Part 3. *Question 3:* What is the internal rate of return (IRR) for the project that includes usability engineering in development?

Solution: To calculate IRR, solve for i in NPV so that NPV = 0.

$$NPV = F_1\,(1/(1+i))^1 + F_2\,(1/(1+i))^2 + ...F_n\,(1/(1+i))^n - C$$

For today, work with units of 1000 to simplify cash values and two decimal points of precision in the PVIF values. For Question 3, the values are:

F_1 = $100,000 or 100 units
F_2 = $200,000 or 200 units
F_3 = $100,000 or 100 units
C = $250,000 or 250 units

Try i = 25%, where PVIF = 0.80, 0.64, and 0.51 for years 1–3.

$$NPV = 100(0.80) + 200(0.64) + 100\,(0.51) - 250$$
$$= 80 + 128 + 51 - 250 = 9$$

NPV is positive, so raise i to lower NPV towards zero. Try i = 27%, where PVIF = 0.79, 0.62, and 0.49 for years 1–3.

$$NPV = 100(0.79) + 200(0.62) + 100(0.49) - 250$$
$$= 79 + 124 + 49 - 250 = 2$$

NPV is positive, so raise i to lower NPV towards zero. Try i = 28%, where PVIF = 0.78, 0.61. and 0.48 for years 1–3.

$$NPV = 100(0.78) + 200(0.61) + 100\,(0.48) - 250$$
$$= 78 + 122 + 48 - 250 = -2$$

So IRR for the three years of the project is between 27% and 28%. The IRR for this project without human factors (14%–15%) might not provide a sufficient return on investment, whereas with human factors the rate of return (27%–28%) would probably warrant a decision to invest in the project.

Question 4: What is the IRR on the investment in human factors on this project?

Solution: To calculate IRR, solve for i in NPV so that NPV = 0. For Question 4, the values related to human factors are:

F_1 = $0 or 0 units
F_2 = $100,000 or 100 units
F_3 = $0 or 0 units
C = $20,000 or 20 units

Try i = 35%, where PVIF = 0.55 for year 2.

$$NPV = 100(0.55) - 20$$
$$= 55 - 20 = 35$$

NPV is positive, so i must be greater than 35%. The answer may be considered complete at this point since the chart ends at 35%.

If you want to know the exact value of i, solve for i such that: F_2 $(PVIF)^2 = 20$.

$$100(PVIF)^2 = 20$$
$$PVIF = 0.2$$
$$(1/1 + i)^2 = 0.2$$
$$(1/1 + i) = 0.45$$
$$1 = 0.45(1 + i)$$
$$1 = 0.45 + 0.45i$$
$$0.55 = 0.45i$$
$$i = 1.22 \text{ or } 122\%$$

Summary and Recommendations

As you begin to try cost-benefit analysis and business case methods:

1. Try one test case.
2. Use low-end estimates of benefits and high-end estimates of costs in business cases.
3. Update your cost-benefit data periodically and when major changes occur in a project or new variables are uncovered.
4. Use the human factors and project cost-benefit data as feedback to improve the use of human factors resource at individual through organizationwide levels.
5. Report your cost-benefit and business case data to the appropriate audiences.

This chapter introduces cost-benefit analysis of usability engineering and encourages professionals in the field to consider this matter. Methods and guidelines for these analyses exist; the current challenge is to begin using these data in project planning and tracking and to develop more accurate measures of the human factors contribution to the success of development projects and their organizations. Development teams working on either internal or external products may be able to reap many positive benefits for themselves and their organizations through attention to usability engineering cost-benefit data and the appropriate use of human factors resource on development projects.

References

Bosert, J. L. (1991). *Quality Functional Deployment: A Practioner's Approach.* ASQC Quality Press, New York.

Brown, J. S. (1991). Research that reinvents the corporation. *Harvard Business Review* **69**(1), 102–111.

Burrill, C. and Ellsworth, L. (1980). *Modern Project Management: Foundations for Quality and Productivity.* Burrill-Ellsworth, New Jersey, 209–223.

Chapanis, A. (1991). To communicate the human factors message, you have to know what the message is and how to communicate it. *Human Factors Society Bulletin* **34**(11), 1–4.

Christian, M. D. (1990). Strategic implementation methodology and cost/benefit analysis for installation of document image processing systems. *Image Processing 90—The Key Issues. Conference Proceedings*, 21–29.

Conklin, P. (1991). Bringing usability effectively into product development. *Human-Computer Interface Design: Success Cases, Emerging Methods, and Real-World Context.* Boulder, Co., July 24–26.

Curtis, B. (1992). Carving a niche in the organizational chart. *IEEE Software* **9**(1), 78–79.

Due, R. T. (1989). Determining economic feasibility: Four cost/benefit analysis methods. *Journal of Information System Management* **6**(4), 14–19.

Galegher, J., Kraut, R. E., and Egido, C. (1990). *Intellectual Teamwork: Social and Technological Foundations of Cooperative Work.* Erlbaum Associates, New Jersey.

Gilb, T. (1988). *Principles of Software Engineering Management.* Addison Wesley, Reading, Massachusetts.

Gordon, L. A. and Pinches, G. E. (1984). *Improving Capital Budgeting: A Decision Support System Approach.* Addison-Wesley, Reading, Massachusetts.

House, C. H., and Price, R. L. (1991). The return map: Tracking product teams. *Harvard Business Review* **69**(1), 92–100.

Karat, C. (1990). Cost-benefit analysis of usability engineering techniques. *Proceedings of the Human Factors Society.* Orlando, Florida, 839–843.

Karat, C. (1991). Cost-benefit and business case analysis of usability engineering. Tutorial presented at the *ACM SIGCHI Conference on Human Factors in Computing Systems.* New Orleans, LA, April 28–May 2.

Karat, C. (1992). Cost-justifying human factors support on development projects. *Human Factors Society Bulletin* **35**(11), 1–8.

Karat, C. (1993a). Usability engineering in dollars and cents. *IEEE Software* **10**(3), 88–89.

Karat, C. (1993b). Cost-benefit and business case analysis of usability engineering. Tutorial presented at the *ACM SIGCHI Conference on Human Factors in Computing Systems.* Amsterdam, April 24–29.

Karat, C., Campbell, R., and Fiegel, T. (1992). Comparison of empirical testing and walkthrough methods in user interface evaluation. *Proceedings of CHI '92*

Human Factors in Computing Systems. Monterey, California, May 3–7, 397–404.

MacIntyre, F., Estep, K. W., and Sieburth, J. M. (1990). Cost of user-friendly programming. *Journal of Forth Application and Research* **6**(2), 103–115.

Mantei, M. M. and Teorey, T. J. (1988). Cost/benefit analysis for incorporating human factors in the software lifecycle. *Communications of the ACM* **31**(4), 428–439.

Martin, J. and McClure, C. (1983). *Software Maintenance: The Problem and Its Solution.* Prentice-Hall, New Jersey.

Pressman, R. S. (1992). *Software Engineering: A Practitioner's Approach.* McGraw-Hill, New York.

Roach, S. S. (1991). Services under siege—the restructuring imperative. *Harvard Business Review* **69**(5), 82–91.

Rosenberg, D. (1989). A cost benefit analysis for corporate user interface standards: What price to pay for a consistent look and feel? In: *Coordinating User Interfaces for Consistency.* (J. Nielsen, ed.), Academic Press, Boston.

Scerbo, M. W. (1991). Usability engineering approach to software quality. *Annual Quality Congress Transactions* **45**, 726–733.

Schlesinger, L. A., and Heskett, J. L. (1991). The service driven service company. *Harvard Business Review* **69**(5), 71–81.

Wasserman, A. (1991). Can research reinvent the corporation? *Harvard Business Review* **69**(2), 164–175.

Wixon, D. and Jones, S. (1992). Usability for fun and profit: A case study of the design of DEC RALLY version 2. Internal Report, Digital Equipment Corporation.

Part II

Approaches to
Cost-Justifying Usability

Chapter 4

Cost Justification of Usability Engineering: A Vendor's Perspective

Kate Ehrlich*

SunSoft, Inc.
Chelmsford, Massachusetts

Janice Anne Rohn

SunSoft, Inc.
Mountain View, California

Introduction

You have just been hired by a medium-sized company to make their products more usable. Prompted by articles in the press praising the ease of use of the competitors' newest product offerings, your company realizes that they can no longer compete on features alone and are looking to you to help them.

The company has hired you, which means they have already made some investment in usability and they are willing to make more. They have already told you that they will fund a usability lab, and you believe there will be money to hire some more people next quarter. They are also somewhat cautious and want to know what benefits they will accrue for their investment. They don't mind spending some money to do the right thing, but they care about the "value" of what they get back. That is,

*Now at Lotus Development Corporation, Cambridge, Massachusetts.

73

they want to know what are the benefits of usability engineering, what it is that usability engineering does to bring about those benefits, and how you plan on measuring (i.e., justifying) the benefits.

Some of the engineers believe that with the help of marketing and good engineering principles, they can build products that will sell well, and be easy to use, and inexpensive to maintain. So what is the additional value that usability brings? The company also cares about the costs of setting up a group to perform usability evaluations. They are aware of the material costs of setting up a usability lab and equipping it with furniture, hardware, software, video equipment, lighting, one-way mirrors, and the like. However, they are actually more concerned about the indirect costs of usability testing on their product-development schedules. They know that usability engineering evaluates the ease of use of products, but they are concerned that this testing will increase their development schedules, causing them to be late in shipping their products.

Usability engineering and other user-centered design[1] activities are becoming a more accepted part of the software development process. As products compete on ease of use and ease of learning rather than just on functionality, companies are beginning to realize that they need to focus more on the users of their products. This chapter will examine the costs and benefits of performing usability engineering in a vendor company.

A vendor company is a for-profit company that obtains its revenues selling products, rather than a company that obtains revenues from selling data or services, or an internal development group whose funding comes from within the company. Although usability engineering methods are and should be utilized in all vendor companies, we will discuss the topic with respect to computer companies, since it is in this context that both our expertise and much of the work in the field of usability engineering is concentrated.

In this chapter, we examine some common stages of acceptance of usability engineering within the company, since these stages often dictate which type of cost-justification, if any, is necessary. We discuss some commonly used usability methods in vendor companies and then examine the costs and benefits of performing usability engineering.

---

[1]We use the term "user-centered design" (UCD) to refer to the overall endeavor of making products easier to use. We use the term "usability engineering" to refer to the specific activities associated with making a product useful and usable, such as performing evaluations and observing customers. We use the term "user interface (UI) design" to refer to the specific activities associated with designing the user interface.

The Increasing Need for Usability Engineering

There are several reasons why practicing usability engineering in vendor companies has become increasingly important. These include economic pressures on companies, and the changing and expanding market of computer users.

Economic Influences

Increasing numbers of companies are moving to the individual-business-unit (IBU) model, in which development teams are separated into functional units that are accountable for budgets and revenues as if they were separate businesses. This segmentation helps the company to identify which products are profitable and also to enforce accountability in spending.

The IBU model typically leads to decreased communication and cooperation among development teams, which can result in a product or product line that is less consistent and usable. The most effective manner of combatting this problem is to implement a centralized user-centered design (UCD) organization that works across the IBUs to ensure that the product looks and works like a single product rather than a conglomeration of efforts.

Another reason for usability engineering is that vendor companies are moving to shorter development cycles in an attempt to remain competitive, which reduces the time available to correct design mistakes. If usability engineering methods aren't implemented from the beginning of the product development cycle, the product will most likely ship before significant improvements can be made.

Additionally, the members of a development team often change between release versions, so the lessons learned from a previous project aren't necessarily passed on to the follow-on project. The existence of a UCD team typically prevents this loss of usability information.

Computer companies also are becoming increasingly aware of litigation possibilities with repetitive-strain injuries (RSIs) and other sources of potential claims from customers. Although performing usability and ergonomic evaluations on products will not eliminate the possibility of litigation, it can reduce the likelihood of producing products that will cause RSIs.

Users Aren't Like the Developers

In the past, development teams found computers easier to design because the users of computers were people like themselves—people who were excited about computers. Now that millions of people use computers, usually as tools to get their jobs or activities done, computer users no longer resemble the development team. In addition to users being more varied in their backgrounds and their needs, companies are trying to capture increasingly larger segments of this varied population with a single product or product line. Usability engineering provides methods to obtain feedback from customers so that the products can meet their needs.

Usability is being touted as the buzzword of the nineties. There is increasing coverage in the press of consumer expectations of high usability in their products (Bond, 1992; Personal Computer Markets, 1993). Vendor companies' attempts at addressing the needs of such a varied population mandate that UCD be an integral part of the product development cycle.

Stages of Acceptance of User-Centered Design

The success of usability engineering depends in part on the receptivity of the product group. (Grudin [1991] has written an excellent review outlining many of the barriers that prevent effective incorporation of good design practices into organizations.) We have observed that organizations vary widely in their degree of understanding and acceptance of user-centered design (Dayton *et al.*, 1993). Those who are more accepting tend to also be more successful in developing useful and usable products. The following are four stages of acceptance that affect the cost-benefit ratio of performing usability engineering.

Stage 1: Skepticism

This stage typifies organizations that have never been involved with UCD. UCD is viewed with some skepticism because it is unclear what benefits it will bring. They fear that inclusion of usability testing will lengthen their product development cycle, causing them to miss their market window. They are very focused on the product features and its development schedule and are less concerned with the usability of the product. Meeting schedule deadlines gets rewarded over quality, user input, or collaboration with other groups.

If a UCD expert is involved at all, he or she is brought in late in the development cycle as a "consultant" with no real influence on the product. That is, the developers may listen to the evaluation of their product but feel they are under no obligation to follow the recommendations.

Stage 2: Curiosity

As organizations move beyond skepticism, they start to become curious about what UCD can offer. They recognize that their products need help and that they might not have the expertise (or perhaps the time) to devote to improving their products' usability. However, they don't quite understand what UI designers or usability engineers do and need some convincing before they are willing to commit money and resources. This group may be open-minded about the benefits of UCD, but needs to be educated about UI design and usability engineering.

In an effort to make their products more usable, management may bring just one UCD person into the project: a UI designer or a usability engineer or someone who is asked to fill both roles. This person has an opportunity to influence some of the overt characteristics of the product but may not be able to change some of the deeper problems that relate to the overall goals and features of the product. Moreover, some of the engineers are reluctant to give control over the design of the UI to someone who is not also implementing it.

Stage 3: Acceptance

The organization understands and relies on the involvement of one or more UCD people on the team. UCD people are part of the team from the beginning. Their role and expertise are well understood and appreciated as an important part of product development. There is a high degree of communication among members of the group.

There will often be more than one UCD person on the team, such as a UI designer, a usability engineer, and a graphic designer. Depending on the breadth of the projects, there may be an additional UI architect who oversees the higher-level conceptual and strategic issues.

Stage 4: Partnership

In this organization, the team is a seamless entity with a single clear product vision and purpose, a high level of communication, and a deeply held commitment to providing products that are not only more usable but also more useful. A lot of time is spent by everyone getting customer input early in the process and often throughout development. The UCD people are not only part of the team but are likely to be "driving" some or all of the project. The onus is on the UCD person to help create products that deliver needed functionality in a way that is simple and easy to use.

This type of partnership is often seen in an advanced-development group. This type of group is charged with exploring ideas for innovative products to a stage of advanced-prototype development, at which point ideas can be communicated to a product group.

Levels within the Organization

The various levels within a company—upper management, middle management, and individual contributors—may be at different stages. All three levels must be in either the acceptance or the partnership stage in order to have an efficient UCD organization that can make a significant difference in the products.

Grassroots Effort

Some companies have UCD champions only among some individual contributors and perhaps some middle management. In order to build the support for usability engineering in these companies, low-cost methods are typically all that can be employed. Preparing a presentation of the numerous benefits, especially those that reduce development costs and increase revenues (see the section on Benefits), is a good method for educating and raising awareness within the company.

In addition to providing education about the benefits of usability engineering, a real example can be very effective. A single project can be selected for performing an informal usability evaluation, such as a simplified thinking-aloud evaluation (see the section called Some Usability Methods). If no budget is available, friends or coworkers can be recruited as participants. To gain the most exposure for the results of the evaluation, a consumer-grade video camera can be used to tape the participants' interactions. Support for usability can build by circulating the videos and the results. If the video is intended to be used as a method to increase awareness, this should be discussed with the development team up-front to avoid any bruised egos.

High-Level Champion

If one or more people in upper management decide that usability engineering is warranted and that it should be funded, the cost justification is often not necessary in the beginning. (Although, since the authors know of no usability engineering groups that are sufficiently funded in companies, this cost justification may be useful after the group becomes established.) This decision by upper management may be prompted by the failure of a product in the marketplace, the loss of a major account due to an unusable product, a decision to change company goals and processes, or the hiring of a high-level executive from a company that already practices usability engineering.

With one or more high-level champions, typically funding is provided to staff a group and build one or more usability labs. The most ideal and cost-effective situation for performing usability engineering is with the backing of all levels of the organization. This enables the group to concentrate on performing the work, rather than spending time justifying necessary changes and convincing teams to implement them. The product teams have significant amounts of control over what is and isn't implemented. If the product team and the usability team share a common goal of creating useful and usable products (as seen in the *acceptance* and *partnership* stages), changes come easily to the product.

Without this understanding among individual contributors and middle management, even funding the usability group and labs isn't enough to improve product usability significantly. The usability team must spend time educating and convincing product teams about the need for and utility of usability engineering. One useful method for demonstrating the need is a usability performance test. The UCD group can design and prototype a new product design for a developing product based on usability and design principles. A usability performance evaluation (bringing representative users into the usability lab to perform specified tasks) can be used to compare the error rates, task-completion times, and other measures of both the original product design and the proposed new design. This type of usability evaluation provides quantitative evidence for demonstrating which components of the designs perform better with various measures.

Usability Engineering Methods

One of the most commonly asked questions in usability engineering is "What are the methods that provide the best cost-benefit ratio?". Although there is still no single answer to this question, a number of studies have helped to define a set of methods that are practical for use in product development and provide demonstrated benefits. Some methods are more beneficial to perform earlier in the development cycle, while others are more suited to perform later in the cycle.

Usability engineering is a young and developing field. Due to increasing awareness of its benefits, new methods are emerging every year, and existing methods are under constant revision. For this reason alone, one of the most important investments a company can make is in developing its employees' knowledge by encouraging participation in key associations and conferences, such as the Usability Professionals Association, ACM SIGCHI, and the Human Factors and Ergonomics Society. New studies emerge each year comparing the relative efficacies of myriad methods.

Usability engineering is most effective if brought in at the very beginning of the product development cycle, during the early definition or requirements phase. For new products, there is no investment in any particular design, and numerous possibilities can be explored at relatively little cost (see Figure 4.1). As design and functionality decisions are made, changes become more expensive to implement. Pressman (1992)

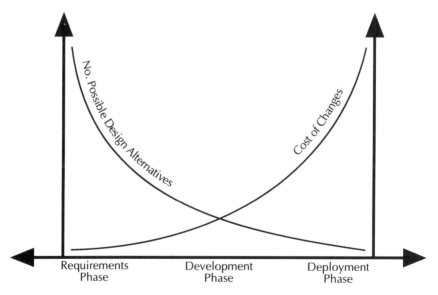

Figure 4.1. The number of possible designs decreases as the cost to make changes increases.

has cited the cost of change to be one unit in the definition phase, 1.5–6.0 units during the development phase, and 60–100 units after product release.

In addition, the usability methods that are typically used in the later phases of product development, when interactive prototypes or working software exist, are better at assessing learnability and usability, rather than usefulness and utility. These latter two characteristics are better assessed by performing customer field studies, surveys, and usability evaluations of comparable products. In a survey of 13 usability engineers, customer site-visit activities, including task analysis, were ranked as three of the top six highest-impact usability engineering methods (Nielsen, 1992b).

From this evidence, it would seem logical that most companies practicing usability engineering have significant resources and skills for implementing these early methods. This is typically not the case. The reasons for this are partially attributable to the origins and the age of the field of usability engineering. The types of methods and frequency with which they are used in companies reflect the development of the field.

The Evolution of Usability Engineering in Vendor Companies

In the past, although most companies utilized some marketing techniques, such as focus groups and surveys, in order to obtain some information about their customers, these techniques were not sufficient for guiding functionality and design decisions for product development. A few companies hired psychologists and/or human-factors professionals to try to improve their products. The methods that were first used in the field of usability engineering and are still in common practice were predominantly derived from methods used in experimental psychology. Techniques adapted from this field, such as those used in user-observation laboratory studies, are used to provide valuable data on learnability, memorability, error rates, ease of use, and subjective satisfaction.

One of the important features of usability engineering is that it concentrates on direct observation of users, rather than on the self-reporting techniques found in marketing. Because people are not accurate self-reporters, more valid information is derived from direct observation of what people actually do than from reports of what they think they do.

Companies utilized these techniques during the later stages in the development process and realized the benefits provided by performing the evaluations. These benefits included the discovery of usability problems and their severity levels so that the problems could be prioritized. However, the practical limitations of performing the evaluations on partially developed products became increasingly obvious. Users were interacting with products that already had many irreversible design decisions, and typically the company either had to slip the product-release date, release the product with the known problems, or some combination of the two. Unfortunately for customers, many companies still prioritize the ship date over solving the usability problems.

The answer to this problem is to use customer-input and evaluation techniques early in the development cycle. Some of these methods were derived from anthropology, sociology, psychology, and marketing. Many other methods have been developed in the increasingly prolific field of usability engineering. These methods are used to study the customers' backgrounds and needs, so that the acceptability and usefulness of the product is addressed in addition to its usability.

Although there are currently over 50 usability engineering methods and activities (Nielsen, 1992b; Muller et al., 1993), interestingly, most vendor companies perform a very small subset of the available methods. Some methods are very cumbersome and time-consuming and aren't found to be very practical in a product-development setting. Others are relatively new and lack sufficient study to demonstrate clear benefits over methods already in use. As in most fields, there is a lag time between demonstration of benefits in research and adoption into common use.

Currently, the most commonly utilized usability method in vendor companies is the laboratory *think-aloud* study, asking participants to perform representative tasks using a prototype or working version of the product, and talk out loud about what they are thinking and doing. Rohn (1993b) surveyed six vendor companies practicing usability methods, and, among the methods used in the companies, think-aloud studies were used 40%–100% of the time. Although this method provides invaluable data, it is typically used later in the development cycle, when the product is already partially developed.

In the 1990s, companies need to allocate more resources and invest in methods earlier in the development cycle. Methods such as customer field studies and product usability comparisons should be common practice. In the early conceptual design stage, numerous designs can be explored inexpensively, and design problems can be corrected before the product is released.

Some Usability Methods

This leads us back to the question of what types of methods will provide the necessary information in the most cost-effective manner. As mentioned earlier, performing studies early in the development cycle is highly cost-effective. Performing early studies is not sufficient, however, and a set of methods should be utilized throughout the development cycle (see Figure 4.2).

The various usability evaluation methods all have their strengths and weaknesses. There are many methods that involve observing and/or gathering feedback from users in order to provide design information. There are other methods that don't involve users, however. These are known as usability inspection methods (Mack and Nielsen, 1993) and are based on the fact that there is already an existing body of knowledge in the form of usability principles that can be used to evaluate products.

Although there isn't consensus on what methods are most efficacious, there is increasing evidence supporting the importance of using different types of methods when evaluating a single product (Desurvire et al., 1991, 1992; Jeffries and Desurvire, 1992; Nielsen, 1993). In planning the usability evaluations for a product through its development cycle, it is important to decide which methods to use and when, so that the resources can be allocated appropriately. These resources include staff, lab time, travel, equipment, skill sets, and infrastructure.

It is important to recognize that all of the methods can be scaled within a range, depending on the budget available. For this reason alone, giving exact dollar figures or declaring that one method is more expensive than another would be misleading. For instance, a customer field study could consist of one person visiting a customer workplace in the same town for a few hours. On the other hand, it could consist of four usability engineers traveling to three countries and performing studies over a five-week period. Implementing a low-budget evaluation is better than none, and implementing a higher-budget evaluation typically increases the validity and amount of the data.

Customer Field Studies

Customer field studies should be performed during the concept development stage to specify the product requirements. From the field studies, user profiles can be generated to reflect the background and characteristics of the target customers. Task analyses should be performed during the field studies to collect data on exactly what tasks are performed and

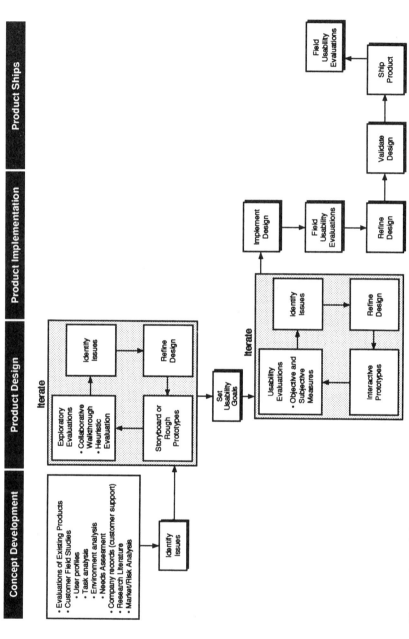

Figure 4.2 Usability engineering methods should be used throughout the development cycle. (Rohn, 1993c.)

84

in what sequence. The analysis of the environment provides a great deal of data about both the physical and the social contexts in which the product will be used. In addition, a needs assessment should be performed during the field study to provide data on what the current customers need and whether or not these needs are currently being met. The customer field studies should also be performed throughout the development cycle, with competitors' products, prototypes, early working versions of the product, and after the release of the product.

Product Usability Comparisons

Product usability comparisons should also be performed during the concept development stage. A great wealth of information that is comparatively inexpensive to obtain can be gleaned from other products with similar functionality. The customers of these products can be surveyed, interviewed, and observed to obtain feedback and usage data on these existing products. By both observing customers in the field and measuring their performance in the usability lab, a great deal of data can be obtained on what works and what doesn't work, and on absolute and relative performance measures. This method isn't effective for assessing innovative solutions or functionality, and it can also be inconvenient and expensive to acquire the necessary products. These expenses are negligible, however, when compared with the cost savings that these evaluations can produce by identifying, and thus not developing, unnecessary functionality.

Exploratory Studies

Simple and inexpensive prototypes or mock-ups provide a good basis for performing iterative evaluations early in the conceptual phase. Collaborative walkthroughs, which elicit feedback from customers on storyboards and other early prototypes, can provide a great deal of information without investing significant amounts of resources. The data collection and analysis in a collaborative walkthrough typically range from one to two weeks.

Heuristic Evaluations

Because products rarely receive sufficient iterations of evaluation and design, there are typically many areas that can be improved by applying usability principles, or heuristics, to the product. This is a very efficient method for identifying problems because it doesn't involve recruiting representative customers, although it does require three to five usability engineers to be very effective. The heuristic evaluation process used at one vendor company typically consumes between 52 to 64 employee-hours. Since the evaluators work in parallel, however, this process consumes only one calendar week (Hammontree, 1993). Given the high number of usability problems that this method typically uncovers, it ranks as one of the fastest and most efficient usability assessment techniques. This method should be combined with observations of real users, so that issues such as the severity of the impact on users can be assessed (Jeffries and Desurvire, 1992).

Laboratory Studies

As data are collected, the design can start to take on more specific directions, and both static and interactive prototypes can be evaluated in the usability laboratory. Subjective feedback should always be gathered through a questionnaire following the evaluation, and is often gathered throughout the evaluation by asking the participants to "think aloud," verbally expressing their thoughts, likes, dislikes, areas of confusion, etc. Other types of studies, such as performance studies to obtain quantitative data, are useful for gathering measures for tracking the usability goals.

When the product can be integrated with the rest of the system (hardware, software, documentation, and packaging), the context and interactions of the components should be tested by performing system evaluations. When the product has been redesigned, it should be tested again to ensure that the new design does improve upon or solve the problem. This validation testing is an important, and often missed, step.

Although laboratory studies range in their time and resource requirements, they typically take three to six calendar weeks to prepare and run the study and then to analyze and summarize the results. There is often more than just one usability engineer working on the study, including a lab coordinator to recruit and schedule the participants. Obtaining representative participants can often be difficult and time-consuming.

Longitudinal Field Studies

Laboratory evaluations are strongest at gathering data on a product's learnability and weakest at evaluating how the product performs as a customer becomes more proficient over time. Longitudinal field studies track customers interacting with the product over time, so that as a customer progresses from novice to intermediate or expert with the product, data can be gathered on actual ease of use. Because longitudinal studies by definition require longer time spans, they are often overlooked for methods that can produce more immediate results, even though the types of information produced are not equivalent.

These and other methods are used in vendor companies with varying frequencies and efficacies depending upon what resources are available, when the methods are implemented in the development cycle, and what level of support comes from the development team and management.

Costs

The total costs of performing usability engineering can be difficult to assess.[2] Unfortunately for those who wish to demonstrate the cost justification of usability engineering, the savings produced by usability engineering are even more difficult to assess (see the section on Benefits for some calculated savings). Another factor that contributes to the difficulty of cost-justifying the expenses for usability engineering is that the costs come out of the current budget, with depreciation costs for capital equipment coming regularly out of the next years' budgets. Even though today's costs can translate into exponential future savings, the lag time and the current imperfections in calculating the savings can make justifying the costs out of next month's budget more difficult. For instance, the UI technologies group at Ashton-Tate waited over 2.5 years before it saw any of its work released into the marketplace (Nakamura, 1990).

Nielsen (1993) surveyed the usability budgets of 31 development projects and found that the median usability budget was about 6% of the total budget, with the median number of person-years devoted to the project at about 1.5. These figures were less than what was deemed to be the ideal median budget relative to the total (10%) and the ideal median number of person-years (2.3). One survey (Usability Professionals Association, 1991) showed that a few companies have an annual operating budget for usability engineering of over $200,000.

Actual costs can vary greatly, depending on the importance of data validity, thoroughness, efficiency, and acceptance of the results (Rohn, 1994). Usability costs can range from a small expense of a cubicle or an office and the cost of the employee's time, to well over one million dollars for multiple high-quality labs, equipment, and employees. If a grassroots effort is being launched (see subsection called Grassroots Effort), typically not much money is available for equipment, tools, and recruit-

---

[2]Because companies sometimes desire confidentiality regarding investments and costs, some of the data contained in this chapter will appear without a reference.

ing representative participants. Under these circumstances, thoroughness, efficiency, and other benefits afforded by a substantial budget must sometimes take a lower priority in order to gain some of the benefits from performing low-budget usability engineering (Nielsen, 1993, 1994).

On the other hand, if usability engineering is ushered into a company by a high-level champion providing a budget and staff positions (see section on the High-Level Champion), the benefits afforded by usability labs and equipment can be achieved in the near-term. More money does not necessarily mean better results, however. A company that invested heavily in equipment and labs without investing in skilled usability engineers would not realize greater benefits than one spending less money on a few skilled employees and less equipment. In addition, there is typically a point at which the return-on-investment curve begins to plateau or fall, when the additional cost is no longer worth the additional benefit.

When estimating actual costs of performing usability engineering, there are initial costs and sustaining costs.

Initial Costs

The initial costs may include: construction of the lab facility, purchase and installation of video and audio equipment, tools, furniture, and the products, such as computers and software.

Products. A sometimes overlooked cost is that of the products themselves. Both internal products under development and external products for product usability comparisons (see section on Usability Methods) cost money. For example, creating a model for usability evaluations can cost thousands of dollars (but save hundreds of thousands of dollars). The cost of products ranges from virtually free to over $100,000, depending on the types and numbers of products being evaluated. For example, if unused computers within a company can be utilized, or if the company has an economical internal purchase policy, the cost for dedicated lab computers may not be significant. For those companies that can afford to purchase competitive products, these types of evaluations are highly beneficial.

Tools. Prototyping and data logging and analysis tools are also costs that are often overlooked. Software for prototyping enables designs to be evaluated in a shorter time frame than writing actual code, and the design is more easily altered. Some prototyping software even generates working code (with various degrees of success). Prototyping applications typically start at over $100.

A highly cost-effective tool is an observation logger, which enables the usability engineer to record the times and types of events that occurred during a usability evaluation. These logging tools, which are typically developed by companies for internal use, can save hundreds of thousands of dollars over time by making data analysis four to eight times more efficient (Hammontree, 1992). Some commercially available logging tools are beginning to be available and may prove to be economical for many companies.

A third category of tools is software that automatically logs what the participant does on a computer, such as keyboard input and mouse movements. This "keystroke logger" can be costly because it must be customized to the hardware platform and the operating system and thus is typically written for in-house use. In addition, unless the software is written with filters so that every event isn't recorded, the logs are typically cumbersome to analyze.

Lab Construction. A dedicated space is an important component to performing efficient usability evaluations. In 1990, Nakamura estimated that the number of usability labs numbered over 100, compared with fewer than 10 in 1985. When starting a usability lab with a limited budget, a single room or even a cubicle can suffice as a lab, with the observer sitting in the same room as the participant. This can work quite well, but does have the disadvantage of not enabling the development teams to watch the evaluations live.

Because this firsthand observation is one of the most effective ways to educate the teams about problems with the design and the benefits of performing usability engineering, most companies that can afford the cost have two rooms with a one-way mirror between them. Of six vendor companies surveyed, all but one had labs with one-way mirrors (Rohn, 1993b). The one-way mirror obviates the problem of the participant feeling reticent to critique the product or feeling intimidated by the presence of the developers in the same room. This also enables the usability engineer to take notes, control video equipment, and perform other tasks that might otherwise be distracting to the participant. In addition, the development team can watch and contribute valuable information to the usability engineer that couldn't be discussed in front of the participant.

Building usability labs can run anywhere from around $1,000 to hundreds of thousands of dollars, not including the cost of the video and audio equipment. Costs can include installing the one-way mirror, special lighting, video and audio equipment, special air conditioning and heating, and soundproofing the walls.

Video and Audio Equipment. Most groups choose to use video equipment to record the usability evaluations so that the sessions can be analyzed. Consumer-grade video equipment can be used to capture audio and gross movements and facial expressions. However, professional-quality equipment is necessary to capture clear screen images and subtle movements and facial expressions. There is typically quite a cost difference, however, and if the budget is under a few thousand dollars for video equipment, it is better to buy a few consumer-grade cameras and decks than to go without.

Several usability labs started with consumer-grade equipment and were able to upgrade as their impact on the products and the company grew. Of the six vendor companies surveyed, the equipment costs ranged from $1,000 to hundreds of thousands of dollars (Rohn, 1993b). If the budget is sufficient to purchase professional-quality video equipment, it is also a wise investment to consult a video expert about the complexities in selecting from the constantly changing technology available. The consultant can often save significant amounts of money by targeting the needs of the lab correctly, and often knows of new equipment that offers greater functionality at a cost savings.

Furniture. Furniture is another category that can vary greatly in cost. Furniture can range from being virtually free, by using existing furniture within the company, to costing tens of thousands of dollars, purchasing special ergonomic furniture that can be customized by each participant. For example, tables with adjustable heights, breakdown tables that store flat, and fully adjustable ergonomic chairs are all beneficial for performing usability evaluations if the budget is available.

Sustaining Costs

Like initial costs, sustaining costs can vary significantly depending on the need for timely and valid information. The sustaining costs may include employees, contractors, videotapes, recruitment of participants, compensation for participants, and upgrades to video and audio equipment, computer equipment, and software.

Employees. The most important investment that a company can make is hiring high-quality usability professionals. These individuals can perform cost-efficient usability evaluations not only by knowing which methods to perform and how and when, but also by knowing usability principles for performing usability inspection methods, such as heuristic evaluations. Nielsen (1992a) found there was a correlation between the number of usability problems discovered in the interface and the quality of the methodology used.

To obtain more accurate feedback on designs, usability professionals who can examine the project more objectively and who know how to design evaluations are required. Given the number of projects and the benefits that performing iterative testing provides, ideally a company should staff for full usability coverage of all projects. Because companies have not staffed usability engineers to cover their product development sufficiently (Nielsen, 1993), trade-offs typically must be made.

As an example, a company has 12 projects that will combine into four products to ship this year. Eight of the projects are deemed most critical, with the other four deemed as very important. Given the type of projects, the minimum number of usability evaluations on the most critical projects is decided to be at least four, and preferably more, before the release date. At least three usability evaluations, and preferably more, should be performed for each important project. Thus, the minimal number of evaluations would be: 8 critical projects × 4 evaluations = 32 evaluations, plus 4 important projects × 3 evaluations = 12 evaluations. The total then would be 44 evaluations of various types that need to be completed this year.

With studies typically lasting from a few days to six weeks, and the average study in the three- to four-week range, each usability engineer would be able to perform an average of ten usability evaluations per year, allowing time for vacation and a minimal amount of other work-related activities. This estimate also assumes that prototypes and products for evaluations are delivered on time, which they often aren't, and that evaluations don't overlap, which they often do. From these estimates, a minimum of four full-time usability engineers and a part-time contractor would be needed to evaluate the products. With more typical amounts of other work-related activities, a minimum of five full-time usability engineers would be warranted.

Contractors. Many companies rely on contractors in addition to full-time staff to perform evaluations. Of six vendor companies surveyed, four regularly used contractors (Rohn, 1993b). There are a number of reasons that full-time employees are typically the better solution. An employee can work on the same project over time, so that the learning curve doesn't have to be repeated for each iteration of testing. Because performing usability evaluations efficiently relies on knowing the company and group processes, the employees are already familiar with the processes, while contractors need to be educated about them. Another disadvantage of contractors is that they are often working on multiple projects for multiple companies, so their attention is divided and their turnaround time is longer. Three of the four companies surveyed that used contractors mentioned having high overhead in training, support, and management of the contractors. However, companies typically are able to hire contractors more easily and quickly than employees, so often necessity dictates the use of contractors. Contractors are also useful when the work overflow is sporadic and can sometimes act as a source of new methods or techniques.

Participants. Recruiting participants from outside the company who are representative of the target users is critical for providing valid data. Coworkers are influenced by company knowledge, technology, terminology, and motivation. Obtaining external participants who match the proper profiles is more expensive and time-consuming than obtaining coworkers as participants, however. Of the six companies surveyed, 40%–99% of the participants used were external (Rohn, 1993b).

Using representative customers as participants adds three costs: designing the screening questionnaire, recruiting, and compensating the participants. The usability engineer should work with marketing and product development to gain information about the types of customers who will be using the product, and design a questionnaire to be used for screening for users who have the desired profiles. Locating and screening users requires either the time of an employee, such as a lab coordinator, or the use of a market-research company or a temporary agency. This can be a very time-consuming process, especially if a database of users and their backgrounds is not readily available. Rohn (1993a) found that without the aid of an existing pool of participants, recruiting often consumed from one to six hours per participant, with an average of 3.4 hours, depending on the particular profiles warranted by the test. Outside agencies typically have more infrastructure and more leads for recruiting participants, but sometimes charge extremely high rates and fail to provide participants who match the requested profiles.

The compensation for external participants can be either monetary or gifts. Of 32 companies surveyed, 17 paid between $10 and $150 per test, with the average compensation being $60 per participant (Usability Professionals' Association, 1991). With many evaluations using between six and 12 participants, and with the average compensation of $60 per participant, $360–720 can be spent on participant compensation alone. Other companies give the participants gifts, ranging from T-shirts and mugs to software. Some companies will pay for transportation and expenses for the participants, including airfare and hotel.

Equipment, Supplies, and Upgrades. In addition to the typical office supplies that any project consumes, videotapes cost from around $2–20 per tape, depending on the format. Most companies don't use the more expensive formats, so that the tapes for a study will cost about $12 or more ($2 × 6 participants).

Because the field of computers is rapidly changing, along with other technologies, it is not uncommon to upgrade the computers, video equipment, and software used in the usability lab (see Chapter 11). Sometimes a single computer upgrade can necessitate an upgrade in software and video equipment. For example, if a computer monitor displays at a different rate than its predecessor, a piece of software used to produce a synchronized picture on the videotape may no longer work. In order to produce a readable image, either the software has to be rewritten, or video equipment that can be tuned to multiple scan rates may be warranted.

Benefits

Incorporating usability engineering into the product development cycle is a win–win situation for both the company and its customers. The company saves time and money by investing its resources more wisely and reducing the likelihood of cancelled projects. The company also benefits from increased sales and lower support costs. The customers clearly benefit by having a product that is both useful and usable.

Benefits to the Vendor Company

Increased Sales. Many vendor companies are seeing a benefit from usability engineering in their sales. Although it may not be possible to tally the exact number of sales that result from improving the usability of a product, companies hear about the relationship between usability and sales from their customers, analysts, and the press. One way to measure the impact of usability is by surveying customers to discover the reasons that they purchased the product.

For companies that are beginning to emphasize the importance of usability in their products, before-and-after sales projections can be used to assess the increased sales attributable to producing more usable products.

For instance, the same factors used to calculate the sales projections for a previous release, without the benefit of usability engineering, can be used to calculate the sales projections for the release with usability engineering. The difference between the sales projections for the new release and the actual sales can be used to estimate the sales due to creating more usable products. When this activity is combined with a survey for customer feedback on the reasons for purchasing the product, the estimates for sales due to increased usability becomes more concrete.

For example, in one company, 20 of the most serious usability problems were fixed in the second release of an application-generator product. The revenues for the second release grew by 80%. This revenue increase was 66% higher than sales projections. Although the role of usability engineering could not be proven, the field test customers repeatedly pointed to improved usability as one of the most significant changes in the product (Wixon and Jones, 1991).

The press and review articles are moving from functionality checklists to emphasizing the importance of product usability. Andersen (1990) found an average of 11.2 usability-related comments per software article. *Info World* assigns between 18% and 30% of its software review articles to three usability factors: ease of learning, ease of use, and quality of documentation, depending on the type of application being reviewed (Nielsen, 1993).

Whereas products in the past competed primarily on features or price, the usability of a product has become a significant selling point. Consider the following quotes from recent computer publications:

> In 1991, the competition among developers to introduce more features into their programs sparked the appearance of steroid-induced software applications: big, bulky, space-eating behemoths. Microsoft Corp.'s Word 2.0, for example, required 15M bytes of hard-disk space; Lotus Development Corp.'s Ami Pro 2.0 required 12.9M bytes. In 1992, though, developers concentrated on what users really want, and their chosen battleground was ease of use. . . . "The emphasis is not on bells and whistles, but on usability," said Ken Schiff, owner of Productivity Through Technology, [Inc.,] a consultancy in [Union City], Calif. "Software developers have discovered that they're not in the business of telling users how they must work." (Singh, 1992.)

> In response to usability studies, vendors of Windows word processors have gained a competitive edge over the past year by simplifying run-of-the-mill tasks such as mail merges. (Rooney and Ferranti, 1992.)

With the release of Quattro Pro for Windows and Excel 4.0, both expected sometime later this year, Borland International, Inc. and Microsoft Corp. will look to extend a technological lead over Lotus Development Corp.'s 1-2-3 for Windows. However, extra features may take a backseat to usability and ease of development, according to users and analysts. Users will be looking for common features that are easier to use and easier to train for. (Lindquist, 1992.)

"Ease of use is what we're concerned about," said Sheldon Laube, national director of information and technology at Price Waterhouse in New York. (Lindquist, 1992.)

Customers are becoming more particular about choosing products that are easier to learn and easier to use. Sales and marketing representatives from several companies believe that most people decide how usable a product is in less than an hour. Satisfied customers not only have brand loyalty and are much more likely to buy the same brand in the future with less researching of the particular product, but dissatisfied customers will be less likely to even consider a brand in the future even if marked improvements are incorporated into the new version or product. Customers also influence their friends and families. Internal corporate studies have varied in the numbers cited, but conservative estimates are that satisfied customers influence four other people to buy the same brand, and dissatisfied customers influence ten other people to avoid the brand.

To sell products in Europe, companies will have to meet European Community (EC) standards. EC has already passed a directive stating that, for all display screen workstations put into service in the EC, "software must be suitable for the task," "software must be easy to use," and "the principles of software ergonomics must be applied." Software companies will have to demonstrate through usability evaluations that their products meet these standards.

Reduced Support Costs. Customer support calls are very costly to the company. Estimates of the costs for a single support call range between $12 and $250, depending on the company. For a company with a low profit margin or a large customer base, a product that is not easily used or well explained can reduce profits by millions of dollars. For example, if a software package sells for $150 and a single support call costs $100, the company can lose money with the sale of that software.

There are numerous examples of how companies can save money by paying attention to even small usability issues before the product gets shipped. For instance, one company released a product that had confusing and misleading error messages. This one category of problems accounted for almost 40% of the support calls, which cost the company an average of $100 per call.

Microsoft, which tracks its support costs, knew that its customers were having difficulty with the print-merge feature on their Word for Windows product. This feature generated more calls to technical support than any other. Moreover, customers spent an average of 45 minutes talking to someone in technical support to get a satisfactory answer. As a result of usability testing and problem identification leading to a revised design, improvements were made to Word for Windows 2.0. The number of support calls dropped dramatically, resulting in a significant cost savings for Microsoft (Reed, 1992).

In another example, Ford Motor Company had developed an accounting system for their small car dealerships. In a usability study they found that the car dealers needed an average of three calls to the help line just to get started. The problem was discovered to be that the commands used to enter credits and debits were designed by the engineers without first consulting users to learn the commonly used abbreviations. As a result of the usability study, Ford changed not only the abbreviations but 90% of their accounting system. The new system was so easy to use that the calls to the help line dropped to zero. It was estimated that this new version saved the company $100,000. This one study more than compensated for the cost of $70,000 to set up the usability lab (Kitsuse, 1991).

Prioritized Product Features. Usability engineering can produce great cost savings for companies by helping to identify and prioritize the product requirements. By performing customer field studies, task analyses, and product usability comparisons, more informed decisions can be made about which features to implement. From these data, the features also can be prioritized by their importance to the customer. For instance, the UCD group that worked on NewWave 3.0 studied the tasks commonly done by their target users and how those customers learned about the tools for those tasks. As a result of these studies, the UCD group was able to recommend that the product be released with a single desktop instead of the dual file and program management strategy in Windows. They also recommended that users be able to use the features in an online help system while they were reading about them. Implementation of this recommendation resulted in a 40% reduction in the time spent revising documents (Nakamura, 1990).

In another example, Ricoh found that 95% of the respondents to a survey never used three key features deliberately added to the product to make it more appealing. Customers either didn't know these features existed, didn't know how to use them, or didn't understand them (Nussbaum and Neff, 1991).

Many of the recently added features in popular PC products are attributed to an emphasis on usability. Lotus, for example, responded to its customers by reducing the size of its Ami Pro product by two megabytes and adding features such as Fast Format which can instantly apply the formatting rules from one highlighted area to another (Singh, 1992).

Reduced Development Costs. The percentage of software code that is devoted to the UI has been rising over the years, with a recent average of 47%–60% of the code devoted to the interface (MacIntyre *et al.*, 1990). Because writing code is costly, reducing both unnecessary features and redesigns of features reduces development costs significantly. Similarly, the cost of redesigns of hardware foam-core models are insignificant compared with the cost of redesigns after the production tools have already been made.

Usability engineering not only addresses the usability aspects of the product, but also the utility and usefulness, providing the methods to gather these data so that knowledgeable decisions can be made. Thus, funding decisions can be made on actual data. With the benefit of these data, the prioritization of projects becomes more defined and easier to perform, reducing the likelihood that the projects will suffer from inconsistent funding. In addition, gathering customer data early and utilizing methods that provide accurate data result in fewer inappropriate design decisions. These problems would otherwise have to be corrected at great cost before releasing the product or not be corrected, resulting in a less successful product.

Most software projects significantly overrun their budget and schedule. Lederer and Prassad (1992) found that 63% of software projects exceeded their estimates, with the top four reasons all related to product usability: frequent requests for changes by users, overlooked tasks, users' lack of understanding of their own requirements, and insufficient user-analyst communication and understanding. From the authors' experiences, the figure of software projects exceeding their original estimates has been much closer to 100%. Many companies are gaining increased awareness that customer input is beneficial to their success, but don't have the processes or in-house skills to incorporate the data into project funding, definition, and design decisions. The implementation of usability engineering techniques have demonstrated reductions in the product development cycle by 33%–50% (Bosert, 1991).

Benefits to the Corporate Customer

Vendor companies often sell large quantities of their products to a single corporation, where an internal group such as an information systems group is responsible for training end users and providing support and general maintenance for the product. Because of this overhead, the cost of training and maintenance can play a significant role in the corporation's buying decisions.

It has recently been estimated that there is a "hidden" cost of supporting PCs of between $6,000 and $15,000 every year for every PC (Bulkeley, 1992). This cost is currently borne by PC "gurus" who help out their colleagues, and is considerably more than the $2000 to $6500 that is typically budgeted for the up-front cost of buying the PCs and networks and employing a support staff. While support organizations may be secretly relieved to have users look after each other, in practice it can become a prohibitive burden on their time for those who find themselves in the role of guru. If products were developed to be more usable and better documented in the first place, there would be less wasted time.

If the software were easier to learn, these peer-support costs would be significantly reduced. A study of MIS managers found that the training time for new users of a standard personal computer was 21 hours, whereas it was only 11 hours for users of a more usable computer (Diagnostic Research, 1990).

Benefits to the End User

Of course, the ultimate recipient of more usable products is the end user. A more usable product can result in higher productivity, reduced learning time, and greater satisfaction. In a study by Snyder (1991), 500 business professionals were asked to identify the characteristics of a computer system that are essential for satisfaction. The most frequently reported characteristic was ease of use. Users have refused to use a program because the manual was too big (Nielsen *et al.*, 1986). In addition, subjective satisfaction typically increases as error rates decrease. Although users are not aware of particular error rates with various products, they typically prefer the products with which they perform more successfully.

Cost-Benefit Trade-offs

In vendor companies, most cost-benefit trade-offs are not explicitly examined. Product teams are typically working against aggressive schedules to ship a product, and including yet another process can seem like a hindrance in meeting their schedule. If benefits can be provided to the teams without high costs, most teams will welcome the incorporation of usability engineering.

Usability vs. Release Date. A key to performing a successful usability evaluation is to identify problems so that they can be corrected before the product ships. If making the changes suggested by the study adds time to the development schedule such that deadlines are missed, then the product might miss an important market window, making it vulnerable to a loss in sales. This can happen if, for instance, the first usability study is done at a late stage of development and reveals fundamental problems that require changes to the architecture as well as feature changes. In this case, the team is faced with the choice of making the changes but delaying completion of the product, or making only a few changes but risking the usability of the product. It should also be noted that, from a design standpoint, it is undesirable to make major changes in the user interface late in development, because a change in one place can have major reverberations in other, often unpredictable places.

"Short and Sweet" vs. Comprehensive Evaluations. An area that has a significant effect on the cost-benefit ratio is selecting the appropriate method for the need. For instance, if the product team has two days to make a decision on a particular design detail, planning and implementing a comprehensive lab observation with 12 participants whose profiles match the target customers' will not help them. Performing a "short and sweet" evaluation with a handful of participants and producing results within the product team's time frame will help them.

On the other hand, the planned and comprehensive lab study may be necessary to evaluate some depth and/or breadth of the product. In addition to the extent of coverage of the product, the preparation time allows for the creation of a well-planned test design and the recruitment of representative participants. This type of study generates more comprehensive and usually more valid data.

If a project has never been exposed to UCD, the most cost-effective usability method to perform first is a usability inspection method, such as a heuristic evaluation, rather than starting with a user-observation evaluation. When usability engineers perform a heuristic evaluation first, known usability problems can be discovered and remedied before bringing in participants for a user-observation evaluation. This reduces the likelihood that participants will spend their time struggling with known usability problems, so that the study can concentrate on problems that are more difficult to predict.

How Much Time to Spend on Prototyping. In an effort to identify usability problems earlier in the development cycle, it is often desirable to develop a prototype that exhibits at least some of the behavior or characteristics of the eventual product. Prototypes have the advantage of being faster to create and easier to change than fully implemented code. But there may be hidden costs. In particular, the time spent creating the prototype, whether by a UI designer, a prototyper, a usability engineer, or some combination of these UCD experts, must be taken into account.

Depending upon the type of evaluation, the degree to which the prototype needs to emulate the product, and thus the time and costs to produce the prototype, may vary. For example, only a few of the product's features may need to be prototyped initially. Another method to reduce the time invested in prototyping is to create paper prototypes initially that can be designed and redesigned easily. Nielsen (1993) discusses many ways to reduce the investments in prototyping.

Whether to Create a Usability Lab. Although creating a usability lab does incur costs, if funds are available, the benefits in time savings and influence make it a worthwhile investment. These benefits fall into four categories: efficiency, data validity, internal influence, and external influence (Rohn, 1993d).

Dedicating equipment and space for a lab enables more tests to be run, since tests don't need to be scheduled around other groups, and time isn't spent reassembling the equipment. Investing in some video-editing equipment enables fast turnaround of highlights tapes with no studio fees. In addition, a dedicated lab with a data-logging system allows for much faster data analysis. All of these factors add up to greater efficiency.

To increase data validity, utilizing multiple cameras and direct screen capture enables better recording and more accurate interpretation of the results. The controlled environment reduces confounding variables, and the lab enables staged simulations to occur in order to evaluate specific scenarios. For example, problems can be intentionally introduced into the interaction so that the team can learn if or how participants recover from these types of problems.

A usability lab is also invaluable for influencing coworkers. The observation room with a one-way mirror allows the development team to witness the evaluations live. The team can quietly discuss the problems as they occur. In addition, highlights tapes can be circulated for greater distribution and more effective communication, and can be referenced for future versions of the same product and similar issues in other projects.

Usability labs are also important for influence outside of the company. Customers who participate have a better impression of the company from the professional appearance and efficiency of the lab. The funding of labs also lets the press and customers know that the company is making efforts to make their products more usable.

How Many Participants to Schedule. One of the most important factors when deciding on trade-offs is the number of participants to use in an evaluation. For each participant, there are incremental costs for recruiting, running the test, and analyzing the data. The challenge is to be able to find most of the usability problems with the fewest number of participants. In a study by Virzi (1990), 80% of the usability problems were found with four to five participants. It should be noted, however, that if the target customers are highly varied in their backgrounds, using four to five participants may not be sufficient. For these types of products, one approach is to segment the customer population into a few general categories, and then to recruit two to three participants per category.

Tips on Maximizing Effectiveness

There are many factors that affect the efficacy of usability engineering, including the resources allocated for performing the work, the stage in the development cycle that the usability work begins, the level of buy-in and teamwork from the organization, and the presence or absence of usability engineering in the formal product-development process.

Getting Buy-in

In addition to the time spent by usability engineers actually performing the usability evaluations to achieve UCD, significant time is also spent gaining acceptance and creating efficient processes. For smaller companies with less formal development processes, in which relationships are more important for getting work done than are formal processes, usability engineers need to spend time educating and building relationships with their colleagues, creating a team approach in order to effect change.

In larger organizations, the buy-in for usability engineering needs to be in all areas—upper management, middle management, and individual contributors—in addition to within formal processes in order to be highly efficient and effective. Even with significant buy-in, several hours per week are typically necessary in order to continue education and public relations so that changes continue to be implemented in an efficient manner.

A very common reaction by coworkers to usability engineering is that it is costly to perform, both in time and resources. Coworkers in the skeptical stage believe that it is an unnecessary and even frivolous cost. Those in the curious stage still believe that it is an additional cost, but are more likely to incorporate at least some evaluation into their product development because they recognize the benefit to their product.

Due to the history of how usability engineering has typically started in companies, this misconception is not surprising. Most often, some amount of money is spent on video equipment, space, and employee time. The next step after making this investment, however large or small, is typically a pressure to perform evaluations on those products that are most critical at that time, which usually translates into those products that are about to be shipped.

Common Pitfalls

One of the most common occurrences in companies is to perform usability evaluations on products that don't have enough time in the schedule to make many or sometimes even any of the changes warranted by the results of the evaluations. Because companies do not have sufficient resources to perform iterative usability evaluations on all of the products, and are often lucky if even one evaluation for the most critical products can occur before they are shipped, it is no wonder that the cost-benefit trade-offs of usability evaluations are questioned. The necessary changes to the products are not being incorporated because the ship date can't slip (or at least typically not for results from usability evaluations), so the potential improvements and resultant increased sales do not materialize.

The practice of performing usability evaluations on products that are close to shipping is often propagated because the next products about to ship become the next "critical" projects to test. Those products that are early in their development cycle and actually have time to incorporate iterative design and evaluations are often perceived as less critical and thus are often ignored until they are closer to shipping.

Working Effectively

Begin Usability Involvement Early. The effectiveness of usability engineering work is highly dependent upon the point at which it begins during a product's life cycle. Early involvement is critical, and it is also where most vendor companies fall short. The cost of change rises quickly as the number of possible designs diminishes rapidly. The cost of fixing problems in the maintenance phase is estimated to be 100 times more expensive than the cost of fixing problems in the design phase (Boehm, 1981; Pressman, 1992). These cost savings not only emphasize the importance of performing usability engineering, but also demonstrate the importance of incorporating the methods early into the product development cycle.

When usability is brought in late into the product development life cycle, as it often is, the changes that can be made are either very limited, very expensive, or both. The design is typically too far along to make significant changes, so early inappropriate design decisions often cannot be changed before the product is released. If usability is involved only during the later development stages, only incremental improvements typically can be made. Thus, the usability of the particular design concept can be improved, but that design concept may be inappropriate to the task.

Invest in Certain Projects. Companies typically do not have enough usability-engineering resources to evaluate their products sufficiently. A longstanding debate in the usability community is depth vs. breadth: whether to concentrate the limited resources on a few important projects or to invest fewer resources into a greater number of projects. One school of thought is that, by concentrating on a few projects, the usability group can then use those projects as examples of the benefits derived from performing usability engineering. Developing before-and-after comparisons will demonstrate the differences that usability engineering can make. This evidence can then possibly result in increased resources. Most usability groups, however, have a difficult time offering absolutely no assistance to a project and typically will attempt to perform at least some form of usability inspection method.

Work as a Team. Teamwork is one of the most critical aspects of being effective. Working as a team both within the UCD group and with the product-development community is imperative to achieving success. Teamwork within the UCD group is important to leverage the range of skills and experiences within the group. In addition, if members of the UCD group are not communicating and coordinated, they can sometimes give conflicting advice to development teams, lowering the teams' confidence in the UCD group. The advice then gives the appearance of being no more than one individual's opinion, which can be quite damaging to a group's credibility.

Working as a team with the product-development community is important for gathering information and obtaining buy-in. By eliciting opinions and information from the development team, better evaluations can be designed. In addition, when the developers are involved in the evaluation process, they are much more likely to accept and incorporate the changes warranted by the evaluation. Often, good interpersonal skills can assure more improvements in the product than many other techniques combined.

Create a Process. Process is key to practicing effective usability engineering in a vendor company. Product development cycles are shortening, and ensuring that usability evaluations are incorporated into the cycle in time to make changes is often a significant challenge. Without a common set of goals and expectations from all involved, even the best-designed of usability evaluations can quickly degrade into a problematic experience.

The following steps will help to create more efficient and successful usability evaluations and results (Rohn, 1993a, 1993d).

Schedule a project-planning meeting. Three factors to increase the efficiency of usability evaluations are: communicating clearly about the deliverables and expectations among all involved, obtaining acceptance from the team for the evaluation plan, and recording and publicizing the results. The first step to ensuring optimal use of resources is a project-planning meeting. All members of the product team who are involved should be invited and encouraged to participate, including representatives from software development, hardware development, documentation, product marketing, and interface design. Each person has his or her own area of expertise and can bring valuable information to the meeting. For example, the marketing representative can provide an idea of who the target customers are.

Equally important, when the team approach is taken, the implementors of the changes are much more likely to embrace the results of the evaluations, rather than being suspicious of them or feeling that their questions weren't answered. If questions aren't able to be addressed at the time, the usability engineer can make that explicit so that the team members are not disappointed when the results are presented. This meeting also helps to increase communication and ensure consistency across the various areas that constitute a product, such as software, documentation, online help, hardware, and packaging. Creating a team effort and eliciting input are critical to performing successful usability evaluations.

Set usability goals. Usability goals should be discussed in the project-planning meeting. The goals are beneficial for reaching a common understanding of which characteristics of the project are important, in addition to being useful for the measurement and tracking of improvements. Goals should be specific and measurable, consisting of the attribute (what is to be measured) and the method for measurement.

Goal levels are often difficult to set without comparative data from similar products. Thus, if software installation times are not known for other products, and the satisfaction levels of the users of these products are not known, then forming a goal level is often no better than a wild guess. It is much more useful to base goals on data. Once the comparative data are known, the team has a much better idea of the usability levels of other products. From these data, the best in each attribute becomes the gold standard.

Goals can be approached similar to software-bug reporting, with different priority levels corresponding to the goal's importance in relation to the product schedule. For instance, a goal for the minimal acceptable level to ship should be formulated, so that performance below this level would either slip the release date or warrant the investment of more resources to fix the problem. This minimal acceptable level should be realistic and achievable. If the current level is too far from the minimal acceptable level given the product schedule, this should be discussed as a team so that it is recognized up front that the problem is with unrealistic expectations, rather than the usability engineering process. The ideal level should surpass the current best level, so that the product has a clear goal. Measurable goals are also very useful to resolve differences of opinion.

Write a meeting memo for review. To save significant amounts of time due to miscommunication, an important follow-up to the product planning meeting is publishing all of the issues, priorities, and goals discussed in the meeting for review by all the attendees. Often people leave meetings with different interpretations of the discussions. A published record enables the team to address any misunderstandings immediately and provides a clear history of the project.

Write a test plan for review. Once the goals and priorities are agreed upon, the usability engineer should write a test plan, complete with schedules, deliverables, dependencies, and contingencies. The test plan should also demonstrate that sufficient time to make changes has been allotted. This record is key to setting clear expectations and reducing the likelihood of bad feelings when problems occur. For example, screening for participants who match a specific profile, convincing them to participate, and scheduling them are all time-intensive activities. Once participants have been scheduled, it is very unpleasant to have to change the dates because the prototype or product won't be ready on time. Calling each participant to see if they can come at a different time is not only time-consuming, it is also disrespectful of the participant's time and willingness to participate, and can result in negative feelings toward the company. To avoid this, there should be a "point-of-no-return" date for participant scheduling, guaranteeing that the test will proceed on the scheduled date. On the date of this "point of no return," the decision should be made whether to proceed as scheduled based on the status of the necessary deliverables. This prevents the test start date from continually slipping, making the process much more expensive than it needs to be.

Create an area for the development team to view tests. No method is more effective for conveying results than enabling the team to watch the studies live. The most powerful message a person can learn is from witnessing the events firsthand. In order to allow the development team to watch the tests without disturbing the test participant, either a one-way mirror must be used to separate the testing room from the viewing room, or the video from the cameras should be fed to a monitor in another room so that the team can watch on the monitor. If large numbers of people want to watch the studies, both methods can be employed, using an overflow room with a monitor for those who can't fit in the viewing room.

Also very effective is enabling the team to watch the videotapes of the studies at their convenience. It is important, however, to emphasize that if the observers are watching only one or a few sessions, what they see may not be representative of the results of the study, so they should treat the observation as a single data point. An additional benefit is derived from eliciting what the observers learned. The observers typically become usability-engineering converts, and also have a better expectation of the procedure for the next set of evaluations. The observers often become more sensitive to UCD and are more likely to produce more usable products in the future. This is very helpful when attempting a grassroots movement.

Create highlights videotapes for certain studies. Editing a videotape of examples of problems is also a very effective means of communicating the results of a study. A highlights videotape is effective not only across the various stages of acceptance, but also across product teams and job levels. The product team may have the time to see several of the test sessions and read the report, but may not be in a position to reallocate resources or make a significant change to the product.

Highlights videotapes show examples of multiple participants encountering the same difficulties with particular aspects of the product, and are quite powerful. These tapes are very effective for showing to executives who can make changes, and are also good publicity for UCD and good justification for the investment in video equipment and resources. For many groups, the acceptance and integration of results is higher with highlights videotapes than with statistical analyses in paper reports.

Give feedback within one day of test completion (Quick Findings). Because product development schedules are so tight, product teams need results "yesterday." To address this need without sacrificing the quality of the evaluations, the results of the evaluation that are known by the usability engineer before analyzing the data should be presented to the entire team within a day of completing the study. These results, or quick findings, include obvious and serious problems, such as frequent or high-impact problems. Trends can be discussed, with specifics deferred to the analysis of the data. This feedback gives the product team the red, yellow, or green light on various aspects of the product.

Write a report. Written reports are still essential for documenting and discussing the various results, possible solutions, and suggestions for follow-up evaluations to further explore certain areas. The report should contain a summary at the beginning describing the project and the results so that people not familiar with the project can benefit from the reading, even if they have limited time to do so. The written report is very important for documenting the design successes and failures, because the same issues are continually revisited throughout the years in product development.

Track the results. A critical step for measuring effectiveness is performing a follow-up with the development team to measure how many of the recommended changes were actually implemented. Letting the development team know at the beginning of the evaluation that a follow-up will occur makes them more receptive to the idea. They are also likely to be more conscientious about implementing changes if they know there will be an assessment. Performing this assessment also helps with the prioritization of projects. Because most usability teams have more projects than they can evaluate, a team who has incorporated many of the warranted changes from a previous usability study will most likely be prioritized over a team who, given similar circumstances, incorporated very few of the changes.

The follow-up is also an excellent opportunity to receive feedback from the development team about what works well and what doesn't for their purposes. The development schedule typically dictates when this follow-up should occur, often one to three months after completion of the evaluation. If only some of the changes can be incorporated due to tight schedules, a subsequent follow-up should occur to ensure that the remaining issues are addressed in the next version.

Summary

This chapter has concentrated on the issues involved in performing usability engineering within vendor companies. Depending upon the size and age of a company, the types of products that it produces, and the competition within its markets, the company already may be a supporter of usability engineering, or may not have discovered it yet. This chapter has discussed the origin of usability engineering efforts in companies, stages of acceptance, and many of the costs and benefits associated with usability engineering. With increasing economic pressures on companies, implementing usability engineering is more critical than ever for reducing development costs while producing products that meet the customers' needs.

References

Andersen, T. F. (1990). *Usability and Software Reviews.* Unpublished report in Danish. Computer Science Department, Technical University of Denmark. Reported in Nielsen, J. *Usability Engineering,* Academic Press, Boston, 1993.

Boehm, B. W. (1981). *Software Engineering Economics.* Prentice-Hall, Englewood Cliffs, New Jersey.

Bond, E. (1992). It's time to take your vendors to task. *Computerworld* (December 7).

Bosert, J. L. (1991). *Quality Functional Deployment: A Practitioner's Approach.* ASQC Quality Press, New York.

Bulkeley, W. M. (1992). Study finds hidden costs of computing. *The Wall Street Journal,* 2 November, B4.

Dayton, T., Barr, B., Burke, P. A., Cohill, A. M., Day, M. C., Dray, S., Ehrlich, K., Fitzsimmons, L. A., Henneman, R. L., Hornstein, S. B., Karat, J., Kliger, J., Löwgren, J., Rensch, J., Sellers, M., and Smith, M. R. (1993). Skills needed by user-centered design practitioners in real software development environments: Report on the CHI'92 workshop. *SIGCHI Bulletin* (July) 25(3), 16–31.

Desurvire, H. W., Kondziela, J. M., and Atwood, M. E. (1992). What is gained and lost when using evaluation methods other than empirical testing. In: *People and Computers VII* (Monk, A., Diaper, D., and Harrison, M. D., eds.), Cambridge University Press, Cambridge, UK, 89–102.

Desurvire, H. W., Lawrence, D., and Atwood, M. E. (1991). Empiricism vs. judgement: comparing user interface evaluation methods on a new telephone-based interface. *SIGCHI Bulletin* 23(4), 58–59.

Diagnostic Research (1990). Macintosh, MS-DOS, or Windows: A synopsis of what MIS managers and business computer users had to say.

Grudin, J. (1991). Systematic sources of suboptimal interface design in large product development organizations. *Human–Computer Interaction* 6, 147–196.

Hammontree, M. L. (1992). *Integrated Data Capture and Analysis Tools for Research and Testing on Graphical User Interfaces.* Presentation at CHI '92, Monterey, California.

Hammontree, M. L. (1993). *Usability Assessment Techniques in Use at Sun.* SunSoft Internal Publication, Mountain View, California.

Jeffries, R. and Desurvire, H. (1992). Usability testing vs. heuristic evaluation: Was there a contest? *SIGCHI Bulletin* (October) 24(4), 39–41.

Kitsuse, A. (1991). Why aren't computers... *Across the Board* (October) 28, 44–48.

Lederer, A. L, and Prassad, J. (1992). Nine management guidelines for better cost estimating. *Communications of the ACM* 35(2) (February), 51–59.

Lindquist, C. (1992). Ease of use may be strong suit of QP/Windows, Excel 4.0. *Computerworld* (3 Feb), 4.

MacIntyre, F., Estep, K. W., and Sieburth, J. M. (1990). Cost of user-friendly programming. *Journal of Forth Application and Research* 6(2), 103–115.

Mack, R. and Nielsen, J. (1993). Usability inspection methods: Report on a workshop held at CHI '92, Monterey, California, May 3–4, 1992. *SIGCHI Bulletin* (January) 25(1), 28–33.

Muller, M. J., Wildman, D. M, and White, E. A. (1993). Taxonomy of PD practices: A brief practitioner's guide. *Communications of the ACM* 6(4) (June), 26–27.

Nakamura, R. (1990). The X Factor. *Infoworld* (19 November), 51–55.

Nielsen, J. (1992a). Evaluating the thinking aloud technique for use by computer scientists. In: *Advances in Human–Computer Interaction.* (Hartson, H. R. and Hix, D. eds.) Ablex, Norwood, New Jersey, vol. 3, 69–82.

Nielsen, J. (1992b). The usability engineering life cycle. *IEEE Computer* 25(3) (March), 12–22.

Nielsen, J. (1993). *Usability Engineering.* Academic Press, Boston.

Nielsen, J. (1994). Guerilla HCI: Using discount usability engineering to penetrate the intimidation barrier. In: *Cost-Justifying Usability.* (Bias, R. G. and Mayhew, D. J., eds.), Academic Press, Boston.

Nielsen, J., Mack, R. L., Bergendorff, K. H., and Grischkowsky, N. L. (1986). Integrated software in the professional work environment: Evidence from questionnaires and interviews. *Proceedings of the ACM CHI '86 Conference*, Boston, Massachusetts, 13–17 April, 162–167.

Nussbaum, B. and Neff, R. (1991). I can't work this thing. *Business Week* (29 April), 58–66.

Personal Computer Markets (1993). Vendors should think more about user needs. *Personal Computer Markets* (February 11).

Pressman, R. S. (1992). *Software Engineering: A Practitioner's Approach*. McGraw-Hill, New York.

Reed, S. (1992). Who defines usability? You do! *PC/Computing* (Dec), 220–232.

Rohn, J. A. (1993a). *Resource Investments for Usability Engineering Methods*. SunSoft Internal Study, Mountain View, California.

Rohn, J. A. (1993b). *Survey of Usability Engineering in Computer Companies*. Unpublished study, SunSoft, Mountain View, California.

Rohn, J. A. (1993c). *Usability Engineering: Increasing Customer Satisfaction while Lowering Development Costs*. SunSoft, Mountain View, California.

Rohn, J. A. (1993d). *Benefits of Usability Labs*. SunSoft Internal Publication, Mountain View, California.

Rohn, J. A. (1994). The usability engineering centers at Sun Microsystems. *Behaviour & Information Technology* 13(1,2) (Jan–Feb), 25–35.

Rooney, P. and Ferranti, M. (1992). Windows newcomers emphasize usability, connectivity advances. *PC Week* (21 Dec), S/29.

Singh, J. (1992). Usability moves to the forefront. *PC Week* (28 Dec), 71.

Snyder, K. M. (1991). Reported characteristics of quality computer systems and usable computer systems. Unpublished IBM report. Reported in Snyder, K. M. *A Guide to Software Usability*. IBM, White Plains, New York.

Usability Professionals Association (1991). Unpublished survey results. Tec-Ed, Ann Arbor, Michigan.

Virzi, R. A. (1990). Streamlining the design process: Running fewer subjects. *Proceedings of the Human Factors Society 34th Annual Meeting* Orlando, Florida, October 8–12, **1**, 291–294.

Wixon, D. and Jones, S. (1991). Usability for fun and profit: A case study of the re-design of the VAX RALLY. *Proceedings Workshop on Human–Computer Interface Design: Success Cases, Emerging Methods and Real-World Context*. University of Colorado, 23–26 July.

Chapter 5

Human Factors Cost Justification for an Internal Development Project

Susan M. Dray

Dray & Associates
Minneapolis, Minnesota

Clare-Marie Karat

IBM TJ Watson Research Center
Hawthorne, New York

Introduction

As mentioned in previous chapters, cost justification of human factors is a powerful tool. Cost justification that is done for an internal development project is the same conceptually as that done for products, but can be focused more clearly on organizationally relevant variables (Karat, 1994). The trick is knowing what these variables should be and gathering background data needed to do the cost-benefit analysis (CBA).

This chapter discusses a case study in which a CBA was prepared for a project that included significant human factors activity. The case is an example of how one project incorporated these concepts. While it is a real case, details have been disguised in the interest of protecting proprietary information.

As this case study points out, there are real and quantifiable direct and indirect financial benefits to the corporation for the development and use of a usability-engineered system as compared with a system without human factors involvement (Dray, 1990; Karat, 1990).

In some organizations, it makes sense to use externally generated information about the value of usability engineering that originates outside the organization, such as that in published studies and books, because it may be perceived as more credible or reliable than that based on studies within the organization. In other companies, including the one presented here, internal data are given more credence and are more compelling. In The Company, an unnamed member of the Fortune 1000, internally generated data are considered to be valid, whereas external experience is viewed less positively. Therefore, in developing the rationale for funding the Help Desk Workstation (HDW) system, an unidentified system built for The Company, the team concentrated on identifying and gathering relevant internal data. In other organizations, this is sometimes reversed. In those cases, finding studies to support claims is a more effective way to garner support for a project. It is important to analyze and understand which method is most effective in a particular organizational setting.

Benefits can be categorized in a number of different areas, including reduced training and software development costs and employee turnover, and increased productivity, work quality, customer satisfaction and morale. (For more information on this, see Karat, 1994.) Each of these benefits can be powerful in different situations. The key analysis must focus on determining which variables are relevant for a CBA of a particular usability-engineered product. This can be assessed by evaluating company documents such as mission statements, value statements, corporate budgets, and strategic plans. In addition, it is important to listen to leaders' presentations both within and outside the company and to watch media releases. Understanding how the proposed product will help to achieve company goals, who the users are, and what the context of use will be are other determining factors.

This chapter will demonstrate how one project team in one company made the case to build an application based largely on the human factors benefits of the system. This approach worked well in this case, and the system was built and implemented successfully.

The Help Desk Background

The Help Desk in The Company serves customers and sales agents alike. It was established five years ago as a "first call for help" to provide information on products and business processes. Sales agents originate over

80% of the calls and often need information on their customers' accounts, as well as clarification of work procedures (such as how to fill out specific forms). Customers usually call for information about their specific accounts.

The Help Desk (HD) answers these questions, based on the on-line and paper information available to them. When they cannot answer the question, they transfer the call to another part of the company. Transferring a call to another person with expertise to answer a caller's question results in increased cost and is a source of dissatisfaction for callers who must wait, then restate their problem to a new person, wait again, and hope for an answer. Reducing call transfers, therefore, is a goal for the agents.

Computer System

The primary computer system that the HD agents used prior to the proposed system that we will discuss was the Client Tracking System (CTS), a mainframe system with a CICS front end built in the mid-1980s. It is based on a very powerful corporate database structure which provides enormous flexibility in data storage and retrieval. It is still the basis for the "engine" of the new system. There are several other systems that also use the same database and are interrelated. HD agents used most of these systems occasionally, but their primary system was CTS. At the time that CTS and the other mainframe systems were developed, there was little focus in the industry on the user interface (UI). With a CICS front end, indeed, the general assessment was that programmers had little flexibility in designing the user interface. Hence, the screens for these systems were derived directly from the database. The user of the system was not shielded from the complexity of the system.

The user interface was a significant problem as a result. It was a major source of delays in answering questions on the HD, particularly by new and less-experienced agents. Screen flows were difficult to remember and inefficient for many of the tasks that HD agents had to do in order to answer questions. The screens themselves did not follow even basic human factors principles for layout or terminology (Smith and Mosier, 1986; ISO, 1993). Instead, they used:

- *Coded screen names* (e.g., KP06 rather than customer information screen): These seemed random to the user and did not use mnemonics, increasing the memory burden for agents.

- *Inconsistent navigation:* Sometimes the agent had to press "enter" to move to the next screen, while at other times, this occurred automatically.
- *Inflexible flows:* Once in a navigation path, agents had to follow it through to the end.
- *Redundant data entry:* Sometimes information carried to subsequent screens, and sometimes it did not.
- *Inconsistent terminology:* Different terms were used for the same information (e.g., "client number" and "customer ID").
- *Cluttered formats:* Screens were extremely "busy," and logically related information was not placed contiguously. Irrelevant and extraneous fields caused confusion.
- *Ambiguous labels:* Many of the field labels were ambiguous, illogical, and/or inconsistent.
- *Vague instructions and help:* Messages were cryptic at best, misleading at worst.

Taken together, the CTS UI had significant room for improvement. Many of these interface issues were a result of the complexity of the database and the CICS screen technology. However, prior to the HDW system, resources were applied toward the symptoms rather than the causes of the usability problems.

Training

The difficulties with the UI resulted in significant training issues for the users of the system. CTS requires dedicated systems training and practice before it can be used. It is commonly asserted that it takes six months to learn the system to a reasonable level of proficiency. For the HD, this required the development of HD-specific training. Agents received two weeks of training when they were hired (primarily on CTS), and each agent then spent time paired with more seasoned agents to learn how to take calls. They did not take calls alone for six months and did not become "proficient" (considered fully qualified) for nine months. During this time, they were monitored by supervisors. The average tenure of the HD agent was just over 18 months.

Paper-Based Reference Materials

Much of the information that HD agents needed was updated regularly, in some cases daily. To deal with this ever-changing information, the HD agents kept paper files, affectionately called "the rack." This paper-based reference book was a foot thick and was individually tailored by the HD agents themselves.

The Help Desk Workstation

HD management was frustrated by these obstacles to quality customer service delivery. Extensive training on complex systems, the ever-increasing volumes of product and procedural information, and the difficulty of accessing it stood in the way of meeting customer service and satisfaction goals. In addition, turnover rates of HD agents soared, further exacerbating the difficulties. As a result of these problems, HD management began to look for solutions, including technology that could better support agents.

Business Analysis and Requirements Definition

Before proceeding, HD management and information systems (I/S) staff worked together to understand the HD business function in order to define requirements clearly and identify improvement opportunities. They made extensive use of measures to develop this understanding and provide a baseline against which to measure outcomes. This latter proved to be immensely valuable in providing information for the CBA.

Examples of measures the team completed include:

- Usability evaluation of existing CTS system use and work flows
- HD agent surveys and focus groups
- Call monitoring
- HD agent observation
- CTS screen flow analysis
- Transferred call tracking and cost analysis
- Evaluation of use of paper documentation
- Survey of sales agents (satisfaction, confidence, etc.)

At this point, it became clear that the key variables for the CBA for developing the new system were reduced costs for staff, transferred calls, and HD printing. Usability engineering was seen as a way to leverage the ability to address these issue areas. As a result, the project was user-driven, rather than technology-driven. This difference in project focus made the project relatively easier to implement, compared with the typical technology-driven project, and much easier to cost-justify.

Technology Review and System Design

Evaluation of the business requirements confirmed that two separate modules would be required. Because of the difficulties with information retrieval, an on-line text management system (called Help Desk Reference System or HDRS) and a graphical user interface (GUI) front end for the existing mainframe systems (called Help Desk Delivery System or HDDS) were proposed. Together these two systems were dubbed the Help Desk Workstation (HDW).

The HDRS is an on-line reference module offering an electronic form of the paper reference material. Product and procedural information is organized and presented in a meaningful, hierarchical structure that was designed by the HD personnel themselves (Gould and Lewis, 1985; Grudin, 1989).

The HDDS provides a GUI front end to the CTS system, allowing users to specify what data they need for a specific business function (such as verifying a sales agent's customers) and how they want to see the data. The long-term plan is to allow HD agents to update the database using the HDDS; this feature will be implemented in the future.

These systems had to be easy to learn and use in order to meet the high-level business goals of improving service and reducing costs. The team made a platform recommendation of a well-known system, based on the GUI and its development environment for the programmers.

Prototype Development and Iterative Design

The HDW project team developed prototypes and conducted iterative usability evaluations of functionality and interface elements. In addition, the I/S project team moved their offices to the HD, where they were in constant contact with HD agents and the context in which they performed their work (Whiteside, Bennett, and Holtzblatt, 1988). This resulted in significant interaction between them with positive impacts on design.

Once a functional prototype was developed, the team conducted formal usability evaluations in the usability lab. This lab followed the same format as the initial usability lab testing on the CTS system. This format consisted of a simulation where a HD supervisor placed mock calls to the evaluating agent, posing as sales agents or customers. The agent then answered the calls using the prototype system.

During the initial evaluation of the CTS system, new agents had struggled to answer questions, and the system appeared to be a major impediment to completing their tasks. In the usability lab evaluation of the prototype, both new and experienced agents were able to use the system quite well with little or no instruction.

Cost Justification

The HDW had been demonstrated in a prototype version, but the decision actually to build the application was a political one which required significant additional support. This project represented a major stake in the ground for a microcomputer platform. In addition, the hardware and software expense was significant because agents previously had only nonprogrammable ("dumb") terminals. The project team developed a CBA that was based largely on the value of the interface in reducing staff costs on the HD (training, supervision, etc.) and transferred call costs. This was a significant departure from previous CBAs in The Company. The cash flow analysis yielded a 32% internal rate of return (IRR). The 32% IRR is a very significant return on investment. Based on these data, the project was approved.

Illustration of the CBA can be made by examining the benefits of the project for the first year after implementation.

Reduced Training

There was a plan to hire 20 new agents in the coming year. The HDW team estimated that, with the combination of the HDW and improved training materials, the time required to train these new hires could be reduced by 35%.

Current: ($4,700/agent) × 20 new hires	$94,000
HDW: ($3,055/agent) × 20 new hires	$61,100
Average annual savings	$32,900

These savings come from:

- Less time spent learning the 250 different screens
- Less time learning differences in the screens
- Less time to memorize screen codes
- Less time required to learn navigation through the system
- Less trainer time to prepare and deliver training
- Less "buddy time" for experienced agents to coach new hires
- Less time updating paper-based reference materials

Reduced Information Organization Time

By eliminating the paper-based reference materials, the HDW team eliminated the labor cost of keeping these materials up to date. It took one-
half hour per week per person to do this task.

Current: ($6.00/week) × 50 weeks × 67 people	$20,100
HDW: eliminated cost	$ 0
Average annual savings	$20,100

By eliminating the paper-based reference materials, HDW estimated the
following savings:

Current: ($0.025/page) × 1500 page manual revisions (6 times/yr) × 67 agents	$15,075
HDW	$ 0
Average annual savings	$15,075

Reduced Supervisory Assistance and Inspection

HDW proposed reducing this by 30%. Average annual savings were
$76,400. These reductions come from reduced time to monitor new
agents and to answer questions from agents due to better support
materials.

Reduced Call Length

The HDW team estimated that agents would spend significantly less time
searching for information with the new system and what this would result in a savings of $148,250, based on the rate for full-time equivalents
(FTE) in this operation. In addition, the number of calls per agent was
expected to increase. This was partially derived from usability lab data.

>   Current: 12.8 FTE/1000 calls
>   78   calls/day/FTE
>   4.43 min/call
>
>   HDW: 11.52 FTE/1000 calls
>   86   calls/day/FTE
>   4.02 min/call

Elements contributing to this estimate included:

- less time trying to recall where things were filed
- eliminated time spent trying to find misfiled items

- less time on each call keying in screen codes and data
- less time jumping between screens
- less time caught in a "flow"

Reduced Transferred Call Costs

Calls were frequently transferred because agents were unable to locate necessary information fast enough. If it takes too long to find information, agents usually transfer a call to avoid having the caller on hold for very long. The longer a caller is on hold, the higher the abandon rate and caller dissatisfaction.

For the HD, callers typically call in on an in-WATS line, and call charges continue to accrue to the HD after transfer until the call is completed. Callers who are transferred have higher dissatisfaction rates because they must repeat the description of the problem, typically after being on hold waiting for the transfer to go through. The agent receiving the transfer typically must also retrieve data, adding to the length of the call. It is therefore important to reduce call transfers as much as possible both to provide better customer service and reduce WATS charges.

Current: transfer rate of 40% @ $0.989/call
Completion rate of 60% @ $0.351/call
Total transfer costs $410,348

HDW: transfer rate of 25% @ $0.989/call
Completion rate of 75% @ $0.351/call
Total transfer costs $345,345

Savings for the first year (postimplementation) $65,003

In addition, the HDW estimated savings to other areas receiving transfers amounting to an additional $997,565 for the first year after implementation. No further detailed information is available on this savings estimate because it was considered to be of a strategic competitive nature.

Calculation of Project IRR and Go–No Go Decision

The system was fully implemented at the end of year 2. Based on the analysis of the average annual savings above, the total average annual pretax operating benefits to the organization for the project were:

Training	$32,900
Organization	20,100
Printing	15,075

Supervision	76,400
Call length	148,250
Transferred calls (HD)	65,003
Transferred calls (other)	997,565
Total	**$1,355,293**

Adjusting for taxes and inflation, the total annual operating benefits over the estimated life of the project (eight years) range from $345,000 in year 2 to $1,321,000 in year 8, as shown in Table 5.1. The total after-tax operating benefits over the estimated life of the project are $6,868,000. Noncash benefits in the form of depreciation are listed for relevant years.

Total project costs, including new development costs, hardware purchase, and maintenance over the eight years of the project, are estimated at $3,561,000 (capital expense and system development in Table 5.1). Itemized costs for each of the eight years are detailed in Table 5.1.

For each year, the net benefit or cost of the project was multiplied by the present value interest factor (PVIF) for the respective year to calculate the IRR. (See Chapter 3 for a more detailed explanation and example of the calculation of an IRR.) The calculation of the IRR for the expected project costs and benefits was 32%.

An IRR of 32% is an exceptionally high return on investment. In most situations, this would warrant a decision to proceed with the project. This was indeed the case in The Company.

Summary

The HDW project was the first at The Company to quantify benefits from reduced training and other UI-related issues in a CBA. The response was largely positive, and the project was ultimately approved.

Today, the HD has implemented the HDW and has realized significant benefits from it. The HD Manager reports significantly reduced turnover, improved caller and agent satisfaction, and an ability to handle significantly increased call volumes without adding staff. The HDW has been adapted for use in other areas of the company and is being considered for use by the sales agents.

While this type of CBA may not be appropriate in all cases, it is increasingly valid where reductions in costs traditionally labeled as "soft" are the primary benefits of the system. Human factors expertise can be extremely important in quantifying these benefits and presenting a coherent CBA to management. Human factors can become part of the criti-

Table 5.1 HDW project proposal CBA summary

(In thousands of dollars)	Year 0	Year 1	Year 2	Year 3	Year 4	Year 5	Year 6	Year 7	Year 8
					Time in Years				
Capital expenditure, net cash effect	(420)								
System development, net cash effect	(445)	(529)	(730)	(339)	(152)	(152)	(198)	(429)	(587)
Annual operating benefits, net cash effect			345	518	1087	1141	1198	1258	1321
Noncash benefits, net cash effect		29	46	27	16	16	8		
Total after-tax cash in (out)	(445)	(500)	(339)	146	951	1006	1008	829	734
Multiply PVIF * IRR @ 32%	1.0	0.76	0.57	0.43	0.33	0.25	0.19	0.14	0.11
Equals	(445)	+ (380)	+ (193)	+ 63	+ 314	+ 252	+ 191	+ 116	+ 81 = 0

Summary: IRR = 32%

cal development path and a significant team player in organizations by communicating the value of usability engineering in terms relevant to larger organizational goals.

References

Dray, S. M. (1990). Cost-justifying human factors support. In: *Proceedings of 34th Annual Meeting of the Human Factors Society*. Orlando, Florida, 832–833.

Gould, J. D., and Lewis, C. (1985). Designing for usability: Key principles and what designers think. *Communications of the ACM* **28**, 300–311.

Grudin, J. and Poltrock, S. E. (1989). User interface design in large corporations: Coordination and communication across disciplines. In: *Proceedings of CHI'89*. (Austin, Texas, April 30-May 4). ACM, New York, 197–203.

International Standards Organization (1993). *Working Paper of ISO 9241 Part 10, Dialogue Principles, Version 2*. ISO/TC 159/SC4/WG5/N155.

Karat, C.-M. (1990). Cost benefit analysis of usability engineering techniques. In: *Proceedings of 34th Annual Meeting of the Human Factors Society*. Orlando, Florida, 839–843.

Karat, C.-M. (1994). A business case approach to usability cost justifcation. In: *Cost-Justifying Usability* (Bias, R. G. and Mayhew, D. J., eds.). Academic Press, Boston, 45–70.

Smith, S. L. and Mosier, J. N. (1986). *Guidelines for Designing User Interface Software*. (Technical Report NTIS No. A177 198). USAF Electronic Systems Division, Hanscom Air Force Base, Massachusetts.

Whiteside, J., Bennett, J., and Holtzblatt, K. (1988). Usability engineering: Our experience and evolution. In: *Handbook of Human–Computer Interaction* (Helander, M., ed.). Elsevier, Amsterdam, 791–817.

Chapter 6

Cost-Justifying Usability in a Contractor Company

Charles L. Mauro

Mauro and Mauro Design
New York, New York

Introduction

To those who practice human factors engineering on a consulting basis, this book represents an opportunity to put into a formal context that which we know to be self-evident: improving usability at any level is a benefit. However, not everyone in industry is so enlightened. This lack of insight is not the fault of industry but more a function of poor market penetration on the part of the human factors engineering service provider. It is constantly a surprise to me that clients "discover" human factors engineering and the associated benefits of improved usability by oblique and chance encounters. In many cases, corporations and government agencies have little or no knowledge of what constitutes a usability problem and, furthermore, have even less knowledge of how to solve such problems.

Certainly the Human Factors and Ergonomics Society has helped get the message out, as has the Industrial Designers Society of America and other affiliated professional organizations. Unfortunately, these efforts have, for the most part, not reached into the core of new product development programs, business schools, software engineering programs, or other critical development entry points. At a series of yearly lectures given at a leading MBA program, less than 5% of the students had any prior knowledge of human factors engineering as a viable discipline for solving critical business problems. The net effect is that most products under development today will not have the benefit of professional usability design, testing, and certification. The overall net loss to industry is literally in the hundreds of billions of dollars. Consider, for example, the following categories of costs that could be directly and measurably reduced (by billions of dollars each) by improved usability:

- Training costs
- System/operator-induced errors
- Service and maintenance costs
- Workplace injuries and lost time
- Waste and loss of energy due to poor decision making in process control applications
- Employee turnover
- Product development costs and better user acceptance
- Product concepts that have serious usability problems
- Long lead times for new product development
- Product liability costs and associated insurance

The cost to the world economy is beyond accurate estimate. The benefits of enhanced usability to our culture and society are so large that they must be seen as central to the advancement of humanity over the next century. These are very big problems with even larger benefits if they are solved in a comprehensive manner.

In an independent consulting firm that focuses on usability problems, the need to cost-justify its services is the key to survival and success. Even corporations who retain such services are slow to recognize usability as a problem central to their concerns. In fact, most clients seek assistance as a result of a serious problem and rarely because of an enlightened product development process.

Defining the Usability Problem

Many clients in the military sector are forced to seek usability design and testing based on standardized requirements and development methods. This captive market has led to the development of a few large consulting firms specializing in military applications. Many of these firms are currently being forced to seek contracts in the private sector where they are finding cost justification a very difficult and complex problem. Often the objectives of the commercial client and the resulting usability engineering methods appropriate for that client are dramatically different from those relevant in military applications. In fact, in most military applications, the problems and objectives arrive on the desk of the human factors or usability team predefined. This is certainly not the case with commercial clients that believe they may have usability problems. In the highest percentage of cases, these clients have at best a fuzzy concept of the problem.

For example, commercial clients typically offer statements such as: "Users are complaining that our manuals are too hard to read" or "our insurance company increased our premiums 300%" or "our 800 support calls are increasing dramatically "or "customers of our newest product are complaining that the old version worked better." All of these are common problems. However, none of them tell the usability team what the real problem is or how to determine the cost, let alone the cost-benefit of solving the problem.

Other common reasons for seeking assistance include: "Our competitor just introduced a new ergonomic design," or "we are changing our interface over to an MS Windows-based system; can you take a quick look at it?". On a more expansive level, some clients have identified improved usability as a key attribute of a new system. In these cases, clients want to define the cost and methods for integrating usability design, testing, and certification into their product development process. These clients fall loosely into a category called "enlightened." This means simply that they are aware of the general benefits of improved usability as a marketable product concept. These clients are generally seeking assistance in usability design, testing, and certification, as well as support for how to integrate usability into their product development process. In all cases, the cost-benefit of solving the usability problems is impossible to determine before careful definition of the problem. If you are seeking assistance with a usability problem, it is critical that you allow the usability team to define the problem before determining the cost benefit. This is a point of special caution that, if ignored, can lead to serious budgetary miscalculations. These miscalculations may involve overestimating or underestimating the fees and benefits involved.

Case Studies from Twenty Years' Experience

Manufacturers seek assistance in the resolution of usability problems for a variety of reasons that appear obvious to them at the time they request help. However, experience has shown that most clients do not have a clear understanding of the scope of their existing problems or the fact that other problems may exist, of which they are not aware. One of the most important contributions that a comprehensive user-centered design process can bring to product development is demonstrating the wide impact that improved usability can have on the financial health of the corporation. The usability consultant is often faced with the problem of determining the exact nature of the client's problems by seeking information in areas not commonly linked in the product development process. By systematically exploring a few key topics, it is generally possible to define within useful limits both the nature and scope of the client's usability problems. The following concerns commonly lead the usability team to establish a comprehensive overview of the problems to be addressed:

Liability
Service and maintenance costs
Customer complaints
Increased complexity in new products
Market competition

Liability

In the early 1960s, after a series of legal precedents, the U.S. courts became pro-plaintiff on issues related to product safety. For the first time, plaintiffs were allowed to attack the design decision-making process of manufacturers. The concept of "design for reasonable use and misuse" became the leading conceptual framework for determining a manufacturers ability to meet the user's needs. Under the legal construct of strict product liability, the courts allowed usability to take center stage in the determination of legal liability. As a result, the bar, both plaintiff and defense, focused on usability as a driving force in litigation. Lawyers immediately understood the importance of well-documented and presented explanations of usability.

In many cases, manufacturers had very poor defense against claims of defective design based on usability. Often, products involved in these claims had never been designed, tested, or certified for usability. At best, these products may have been reviewed by a safety committee for compliance with existing safety standards and regulations. As any corporate counsel now knows, compliance with industry standards is only one test that the product will face in the courtroom. The legal system holds manufacturers to a far higher standard when the question of usability is at hand. In many cases, the requirement for the manufacturer to "design for reasonable use and misuse" is the overriding requirement. Disproving such a claim is complex and difficult if the product has not been created with professional usability methods that will stand up under cross-examination.

As a result, plaintiffs' attorneys have often retained the expertise of professional human factors engineers to evaluate the usability of the product. These evaluations often proved devastating and provided the jury with tangible information and analysis on how the product should have been designed for usability. This sort of reverse engineering was often the first time that manufacturers had been exposed to human factors engineering. In cases where design for usability has been a formal part of the development process, manufacturers have a much better chance to reduce the size of claims, if not win outright. The cost-benefit of this approach is staggering.

The Costs. Cases involving serious injury or damage resulting from claims of defective design will cost a minimum of one million dollars to bring to trial. These costs include legal fees, experts, discovery, documentation, and more. This first million does not cover the cost of person-hours for corporate staff preparing to testify, producing documents, meeting with counsel, and expenses for travel, etc. In a complex case, these costs may easily exceed the original one million dollar estimate. Add to the previous losses in legal fees and corporate person-hours the long-term effect of not having management, engineering, and design staff working on critical new product development projects, but instead working to support litigation. This last cost has a direct impact on return on investment (ROI) and may be the largest expense affecting the long-term health of the corporation.

Such costs are difficult to predict. Taken together, these three sources of costs may easily total three million dollars as a minimum. And they are not the full story. Many cases go far beyond this amount. Jury awards are added to litigation costs. Other punitive damages may also apply. Even in the case of high fees, costly internal expenses, and a sizable jury award, the problem is not over. When a product is found defective by design, a whole new issue arises: repeat litigation. Certain products have actually spawned entire industries of attorneys, experts, and documentation specialists. The cost to the corporation in these cases is enormous since they must self-insure after a certain point and may have to carry the cost of litigation themselves.

The cost-benefit of designing for usability is so overwhelming when seen from this perspective that it is hard to imagine why more corporations do not adopt a comprehensive program for addressing the usability problem. The answer probably lies in the accounting and budgeting methods of corporations. Of all the costs just discussed, only one shows up as a line-item expense: insurance premiums. All other costs are either not documented, paid out of reserve accounts, or channeled through corporate legal expenses which often do not have strict reporting or budgeting requirements. As a result, many corporations never see the true cost of litigation. If they did, they would be shocked, as would their shareholders. By comparison, the cost of a thorough usability design program for a product would be at worst only a small fraction of the cost of even a normal litigation proceeding. In many cases, corporations could easily hire a top-quality human factors staff, construct a testing lab, rewrite their product development procedures, and educate their product development managers for a small fraction of the potential cost of litigation. The long-term benefit of ROI would be hard to equal in any other area of corporate development.

The Benefits. Certainly, there is no absolute guarantee that designing for better usability will dramatically reduce litigation costs, but the probability that it will is very high. For example, plaintiffs' attorneys always assess the strength of a defendant based on what they discover by way of formal test results, design alternative documentation, and the background of those responsible for usability design and testing. It is hard to imagine that a plaintiff's attorney would push to trial knowing that a corporation had employed professional usability engineering methods in the design of their products. They would certainly look for an easier case that would involve less costly opposing experts and easier evaluation of the product. In this way, usability becomes a litigation deterrent and a source for improving the safety of the product. Both of these factors mean a very large potential savings for the corporation.

Service and Maintenance Costs

It is estimated that a typical call to a software support line costs the manufacturer between $4.00 and $10.00 per call. This cost includes the salary and benefits of the employees, facilities, insurance, computers, training and updating, and maintaining the customer database, user registration cards and correspondence, telephones, and more. Furthermore, once customers call a first time, they will be much more likely to become repeat or, worst of all, frequent callers. The cost of these seemingly necessary calls can drive the profitability of a product down so far that it is impossible to break even on development costs, let alone show a profit.

With the wide proliferation of user support lines, these costs are becoming increasingly critical to the long-term success of software and hardware manufacturers. In many cases, the use of customer support lines could be reduced dramatically by designing the software from the beginning for better usability. It is often possible for software under development to be subjected to usability evaluation before it reaches the alpha or beta testing so that critical incidents can be identified and reduced or eliminated. The net effect on profitability can be significant.

In the simplest case, it is possible to conduct a critical incident analysis of the software for the specific purpose of identifying usability problems that can lead the user to make that first, important call. Such a study can be highly cost effective when viewed against the cost of customer service calls. This type of usability study does not strive to identify in a comprehensive manner all aspects of the user interface that can be improved. Instead, the purpose of this type of usability study is to identify in as direct a manner as possible the *critical* problems that can lead to overuse or misuse of the customer support lines. Often, the human factors consultant must recommend this approach based on the clients lead-time constraints, budgets, and overall product development objectives.

Case Study: The Case of the Problem Printer Driver. A leading manufacturer of printers released a product that had only one serious usability problem. The difficulty was present in the installation and operation of the printer driver software. However, this problem was so difficult to solve that over 50% of the first 100,000 users called the customer service line. The cost was nearly a half a million dollars *per month*. The secondary and equally important problem was the poor reputation created for the manufacturer due to overburdened phone systems. Many users had to call over several days to reach a customer service person. The manufacturer was also forced to correct the problem by sending the customers new diskettes with a letter of apology at a cost of $3.00 each. By this time, the distribution of the printer was well in excess of 200,000 units.

The total cost of replacing the printer drivers was $900,000. It was very clear upon analysis that the problem could have been identified and corrected at a fraction of the cost if the product had been subjected to even the simplest of usability testing. It is interesting that the printer's usability was originally tested internally by the engineering group responsible for development of the product; of course, they did not have a problem with the driver software.

Increasingly, manufacturers are discovering the benefits of reduced service and maintenance costs brought about by improved usability. However, in many cases, manufacturers and developers are not aware that service and maintenance costs can be reduced dramatically by improved usability. It is critically important that the usability team seek detailed information on the client's service and maintenance records before attempting to identify the scope of the problem or propose methods or budgets. Waiting to identify usability problems by monitoring customer support calls is like fixing a leak in the hull of a boat that has already sunk. Once the product is in the hands of the user, the cost of fixing the problem will always exceed the cost of a comprehensive usability design and verification program.

Customer Complaints

Manufacturers of most products maintain a file of customer complaints. Some files are very comprehensive; others are quite informal. The identification of usability problems should always include a review of customer complaints. Occasionally, manufacturers will seek assistance in resolving usability problems based on these types of complaints. In these cases, the usability problems are generally so overwhelming that complaints are a small part of the problem. The most interesting aspect of customer complaints is that they are nearly impossible to measure in conventional terms. The cost to the corporation is qualitative and indirect, showing up in terms of low repeat customer ratios, poor peer recommendations, and generally poor customer relations. These factors have their greatest impact on the long-term profitability of the corporation. Rarely are there any mechanisms set up to measure these variables in a manner that is useful to product management.

The general assumption is that customers' complaints are a problem to be dealt with by replacing the product or making an occasional follow-up call. In cases where the product has in some manner failed mechanically or is otherwise defective in operational terms, this approach is acceptable. However, it is very rare for a manufacturer to receive a customer complaint that focuses on usability. Most consumers will not file a complaint on poor usability. The reasons for this are subject to much debate. However, it is clear that customers do not yet return products because they are difficult to use, but that trend may not continue forever as consumers become generally aware that products do not have to be so difficult to use or maintain.

Case Study: The Case of the Digital Watch under the Couch. A leading manufacturer of digital watches produced and sold a watch that was so difficult to operate that the end user perceived it as a mechanical failure. When faced with the possibility of changing the watch's time, the user was referred to a miniature operator's manual of some 30 pages. The task was so complex and procedure-specific that most users could not change the time on their watches even after persisting for more than 15 minutes, using the manual as support. When faced with the task of setting the alarm function, they had a similar experience. In a study conducted to identify usability problems, respondents stated that they simply could not set the alarm or, more importantly, turn it off when it rang. In several cases, respondents stated that they actually put the watch under the living room couch cushions so that it would not wake them up when it went off at night. They could not reliably set the alarm or manage its operation.

The manufacture did receive a significant number of watches back with claims that they were broken. However, when the watches were tested, they were operationally sound. This is clearly an extreme case of poor usability design. However, it does demonstrate that users must often be driven by poor usability design to the point of believing that the product is actually mechanically defective before they will log a customer complaint or return the product for refund or repair.

Usability problems of this magnitude will usually kill a product and sometimes its manufacturer within one or two product life cycles. This product went to market without any usability testing except that undertaken by the product development team itself. The general rule in human factors engineering is that if usability problems are being mentioned in customer complaints then the problems are probably very serious. Examination of customer complaints can be a useful means of identifying critical usability problems. However, they oftentimes can be and are deceptive.

While the benefit of reduced customer complaints seems self-evident, the real message here is that manufacturers should never refer to a lack of customer complaints related to usability as a measure of the quality of their product's user interface. Furthermore, if customer complaints do begin to show up, manufacturers should pay attention and act immediately to identify problems through the use of human factors testing. If they don't act, the next correspondence they receive may be from a plaintiff's attorney. They can also expect the sales of the product to drop precipitously as customers approach the phase of secondary purchase decisions. In markets where peer recommendations are a critical factor in purchase decisions, problems of this scale will kill a product unimaginably faster.

It is the responsibility of the human factors consultant to identify and analyze problems for the client by examining customer complaints. Clearly, this should never be the only criterion reviewed to determine usability problems, but only one of several defined in this and other chapters in this book.

Increased Complexity in New Products

Increasing product complexity is a very real predictor of usability problems that the human factors consultant must examine if they are to provide the client with critical support in developing an effective usability policy for new product development. Increasing complexity is rarely understood by the development team as they upgrade software packages or create new products. In many instances, the product development team is too close to the software to realize how seemingly minor changes in operational structure combined with new features affect users' ability to use the product effectively.

A critical component in identifying the scope and nature of the complexity problem is examining in detail the product's previous generation while reviewing the proposed new user interface. This is an especially critical issue for products that have a large installed user base or are adding significant new features. In the event that the product meets both criteria, considerations of negative transfer and access to new features are absolutely critical. This kind of cross-correlated task analysis is essential in determining what aspects of the user interface must be retained in the new version. Unfortunately, the findings of such studies often run against the desires of the development team to create a new and exciting user interface.

The training equity that users have invested in a software package cannot be discounted in the design of a product upgrade or a new product. Major corporations have lost significant market share by ignoring or discounting the equity that a user group has established in a software package or user interface structure. Regardless of all the theoretical discussion surrounding the definition of operational complexity, it is clear, based on practical experience, that adding significant new features to a user interface while also dramatically changing the existing interface is courting disaster in the marketplace. This does not mean that every software manufacturer should copy the user interface of the market leader, but it does mean that the design of an effective, highly usable interface is a complex problem that must consider the users' capabilities and limitations as the starting point, not an afterthought. The main theme is to capitalize on the users' previous experience combined with new features that have real functional value. While this approach seems self-evident, it is rarely followed.

Case Study: Dusting off Old Reliable. A number of years ago, a world leader in sewing machines came to my firm for an usability analysis of a new microprocessor-based sewing machine. The new device offered the user a highly attractive user interface, including touch selection of stitch patterns. The engineering team had used the newest technology to automate some aspects of the sewing process, mainly stitch selection. Other operational requirements, such as threading the machine, making button holes, and other frequently used features, were also changed slightly but were not automated. When we recruited and tested the first round of users, we discovered a very interesting fact. Many of the users stated that they frequently kept their old machines out and in working order so that they could switch to the old machine if they needed to do something quickly. The longer that the user had experience with the new machine, the more likely they were to abandon the new machine altogether. In fact, several users had actually put the new machine away and returned to using their old machines exclusively. This transfer to the old machine usually took place after many hours of attempting to use the new machine to do what the old machine did supremely well, namely, sew a few simple stitches, make button holes, sew a button, and other high-frequency tasks.

Upon the execution of a professional usability analysis, it was discovered that the development team had chosen to automate aspects of the device that were operationally insignificant. They left the key functionality buried behind a facade of slick covers and difficult operating procedures. By poor usability design, they dramatically increased the operational complexity of the product at a time when women had less and less time to learn to sew due to increased demands on the family structure for a second income.

For example, an error analysis of a critical operational task, threading the machine, produced very interesting and insightful results. Novice sewers tended to make the same kinds of errors in threading the machine as did more experienced users. However, the novices left a much higher percentage of their errors uncorrected. At one critical point in the thread path, these uncorrected errors caused the machine to jam. Because of the design of the machine's thread path, it was very difficult to clear the jam. Even when prompted to unclear the jam using the troubleshooting portion of the operator's manual, the novice users could not fix the machine. The user interface had failed; the user was stuck.

The benefit of designing for reduced operational complexity can have tremendous impact that can be directly measured in terms of profit and loss. In the case of the sewing machine's jammed thread path, the human factors team did not stop at identifying the problem. In addition, they examined in detail the impact that such an operational failure might have on the success of the product and more broadly on the corporation. By examining the warranty for the product, they was discovered that the manufacturer would come to the user's home to fix the machine any time in the first 90 days of ownership (i.e., novice user prime time.) By gathering service and maintenance records from field offices, they found that over 50% of the in-home service calls were attributed to jammed thread paths. The estimated cost to the manufacturer: over one million dollars a year in North America alone. The usability study resulted in the redesign of the threading procedures and related thread path which reduced the number of jammed machines by more than 90%. The cost saving worldwide was several million dollars a year.

If the product had been subjected to a usability testing program prior to production, the problem would have been identified and corrected. Furthermore, the effort that went into creating a new user interface for insignificant features would have been redirected, and millions of dollars in development and production costs would have been far better utilized. This product never produced a profit and may have cost the manufacturer a world leadership position in this product category. Simply knowing how to evaluate the relationship between new features, past experience, and basic operational requirements of a product is one of the greatest contributions that a human factors consultant can bring to the product development process. The overall ROI can be staggering.

One important aspect of the new sewing machine was that at first impression (the most important impression when it comes to purchase decisions) it actually *looked* easier to use than the older version. This "designed to *look* easy to use" factor is a critical problem for the designers of complex user interfaces. In fact, much of the human factors literature on screen design and layout is incredibly narrow and accepting in its belief that simple is better.

Experience shows that screen designs need to be different based on the skill base and operational goals of the user. I have seen visually complex screens that were highly error resistant, easy to train, fast, and operationally satisfying to use. At first glance, none of these screens would have won awards for graphic design. That is not to say that they were bad designs but simply that they did not follow the naive modernist dictum that simple is better. One of the most difficult issues to resolve in the design of a highly "usable" interface is the notion that graphic layout can and does allow the manufacturer to create the *impression* of operational simplicity. As with the case of the sewing machine, in the long run, these half-truths do not leave the customer with a warm and fuzzy feeling toward future generations of the product.

Market Competition

Frequently, a corporate client may not be aware that significant improvements in usability can lead to increased sales and market share. The basic perspective of the typical corporate client is to view usability enhancements as a necessary evil that must be addressed only if they have very real safety or use problems. However, an increasing number of corporate development groups are being made aware that enhancing usability can and often does produce directly measurable results in terms of market share and sales.

The most interesting aspect of this issue is that a product development group rarely identifies improved usability as a major project objective when seeking assistance from an outside human factors consultant. It is the role of the usability expert to identify and propose improved market share and sales as a primary benefit of the program. Clients are often actually surprised that these absolutely critical variables can be directly effected by usability enhancement.

Cost implications of improved usability depend on a number of factors, including, but not limited to:

- The maturity of the market for the product or system
- The competition's emphasis on usability as an aspect of competitive edge
- The presence of an industry standard interface (very rare)
- The costs of training and updating
- Demands for significant ROI based on automation
- Demands for significant ROI based on job elimination

Any one of these factors can signify an opportunity for the client to sell usability as a significant product feature. The difficulty is convincing the client that he or she should fund a larger project so that the user interface performance of the primary competition can be documented as a benchmark for program enhancement. The development of a detailed understanding of the usability performance of the client's products plus the primary competition is absolutely essential if the client wants to realize a significant improvement in market share and sales as a result of enhanced usability.

Often the detailed examination of the competitive products can add 40% to 60% to the early phases of a usability program. However, these costs are often insignificant when viewed against the opportunity to improve market share or sales by even a very small percentage. There are many secondary benefits as well, including the opportunity to understand how users actually interact with the competitors' product and why they have purchased the product in the past. Such information is rarely part of a marketing plan or product development objectives.

Case Study: Battling for Market Share in Process Control. In the early 1970s, a group of young engineers left a leading manufacturer (Company A) of process control computers to form a new business (Company B) focused on providing computer automation to the paper-making industry. The first generation of Company B's product was very successful, becoming, within a few years, the market leader in terms of market share, gross sales, and profits. This first product line focused on automating a few basic aspects of the paper-making process, most of which did not require direct human interaction on a real-time basis. Company B grew rapidly and made the original development team and management wealthy.

As is always the case, a successful product launches competitive products, and a third company (Company C) was formed by engineers who left Company B. They created a new system to compete head to head with the main product of Company B. However, Company C offered the industry a new user interface that was marginally easier to use, for a lower price with more automation. They began to take market share from Company B.

During the following two-year period, the Company B designed and developed a new system that offered far more automation but maintained much of the old interface design, which was very difficult to use. As the new systems began to come on-line, customers noticed an actual drop in the productivity of their work crews. This, of course, did not make for happy customers. It was during this phase that Company B began to lose more market share and to develop a questionable reputation in a very tightly controlled industry. In a last-ditch effort to identify the problem with their new system and with the hope of creating a rapid fix, Company B sought assistance from a human factors consulting firm.

After only two site visits and a preliminary task analysis, it became obvious that the new system was exceptionally difficult to use. Furthermore, the new computer took the user out of the decision-making process at critical points when the machine crew had to make rapid decisions about the status of the process if the paper being produced was to remain within specification. As a result, the machine crew would often purposely take the computer off-line and record the event as a computer malfunction. In fact, nothing was wrong with the computer itself except a totally unusable user interface. The net effect of this was a miserable reliability record and a series of very unhappy customers who did not see any reason why their considerable investment was not returning a better product at a lower price.

It is very important to realize that it is frequently possible to identify clearly the important usability problems in a relatively short period of time. On the other hand, it often requires much more effort to convince the client that a new user interface is the answer. In this case study, the client immediately understood the need for a new interface and adopted a user-centered design approach in creating new code for the next-generation system. The program received support from the highest levels of management and was given top corporate priority. Information gathered from field interviews and related observations identified many additional problems and areas of innovation for the client's system and for the overall process of successfully integrating advanced computer control systems with human intelligence to produce a better product at a lower cost.

There are many excellent reasons to integrate usability engineering into the product development process. However, none are so powerful or will be so easily understood by the executive suite as the benefit of creating a marketable product that will increase market share and profits. In any product development effort, the consultant will serve the client best by positioning usability improvements in ways that can be leveraged by the client to increase the sales and profits of the product.

In the paper industry example, the benefit to the client was immediate and significant. From the earliest stages of development, the new user interface was seen as a means for the client to regain market share and return to profitability. The client's advertising agency frequently sat in on presentations by the human factors team. Improved usability became the centerpiece of the new product marketing strategy. Formal usability testing and design became central to the product development methods of the client, thus reducing product development lead time.

The new product, with a completely redesigned hardware and software interface, was introduced with improved usability as its main marketing strategy. Within one year, the product had recaptured all lost market share and gathered new percentage points. The user interface became widely regarded as the best in the industry and is now a de facto standard. The client returned to high levels of profitability and was acquired by a world leader in process control computers.

It is safe to say that improved usability was the central driving force in this important case study. However, none of the benefits listed here would have been realized if the management of the corporation had ignored the importance of human factors engineering in the design of their new products. It is unfortunately more common for manufacturers to discount the importance of usability and focus instead on cost, features, or time to market.

The product discussed here was able to increase market share while maintaining a high profit margin. Dramatically improved usability allowed the client to maintain their position as the premium producer of process control computers for the paper-manufacturing industry.

Marketing Usability: Determining What the Client Needs

As can be gleaned from the preceding case studies, it is apparent that professionally executed design for enhanced usability can and does produce very tangible benefits for the corporate client. In most successful projects where improved usability is adopted as a critical product development objective, it is because the human factors engineer or consultant has been able to document the benefits effectively in a manner that can be understood by the product management team. This is often no simple matter and requires that the consultant have excellent intuition and experience in solving complex usability problems. This is not a business for newly minted graduate students or narrowly experienced human factors engineers. The human factors consultant is retained by corporate clients for one primary reason: to fix the problem. They are not hired for any of the other frequently observed reasons, including:

- To prepare reams of useless task-analysis data showing obvious problems.
- To interview customers to make them feel that the client cares about their problems.
- To convince a stubborn software manager that his or her approach is outdated.
- To get some quick ideas so that they can claim that their new product is "ergonomic."

Asking the Right Questions

All of these reasons are common and will surely lead the client and the contractor to a unsatisfying conclusion. The critical problem is: How does the usability team identify the problems whose solutions would have real value to the client?

Testing for Program Objectives and Consensus. Most successful projects start with a detailed interview with the product development team. In my firm, these interviews are always conducted by a partner of the firm and are on an individual or small-group basis. Each of the client's departments is interviewed individually. The purpose of these initial interviews is to *identify the project objectives and test for consensus.*

By interviewing each product development discipline, including marketing, sales, software engineering, hardware engineering, production, training and instruction development, service and maintenance support, and senior product management for both the product and the division overall, it is immediately apparent if the team has a well-thought-out set of performance objectives for the product and, most important, if the team agrees that usability is a critical, high-priority issue. In more than 80% of the initial interviews, a significant disagreement and lack of consensus on basic project objectives, including the judged importance of enhanced usability, are apparent. Clearly, this issue goes beyond usability to basic product development methods.

If the group does not have a clearly defined set of program objectives and wide agreement on the importance of enhanced usability, it will be impossible to implement a user-centered design approach for the client. While it is often painful, the best plan of action when lack of consensus and poorly defined objectives are revealed is to document the sources of conflict and ask the client to work with the human factors consultant to resolve them. This process often adds significant up-front costs to a program and can also affect lead time and production schedules. Some clients insist on proceeding without consensus. In these instances, the client rarely benefits in a significant way from a professional human factors engineering effort. An experienced human factors consultant may decide not to proceed with a program with these problems due to a reduced probability for success.

If the client resolves the discrepancies, the usability team is then faced with the interesting and complex task of defining the problems and proposing workable solutions. Knowing what questions to ask in the succeeding phases of the program has been the subject of much controversy and little structured information. However, one factor seems to be universally true: the timing for defining critical usability problems. The usability team must know the operation of the system or product better than any user and even better than the engineer who created the product. This means simply learning to use the product in depth for a foreseeable range of uses and misuses. If the team has done their work effectively in a structured manner, the proper questions will be readily apparent. Unfortunately, there are no short-cuts in this process. The cost of such an approach is far outweighed by the quality and quantity of insights produced by the human factors team. The case studies presented in this chapter were all executed according to this general method.

Knowing Where to Look for the Real Problems and Benefits. In the sewing machine case study, the critical insight that produced the greatest benefit to the client was establishing the link between thread path design, the uncorrected errors of novice sewers, customer warranty agreements, and instruction design. None of these areas in itself would have produced the best return on investment for the client. However, taken as an interconnected system of issues, it was clear that this was a problem worth addressing. The critical method for identifying such interactions must be considered the task analysis, combined with the knowledge and experience of the human factors team. If the team has a basic task analysis that includes branches for exploring the users' interactions with all aspects of the corporate support system, then it is more likely that the real problems will surface and be addressed. Certainly, nothing will happen no matter how insightful your investigations are unless the client is ready and willing to embrace professional human factors engineering methods, costs, and questions.

Building a Support System within the Client Organization

All successful usability programs start and end with a person or persons in the client organization that are militantly committed to enhancing the usability of the product or system. There is no exception to this statement for the successful human factors consultant. If you don't have an ally, you don't have a program. Assuming that you do have a champion within the client company, it helps if he or she is highly placed both functionally and politically. If not, it is absolutely essential that a support system be put in place that can drive a successful program. There is only one way to do this: Sell the benefits to upper management through the use of the general cost-benefit techniques outlined in other chapters of this book and in case studies such as those outlined in this chapter. As the project progresses, the quality of the work put forth by the usability consultant will speak for itself.

Identifying Lose/Lose Situations. No matter what some clients say, it is clear from the beginning that their corporate culture will not support human factors engineering as a means of enhancing usability. Knowing whether a corporation can and will support a use-centered design approach is vital since it will save everyone involved critical time and money. There are two "red flags" to watch out for:

(1) Does the client corporate culture view the customer or user as basically "dumb"? By this, I mean are customers seen as a necessary evil, and is it really their own fault that they cannot think through the use of the product or make sense of its related instruction manual? The most important operative phrase here is that the client would like to make the product "idiot proof." This is often a clear sign that the client does not understand or have the proper attitude for creating user-friendly products. Stay away.

(2) The second red flag is a client's desire to have someone validate or "rubber stamp" the usability of the product or software package after it has already been designed and developed by the engineering staff. This is a clear lose/lose situation because, even if you do succeed in identifying and proposing solutions to complex usability problems, you will never survive the product launch as a contractor. Yes, when you are finished, the client will be committed to a human factors engineering approach. Yes, they will pay your bills. Yes, they will even give you credit for a job well done. However, you will be replaced post haste by in-house usability staff that will report to the director of software engineering. This is like the proverbial wolf watching the hen house. In successful usability programs, human factors *never* reports to engineering.

Summary

The preceding case studies and related comments have been drawn from more than 20 years' experience as an independent human factors engineering consultant. During that time, there have been staggering improvements in the design of hardware and software. The relative cost of computing power has dropped so fast that it is now hard to imagine where it will all lead.

Conversely, advances in user interface design have not been nearly so dramatic. The reasons for this are beyond the scope and objectives of this chapter or book. However, it is safe to say that what improvements have been made in user interface design have benefited users and manufacturers in substantial and even dramatic ways, both tangible and intangible. As the next generation of computing power emerges from the development labs, we can hope that some significant portion of the new computing power will be channeled toward improved usability for all products, large and small, complex and simple. The key to this may well be the successful application of cost-benefit analyses at opportune moments in product development organizations. The various case studies cited in this and other chapters in this book can in turn be an important supporting piece of any such cost-benefit analysis.

Part III

Case Studies

Chapter 7

UPAR Analysis: Dollar Measurement of a Usability Indicator for Software Products

Mary E. Cox and Paige O'Neal

IBM Corporation
Research Triangle Park, North Carolina

Wayne L. Pendley

IBM Corporation
Austin, Texas

Introduction

Usability is essential to the success of any software product. Currently, the techniques used to achieve a highly usable product are primarily applied in a laboratory environment, providing minimal contact with the real world of users. This chapter presents a new method for connecting existing customer feedback with more traditional forms of usability work. This chapter also proposes a much-needed translation of usability measures into the language of dollars and cents.

The basic method involves conserving existing field data, tracking counts of these data to compare usability at the product-level, and analyzing these data by task for more precise user interface work. The method is very cost-effective and ensures that usability work is in line with customer priorities.

Why Measure?

It is sometimes said that in order to manage something effectively one must be able to measure it. All things are not measured with the same precision, but, if a resource is to be managed successfully, one must know when that resource is in adequate supply and when it is lacking.

The development of a software product is a complex process with many variables. Usability measurement is needed as a source of feedback to direct the iterative design of the user interface.[1] For some time, usability has been measured in various ways, but the goal has always been to ensure a highly usable product through early test evaluation and iterative design of the user interface. This goal can be better realized if one starts test iterations from known customer priorities.

Usability management requires feedback for the same reason that a person practicing archery does. People must know their "hits" from their "misses" so they can adjust their aim to the target. Usability management without measurement is like practicing archery in total darkness. Without the ability to measure one's progress, one aims blindly, not knowing what the target is or where. The arrows are shot, and they fall where they may. By chance, a few may hit the target. But unless the hits significantly outnumber the misses, customers will go elsewhere.

Ideally, usability measures should reflect how usable the product is to all possible customers in their natural environments. A serious risk with conventional efforts to manage usability is that usability measures may not adequately represent the entire customer population. Most usability tests are conducted by simulating an arbitrary subset of product tasks in the artificial setting of a laboratory. Due to these factors, usability tests face serious obstacles:

- Obtaining test participants that represent the real users of the product.
- Securing a representative sample that will be predictive of how the total population will evaluate the product.
- Selecting the tasks that are most critical to the usability needs of real customers.
- Writing test scenarios that accurately represent real task situations that a user will encounter in the customer environment.

---

[1]The user interface is the hardware, software, and information packages that allow a user to interact with and perform operations on a system, program, or device. For software systems, the user interface includes all signals and information that the system presents to the user and the provisions in the system for the responses of the user.

• Predicting which of the menus, commands, displays, and publications are most critical or most often used in a real customer environment.

The problem, in short, is that the laboratory is not the real customer situation; test participants are not the total user population; and laboratory simulation may not accurately approximate the concerns of the real world. Testing the wrong people or the wrong tasks will yield very poor guidance for product development.

So, should usability testing of products be eliminated? Absolutely not. The user interfaces of products must be tested with the precision and control that is only possible in a laboratory setting. However, it is essential that usability test administrators and facilitators should constantly strive to better the methods used to select the people, tasks, user interface features, and scenarios for usability tests so that they more closely reflect real-world situations for real customers.

In addition to improving these current methodologies, it is also necessary to supplement usability efforts in a way that will represent real customers performing their actual tasks in their own environments. It is proposed that this can be accomplished by measuring user errors.

Measuring User Errors

What is a user error? A user error begins when a customer contacts the software service personnel because that customer is convinced a product is failing. The customer problem is documented by the service personnel in a database and is tracked until a resolution is reached. When a problem is "closed" in the service database, it is summarized and categorized in the database as either a defect-oriented problem or a non-defect-oriented problem. A defect-oriented problem can be tracked down to a defect in the product code, whereas a non-defect-oriented problem is not associated with a defect in the product code. Non-defect-oriented problems are often associated with poor product design that causes users to make mistakes when interacting with the user interface of the product. These mistakes made by the customer are termed "user errors."

Multiple user errors with the same user interface may indicate that the user interface needs improvement. Analyzing user errors gives an organization an opportunity to align its usability work with their customers' real-world usability problems.

The process of analyzing user errors is called the user errors problems analyzed and reported (UPAR) process, which is a specialized system for performing causal analysis on user errors. Once user errors have been analyzed using the UPAR process, they are termed UPARs.

UPARs are indirect indicators that collapse many aspects of usability (overall ease of use, nuisance factors, interference from competing interfaces) into a single number—the service cost per license spent on user errors. UPAR tracking is one way to summarize many dimensions of product usability into a single, meaningful number for a given release of a product. The UPAR indicator is not perfect, but it is a cost-effective way to make comparisons of usability between products and between different versions of the same software product.

Counting UPARs will not provide usability improvements. Although UPARs are sensitive enough to compare product usability at the release level, they are not sensitive enough to tell us which aspects of a product's user interface need work. To improve usability, more precise analysis of the user errors must be fed back to user interface design and laboratory testing. This is accomplished in the task level of the proposed system, which will be described later.

Why Dollars?

Dollar measurement is desirable because it uses a familiar unit of measurement directly related to the cost of doing business. One way to assist communication is to use measurement units that are already familiar to the people who will be using the results. Measures used in surveying are familiar to surveyors, pharmacists, and statisticians. But "square poles," "drams," and "R-square" units mean very little to most people who make decisions on software development. It is the duty of the speaker to use a language that is understood by the listener. Cost measurement in dollars is a familiar language in the business community.

Cost measurement also demonstrates the importance of usability work. Some people still wonder if the emphasis on usability is deserved. Occasionally, individuals even suspect that usability is a matter of window dressing or showmanship and is not as important as internal design. When usability is measured in dollar terms, the magnitude of usability problems becomes more apparent. When skeptics see even small portions of the costs created by poor usability, their doubts disappear.

Dollar measurement also makes resource decisions simpler. The effort to develop a software product and modify an existing user interface has a real dollar cost. Clearly, it is easier to decide how many dollars to spend on usability if one has some idea of the dollar value one can expect in return. Why should people agree to purchase a service if they have no idea what value that service will provide?

Service Costs and "User Errors"

The dollar cost of user errors can be estimated by multiplying the number of hours spent on servicing user errors by the service cost per hour. In addition to the service cost incurred by the company responsible for servicing the product, there is also an additional cost to the customer in terms of network outages and problem diagnosis before the problem is reported to service.

It is clear that service costs reflect an important part of the overall usability of a software product. From this finding, one can conclude that the most problematic tasks define valuable usability objectives and give more accurate direction to early usability design.

UPAR Process

The UPAR process consists of two levels to measure usability in dollars: (1) the product level, and (2) the task level.

The product level tracks customer feedback from the most similar product releases in the field. This level provides a rough usability indicator and establishes the global priority of usability work for the product.

The task level identifies the specific issues that guide user interface design and provide real-world scenarios for more controlled laboratory testing.

The output of this two-level system is a new source of customer information to help guide conventional usability activities.[2] Emphasizing both laboratory testing and customer feedback provides a complementary balance of strengths and weaknesses: Customer feedback will accurately represent the customer world and signal shifts in priority over time. Laboratory measurement, guided in part by field-validated priorities, will provide the control and precision lacking in field measures.

It is proposed that products:

- Track their dollar costs for servicing user errors.
- Classify the cause of these user errors by the task that the user was attempting.

---

[2]Existing sources of customer feedback include field surveys, direct interviews during customer visits, and customer requirement gathering sessions or conferences (i.e., SHARE/ GUIDE for IBM customers).

- Analyze the most problematic tasks at a detailed, subtask level to direct selection of the laboratory tasks and behavioral measures for the early usability testing and walkthroughs of products.

The Product Level: The UPAR Ratio

For each product, the simple ratio of user error service cost divided by the number of product licenses yields a single number. This resulting number adjusts user errors for the number of licenses reporting problems by obtaining the cost of servicing user errors per product license.

Dealing with Sources of Error

While the UPAR indicator does contain usability information, like all measures, it also contains error. The major sources of error are discussed as follows.

(1) User errors are a subset of total usability problems. As previously stated, important parts of usability are not included in the user error data. So, this system should only be a supplement to other data collection procedures and should not replace efforts to gather information on more subtle usability failures.

(2) User errors include random human error that is not associated with product design. In fact, the user error category was originally intended to capture service events that were only random human errors. UPAR tracking assumes that, when one product has significantly more UPARs than another, something nonrandom about the more error-prone product is playing a role. But the UPAR ratio does not separate the random errors from the error-prone aspects of the user interface. The quantity of random human error is separated from the UPAR counts in the task-level portion of the proposed system.

(3) UPAR ratios do not reflect the differing extent of user interface in products. While the UPAR ratio's divisor provides some adjustment for the number of users interacting with the product, no correction is made for the fact that some software products have more extensive user interface than others. When comparing products with differing levels of user interface, a correction should be made to allow for this difference.

(4) The user error closing code is sometimes assigned inappropriately. Some service problems are coded as user errors when they should have been closed as defect-oriented problems. Others are coded as user errors

when they should not have been charged to the product in question at all. A simple counting of UPARs will not separate the erroneous user errors from those meeting the full criteria for that closing code. The task level of the proposal identifies the proportion of the records that are erroneously coded as user errors. This information can also be fed back to service personnel to improve closing code accuracy over time.

The Task Level: Guiding Usability Improvements

User errors can be categorized by the task and subtask that caused the problem. Comparing the relative frequency of the causal tasks and subtasks reveals which are posing the most difficulty for users. The user interface for these problematic tasks can then be given high priority for redesign and laboratory testing. This linking of field data to the laboratory usability test removes uncertainty about which tasks, scenarios, and pieces of the user interface to test. The customer data allow one to focus laboratory effort on the portions of the user interface that are costing a company and its customers the most money.

At the product level, the signal of a productwide usability failure was a UPAR rate significantly higher than comparable products. Here at the task level, the task analysis may signal a failure in a portion of the user interface even when the overall UPAR rate is not high. If a few tasks are consistently associated with many user errors, then the user interface provided for those tasks should be improved. The tasks identified as problematic are used to identify usability objectives, alter user interface design, write usability test scenarios, and weight measurable criteria for usability testing. The next section describes the method used to implement a UPAR project at the task level.

Method: Four Basic Steps

For each UPAR project, an interdisciplinary team needs to be formed. The requirements for each team member are to be:

- Technically familiar with the product at a fairly broad level,
- Interested in usability,
- Able to take the customers' perspective,
- A good communicator, and
- A team player.

Usually the team is composed of representatives from Product Assurance, Information Development, Product Planning, Design, Service Planning, and Human Factors.

The UPAR method consists of the following four steps:

(1) *Collect raw data:* From the service database, it will be necessary to pull all customer problems closed as non-defect-oriented problems that fit the previous definition of user error. Each problem record should document all activity on that particular problem and contain a description of the problem, along with diagnosis information and the final resolution.

(2) *Code the data for analysis:* Once the user error data are located and pulled from the service database, the next step involves reviewing and summarizing the problem information. It is helpful to code the text information in a format that allows for easier review and analysis.

For each problem record, each member of the interdisciplinary team reviews each problem record and codes the following information:

- Causal task (task user was performing when the error was made).[3]
- Causal subtask (subtask user was performing when the error was made).[4]

After adequate review time, a meeting of the interdisciplinary team is called to reach a consensus of an appropriate causal task and causal subtask for each problem. The goal of this meeting is to use the blend of different skills and technical perspectives in the team to better identify and understand the causal tasks and subtasks.

All of the information for each user error should be consolidated in an on-line data file in a format suitable for statistical analysis software. At a minimum, frequencies of causal tasks should be performed on the coded data.

(3) *Analyze the coded data:* In order to analyze the coded data from step 2, another meeting of the interdiscliplinary team is needed. From the frequency analysis performed on the causal tasks, the group identifies the top-priority causal tasks that merit the most focus. Usually, two or three of the causal tasks account for the majority of the user errors.[5]

---

[3]The causal task is selected from a predetermined list of product tasks (i.e., installation, customization, resource definition, performance, diagnosis, operations, maintenance, etc.).

[4]The subtasks were created by the action-object descriptions found in the problem text. Often this coding is verbatim from the user error problem description.

[5]If the user errors are more or less evenly distributed among the causal tasks, then other criteria can be used to select the causal task(s) that need to be addressed.

Once the top-priority causal tasks are chosen, then the team examines all of the causal subtasks within these chosen tasks. Next, the team sorts the causal subtasks into related clusters that provide more contextual detail on the top-priority causes of the user errors. This causal subtask sorting is best accomplished by the entire team. First, a set of index cards is prepared for each top-priority task, with each card containing the subtask description for one problem. The cards are manually organized into groups or clusters according to problem similarity. It is important to allow for flexibility between grouping of causal subtasks. Two subtasks might be grouped together because they require the same skills from the user or because the subtasks involve the same portion of the product's user interface. The goal of this organization process is to cluster similar subtask descriptions together so that the same problem will not be addressed more than once.

All options should be considered and discussed until the team agrees on the clusters. Once the clusters are formed, each group of cards is coded with its cluster name, and the new codes are added to the soft copy data file for on-line processing.

(4) *Conduct causal analysis:* The goal of the final step of the UPAR process is to understand the exact causes of the user errors associated with the high-frequency causal subtask clusters. In addition, specific design recommendations for the user interface are made that will eliminate these problems.

In order to identify the highest-priority causal subtask clusters, frequency analyses should be performed on the subtask clusters (from step 3) for each of the top-priority causal tasks. Next, brainstorming techniques are used to (1) determine the exact causes of these problem clusters and (2) generate design changes that would eliminate these errors in the future. In the brainstorming session, the interdisciplinary team should answer the following three questions for each high-priority subtask cluster:

- *What caused the error?* The team assesses each cluster, one at a time, and identifies specific reasons why users repeatedly make similar errors at this point. All clusters are listed with these reasons for the entire team to see, review, and revise.
- *What changes will eliminate these errors?* The team suggests changes to eliminate the errors in each cluster. These suggestions might involve redesign of the user interface, automation of the task, or other changes. The same change might resolve multiple errors. All changes are listed beside their errors for the entire team to see, review, and revise.

- *What actions are needed to make these changes?* Here the team makes specific plans to carry out each of their recommended actions. They identify the resources required and the parties controlling those resources. The team assigns persons to present the findings to the controlling parties and gain their support for the recommended actions.

Successful causal analysis will require a wide range of expertise so it is very important to have the entire interdisciplinary team participate in these meetings. In addition to the interdisciplinary team, one may want to explore the possibility of including customers in the causal analysis meetings.

UPAR Pilot Project

In 1986, Human Factors at the Research Triangle Park Programming Laboratory in Raleigh, North Carolina initiated a six-month pilot project for UPAR to:

- Emphasize using existing customer feedback of the UPAR process as a major source of usability information,
- Recommend establishing an interdisciplinary team to study usability, and
- Link usability to direct service costs.

An interdisciplinary team was formed to conduct the pilot project. The resulting team was coordinated by Human Factors and included representatives from Product Assurance, Information Development, Product Planning, Design, and Service Planning. The pilot project was conducted from November 1986 to April 1987, and the previously mentioned four basic steps of the UPAR process were followed.

Results and Recommendations

Figure 7.1 shows the percentages of user errors for each of the six causal tasks. Our analysis of the problem summary data showed that two of the six causal tasks (Task 1 and Task 2) accounted for 60% of all the user error problems. Those same two tasks accounted for 62% of the hours that Service spent resolving the user errors.

In Task 1, the causal subtasks could be sorted into six subtask categories. Figure 7.2 shows the percentages of user errors for each of the six

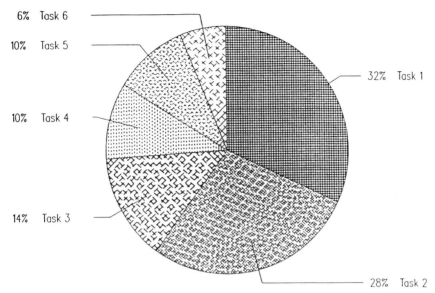

Figure 7.1 User error percentages for the six causal tasks.

subtask categories. Of those six subtask categories, two accounted for 71% of the user error problems in the causal task.

For Task 2, seven subtask categories were identified. Figure 7.3 shows the percentages of user errors for the each of the seven subtask categories. Two of the subtasks accounted for 52% of all user error problems within that causal task.

The four high-frequency subtask categories accounted for 63% of the user errors in the two high-frequency tasks (Task 1 and Task 2). These same four subtask categories accounted for 37% of the user error problems across all six of the causal tasks.

Causal analysis was performed on these four high-frequency subtask categories. The interdisciplinary group agreed that all four subtasks required customers to make complex arithmetic computations and to sort and remember large amounts of information. These requirements provide many opportunities for human error. The product did not provide any error-checking of the user-input values. Days, weeks, or even months might have passed before the error caused a noticeable problem. When the problem finally appeared, problem diagnosis proved difficult and costly to both the customer and IBM.

Changes to the user interface design were recommended for each of these four subtask categories. These recommendations included product changes, creation of additional software tools, and changes to the publi-

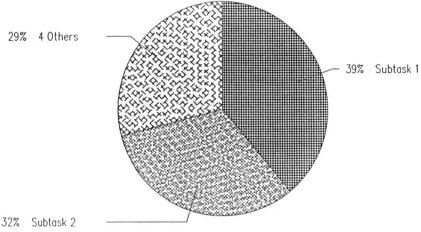

29% 4 Others

39% Subtask 1

32% Subtask 2

Figure 7.2 User error percentages for the six subtask categories in Task 1.

cations. The recommendations addressed the concerns of human information processing, system error checking, and timely system feedback. The results and recommendations were presented to the product's designers, developers, planners, and information developers, and to their managers and the product manager.

Since the pilot project, many other software products and one hardware product within IBM have successfully used the UPAR process to identify and recommend design changes for usability problems.

Benefits of a UPAR Project

Anyone who has ever conducted a field survey knows how much effort is required to collect the data. The beauty of this proposal is that the data already exist. This type of data is routinely collected but is often discarded. The cost of conserving these valuable raw data is very small compared to the cost of collecting equivalent information from scratch.

User errors are a practical and valuable source of usability information. The UPAR process provides in-depth analysis of user errors that may not be uncovered in a typical usability test. In a normal usability test, the amount of time and the number of participants and of tasks that can be tested are limited. UPAR analyses can provide feedback from the

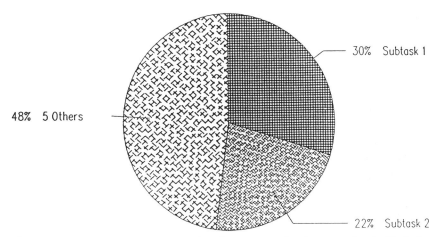

30%   Subtask 1

48%   5 Others

22%   Subtask 2

Figure 7.3 User error percentages for the seven subtask categories in Task 2.

entire customer population, performing all tasks across a longer period of time.

The information gathered from this process can provide direction to several groups within a company. It can help guide Human Factors in preparing usability plans and objectives, designing usability tests, and setting priorities for future usability work. Information Development can benefit from the identification of specific chapters and sections within manuals where usability problems exist. This identified information can point to areas in the product library where additional documentation or testing is needed, as well as where the content and organization of the library could by improved. The results can also assist product planners to determine the priority level of the many customer requirements submitted.

The analysis of user errors from service databases can also help reduce service costs. The design changes may not reduce total service charges over time; the user interface will change, and new features may create new user errors. But bringing usability work in line with customer feedback should keep efforts directed properly as that feedback changes. While future total service costs may grow, eliminating the existing problems should certainly reduce the future service costs far below what they would have been without such management.

A major strength of this method is that it can be applied by any group to any software product that tracks user errors in customer service records. The analysis can be carried out for each release of a product to track improvements over time.

Summary and Conclusion

A two-level system is proposed to supplement existing usability management. The product level tracks customer feedback from the field for dollar measurement and usability priorities. The task level better identifies these priorities and integrates the results with user interface design, usability objectives, usability walkthroughs, and more controlled laboratory testing.

While the UPAR method does not address all usability concerns, it allows organizations to measure a part of a product's usability progress in dollar terms. Design improvements based on the UPAR findings can reduce operating costs while addressing some of the most costly usability problems experienced by customers.

Chapter 8

Cost–Benefit Analysis of Upgrading Computer Hardware

Deborah J. Mayhew

Deborah J. Mayhew & Associates
West Tisbury, Massachusetts

Introduction

The following case study is hypothetical but based on a real example from the author's experience.

The customer service department of the XYZ Company was considering replacing the 3270 terminals ("dumb terminals") used by its customer service reps with IBM personal computers (PCs), in particular, with PS/2 model 70s with a mouse, running OS2. There is a substantial cost associated with purchasing so many PCs, and XYZ Company wanted to know if there would be any significant return on investment (ROI) to justify this cost.

One way to estimate such an ROI would be to perform a cost-benefit analysis where the benefit is derived by calculating the dollar value of *increased user productivity* that might be enabled by PCs as compared with dumb terminals. This quantified benefit of increased user productivity could then be compared directly with the cost of the PCs.

The discipline of usability engineering offers data and methodologies for predicting objective, quantitative differences in the human performance that can be expected to result from user interface design alternatives. Some user interface design alternatives are implementable on PCs, but not on dumb terminals. Examples include:

Windowing
Graphical display of information
Color (some dumb terminals offer color and some do not)
Alternative input devices such as mice
Point-and-select dialog styles
Multiple fonts and text styles
Boxes and borders
More flexible and powerful scrolling
Faster response times

Thus, it is possible to perform a cost-benefit analysis that estimates the increase in user productivity made possible by user interface design alternatives such as these.

Note that although it is undoubtedly possible to improve user performance on many systems just by making improvements to the user interfaces currently implemented on dumb terminals, XYZ Company was interested in the benefits that could be realized through PCs *over and above improvements that could be realized by redesigning interfaces for dumb terminals.*

A usability consultant was retained by XYZ Company to perform such a cost-benefit analysis. The rest of this chapter summarizes the consultant's final report.

Cost-Benefit Analysis of Upgrading Computer Hardware: A Case Study

Executive Summary

The final conclusions of the cost-benefit analysis performed for XYZ Company are as follows:

- The *total estimated benefit* in overall increased user productivity of replacing current dumb terminals with PCs is $2,204 per user per year.
- Assuming a per-user cost of $5,000 to purchase and maintain PCs (two users on two different shifts will share one PC), this represents a payback period of about 2.27 years.
- Assuming 2000 users, this represents an ROI of $12,040,000 over a system lifetime of five years.

The details of this analysis are explained in the section called Detailed Analysis that follows.

A few general comments regarding these conclusions are presented here. First, note that the cost figure in this analysis includes only the cost of purchasing PCs. It does not include the cost in interest of borrowing money to purchase the PCs. On the other hand, it also does not take into account the tax deduction realizable from the purchase.

And it is also true, of course, that redeveloping current application systems to take advantage of the user interface capabilities of PCs will cost a substantial amount of money as well.

However, the total cost of interest and software development will probably not approach 12 million dollars, so that a cost/benefit analysis that included the total cost of replacing dumb terminal-based systems with well-designed PC-based systems would, in all likelihood, still show some significant, positive ROI over a five-year period.

Also note that one alternative that XYZ Company has is to keep the existing hardware (dumb terminals), but invest a certain amount of money in redeveloping optimal user interfaces on that hardware. One could perform a cost-benefit analysis where the cost was software development cost (rather than hardware cost) and estimate the benefits that would be realized in user productivity. There is little doubt that a significant ROI would be revealed by such an analysis. However, the ROI calculated in *this* analysis reveals a ROI *independent of, that is, above and beyond, this potential ROI.* That is, if one directly compared both the costs and benefits of redeveloping software user interfaces on existing dumb terminals vs. both purchasing PCs and redeveloping software for them, there should be an overall ROI of close to $12 million more for the latter option. Consider the following hypothetical scenario to see how this is so.

Suppose that the cost of redeveloping software user interfaces for existing dumb terminals was $1,000 per user, and the benefits in user productivity from doing so was $2,204 per user (a comparable improvement to the one we calculated for PCs, but based on different types of improvements to the user interface not constrained by hardware). The payback period would be roughly 2.2 years, and the ROI over five years would be $4,408,000 ($2,204 × 2000 users × 5 years) − $2,000,000 (2000 users × $1,000) or $2,408,000.

Now suppose that the cost of purchasing PCs and redeveloping software is $2,000 in development plus $5,000 for PCs or $7,000 per user. The benefit now is $2,204 realized from the improvements that could have been made on dumb terminals plus $2,204 above and beyond this in improvements only realizable on PCs. Thus, the total benefit is $2,204

× 2 or $4,408 per user. Now the payback period is 1.6 years, and the ROI over five years is $44,080,000 ($4,408 × 2000 users × 5 years) − $14,000,000 (2000 users × $7,000) or $30,080,000. Factoring out of this the ROI that could have been realized by just redeveloping software user interfaces on dumb terminals gives us $14,000,000 ($44,080,000 − $30,080,000), close to the ROI of $12 million calculated in this report for purchasing PCs. *That is, the $12 million ROI calculated here represents an ROI independent of, above and beyond, any ROI realizable just by redeveloping software for dumb terminals,* but without factoring in the cost of software development.

It is worth noting here that part of the cost of development *must* be associated with investing time, money, and resources in user interface expertise and methodologies to insure that the *potential* benefits assumed in this analysis are in fact realized. It is very important to realize that many applications developed on PCs fail completely in providing *potential* productivity gains because the appropriate expertise and methodologies are not employed during the software development process.

Two other points regarding this analysis are in order. First, the costs of upgrading to PC-based systems have been estimated quite simply in this analysis. It is recognized that other cost factors are associated with upgrading to PC-based systems besides purchase price, but it seems unlikely that these costs would change the final conclusions of this analysis in any substantial way. The cost of redeveloping software was already addressed. It does indeed take a bite out of the estimated ROI, but not so significant a bite that the purchase of PCs becomes unjustified.

In addition, there will be some cost in retraining users to use the new system. However, there would also be retraining costs associated with upgrading current dumb terminal software, so it seems reasonable to simplify our calculations by excluding this cost.

It might also be argued that there will be costs associated with providing a Help Desk to support PCs. However, this potential cost has been factored into the high estimate of maintenance that we have used in our analysis ($800 per year per PC for five years). And, one might raise the possibility of installation costs. However, this cost is often borne by the vendor and included in the purchase price, and we have assumed this.

Thus, although we recognize that we have not directly considered all of the many categories of costs associated with upgrading to PC-based systems, we believe that they would not substantially change our main conclusion, that some significant ROI would be realized through such an upgrade.

The second important point is that we have performed our analysis in the context of only one group of XYZ Company users: customer service representatives. There are other equally large groups of users within XYZ Company. An overall ROI could most likely be realized by providing these users with PC-based systems as well, multiplying the ROI calculated here severalfold. That is, the potential ROI of upgrading *all* XYZ Company users is several times larger than this analysis alone suggests.

Thus, although this is a fairly simple-minded analysis as far as both costs and benefits are concerned, the results strongly suggest that the purchase of PCs would be easily justified in a bottom-line sense.

Detailed Analysis

The remainder of this report explains in detail how the costs and benefits in this analysis were estimated.

At the highest level, the cost-benefit analysis may be summarized as follows:

Total benefits:	**$2,204 per user (per year)**
Total costs:	**$5,000 per user (one-time cost)**
Payback period:	2.27 years

Benefit per year after payback period:

$2,204 per user $\times$ 2000 users = $ 4,408,000

ROI in five years: Benefit = $2,204 $\times$ 2000 $\times$ 5 = $22,040,000

Cost = $5,000 $\times$ 2000 = 10,000,000

ROI =	**$12,040,000**

The summary values of this analysis are based on three components: calculated costs, established parameters, and estimated benefits. These are described in the following sections.

Calculated Costs. In the case of this analysis, the calculated costs are straightforward and easy to calculate. The cost of each PS/2 model 70 with a mouse, running OS2/PM ($6,000), plus maintenance ($800 per year for 5 years = $4,000) was determined by XYZ Company to be $10,000. Given that two users on two different shifts will share a PC, the per-user cost for each PC would be $5,000.

Established Parameters. A number of parameters, unique and specific to XYZ Company, provided the basis for this analysis. Parameter values were provided by XYZ Company staff. They are best guesses, rather than precise values. All that really matters for the purpose of performing the analysis is that these parameter values represent conservative estimates that everybody can accept as reasonable and likely. It is not necessary that any or all of them be highly accurate.

Some of these parameter values were quoted directly by XYZ Company staff, and others were derived from values quoted by XYZ Company staff.

The parameters used in the analysis were as follows[1]:

Total number of users:*	2000 (2 per workstation)
Average user's fully loaded hourly wage:*	$20.00
Number of users trained each year:* (turnover rate = 50%)	1000
Typical number of weeks spent in a system training course (per user):	11
Cost per user of training course:*	$8,000
Average number of days a user works in a year:	230
Average number of screens processed per user per day:*	800
Average expected system lifetime (in years):*	5
Cost per PC:	$6,000 ($3,000 per user)
Maintenance per PC over 5 years:	$4,000 ($2,000 per user)

Estimated Benefits. A number of assumptions regarding benefits were made. First, *basic assumptions* regarding the potential benefits offered by PCs for users with the specific characteristics of XYZ Company users were determined. Then, *specific estimated benefits* based on the unique parameters of XYZ Company were derived. These are discussed in turn as follows.

Basic Assumptions   The basic assumptions of this analysis are that better user interfaces made possible by PCs will result in

Benefit Type	Benefit
Decreased training time (users and trainers combined)	1/11 less training time per user
Increased productivity	1.5 seconds less per screen
Decreased errors	3% fewer errors 10 seconds per error

---

[1]Note that if any of the parameters marked with an asterisk are underestimated, then the total benefits would be even more, while the costs would remain the same.

as compared with optimal user interfaces on dumb terminals.

XYZ Company is asked to accept these assumed potential benefits as reasonable and likely minimum general benefits, rather than as precise, proven, specific benefits. Research simply does not exist that would show reliable comparative performance figures for specific applications on dumb terminals vs. PCs.

However, there is ample research showing measurable and significant performance advantages of specific user interface design alternatives that are implementable on PCs but not on dumb terminals. PC capabilities enabling these potential benefits were summarized by XYZ Company staff as follows:

Graphics
Multiple screen fonts
Multiple text styles (e.g., italic, outline, shadow)
Boxes/borders
Color
Faster system response times
Mouse
More flexible scrolling and paging
More flexible cursor movement
More flexible design of input areas
More powerful field editing capabilities
Windowing
Dynamic instruction line
Point-and-select dialog style
More efficient, effective on-line help
More intelligent error handling

These benefit assumptions are based on studies of such capabilities. A rationale for these benefit assumptions follows.

Available studies that explore the benefits of PC capabilities typically vary one narrow aspect of design (such as fill-in field design, windows, color, or response time), keeping all other design variables constant, and measure human performance on some simple, well-defined task.

From these studies (a representative sample of which are summarized in Chapter 2, Tables 2.2 and 2.3), we can extrapolate to make some reasonable predictions about the order of magnitude of differences that we might expect to see in user interfaces implemented on PCs vs. interfaces on dumb terminals.

Note that these studies reveal productivity improvements that can be realized through only one design alternative when all others are held constant. That is, they compare two interfaces that vary in only one way, such as color or windows. Thus, they provide results generalizable to comparing *optimal* interfaces on PCs to *optimal* interfaces on dumb terminals. Since we are trying to calculate the ROI on PCs *above and beyond* any ROI that could be realized by redesigning user interfaces on dumb terminals, these data are appropriate as guidelines for our estimates.

For example, one study (see Chapter 2, Table 2.2) found that for a relatively complex task involving many files, screens, and interactions, overlapping windowing allowed users to perform 150 seconds faster as compared with simple, tiled windows. Other studies show that, on the average, adding color to a screen allows users to perform certain simple search tasks two to four seconds faster as compared with monochrome screens (see Chapter 2, Table 2.2).

We can imagine a typical application and complex task involving, say, three screens, each of which must be searched for information. Dumb terminals do not allow overlapping windows. Most don't allow color (50% in XYZ Company's case). These capabilities are both available on a color PC. Thus, in principle, users ought to be able to perform a complex task 150–156 seconds faster on the PC. That is, color will allow the user to search a screen two seconds faster, and there are three screens. Being able to display the three screens as overlapped vs. tiled windows will allow other aspects of the task (such as compare, edit, verify, etc.) to be performed 150 seconds faster. Thus, PCs may show an advantage of 150 seconds over color dumb terminals and 156 seconds over monochrome dumb terminals on such a task.

Assuming that both interfaces are equally well designed so that the only real difference is the availability and effective use of certain hardware capabilities such as color and windowing (other things are always held constant in such studies), we can safely predict that for a fairly complex task in our hypothetical application, the PC provides a potential performance advantage of over 2.5 minutes per complex task as compared with an *optimal* user interface on a dumb terminal (which current XYZ Company systems do not have). Although no study shows this particular 2.5 minute performance difference on the two types of hardware directly, the data we do have suggest that this is a reasonable prediction. And it is a prediction of an improvement *over and above* improvements that one could make to existing interfaces on dumb terminals.

The basic benefit assumptions in the cost-benefit analysis described in this report were made in this fashion, based on the wide body of published research data that exists and on the consultant's 12 years' experience working with and studying software user interfaces.

A sample of the research data that provide part of the basis for these benefit assumptions is included (see Chapter 2, Tables 2.2 and 2.3) to give the reader a basic sense of the order of magnitude of performance differences that can result from variations in user interface design. There is not enough detail in this summary to explain the method and results of each study completely, but this is not the purpose.

The main conclusion from these sample studies for our purposes is that individual design alternatives available on PCs, but not on dumb terminals, generally seem to improve performance on simple search/ select tasks (i.e., on single screens) by a few seconds, on simple tasks by as much as one or two minutes, and on complex tasks by anywhere from one or two minutes to as much as one-half hour, depending on the complexity of the task.

These are improvements provided by *individual* design alternatives, such as windowing, effective on-line help, color, pointing devices, etc. Since PCs add *all* these capabilities, as compared with dumb terminals, there would presumably be some additive effect of using all of these design alternatives, although probably not a simple one, since the cognitive processes that they facilitate may overlap somewhat.

In sum, for the purpose of this cost-benefit analysis, it seems entirely reasonable to assume that, given a PC providing graphics, an input device such as a mouse, color, multiple fonts and text styles, boxes and borders, windowing, effective on-line help, improved response time, more flexible scrolling, cursor movement and input field editing capabilities, more effective feedback, alternative dialog styles such as direct manipulation (i.e., point and select), and certain other display capabilities such as effective fill-in field indicators, simple search/select tasks (involving a single screen) might be on the average 1.5 seconds faster as compared with an optimally designed dumb terminal user interface.

We could also assume that the additional PC capabilities will decrease the time for users to perform simple tasks by as much as 5 seconds and complex tasks by as much as 15 seconds as compared with an optimally designed dumb terminal user interface. These are extremely conservative assumptions, given the data summarized here, and as such seem reasonable for the purpose of carrying out a convincing cost-benefit analysis.

Part of the reason for being so conservative in making benefits assumptions is based on user characteristics. According to XYZ Company staff, many customer service representatives have low job experience, general computer literacy, and educational level. These types of users are more likely to benefit from user interfaces that exploit the capabilities of PCs. On the other hand, they also have positive attitudes toward computers, high typing skills, extensive training, and very high frequency of use. These types of users generally perform fairly efficiently even on poorly designed dumb terminal interfaces and thus may benefit less significantly from user interfaces that exploit PC capabilities.

Many users in the studies cited (see Chapter 2, Tables 2.2 and 2.3) have more of the former than the latter characteristics, and this may in part account for larger performance advantages than we have chosen to assume in this analysis. These studies might have found less of a performance advantage with users who were similar to XYZ Company users, so smaller performance advantages than are generally cited in these studies seem like a more reasonable assumption to make in this analysis.

The basic benefits assumptions laid out earlier in this section and the rationale just outlined for them are part of the basis for the specific benefits estimates made in the cost-benefit analysis described in this report. This discussion focused on providing a rationale for assuming *increased productivity* benefits. Other categories of benefits, namely *decreased training time* and *decreased user errors*, are also assumed. The reader is asked to accept that these assumptions are also based on the consultant's familiarity with research results focusing on these measures (i.e., learning time and error rate/time). Complete discussion of research relevant to these benefits is beyond the scope of this project and report.

Specific Benefit Estimates   Given the basic assumptions regarding the *general* potential benefits offered by PCs, *specific* benefits in the case of XYZ Company are estimated as follows:

Benefit Type	Benefit per User per Year
Decreased training time (Users' and trainers' time combined)	$ 364
Increased productivity	1,540
Decreased errors	300
Total:	**$2,204**

These benefits were derived as follows, based on the unique parameters provided by XYZ Company laid out earlier.

1. **Decreased Training Time** (users' and trainers' time)
   Established Parameters:
   $8,000 spent per user in training (includes cost of users' and trainers' time)
   11 week training course
   1000 users trained/retrained per year (1/2 of total number of users)

General Benefit Assumption:
Training program reduced by 1 week or 1/11 due to easier-to-learn, easier-to-teach user interface: 1/2 week in system training time, 1/2 week in task training time

Specific Benefit Calculations:
Dollars saved $= 1/11 \times \$8,000 \times 1/2 = \$364$

Total: $364 per user per year

A software system that is easier to learn is easier to teach. PCs provide user interface capabilities that can make a system easier to learn. Windowing, intelligent prompting, point and select, graphics, color, and effective on-line help can all make a software system much easier to learn. A variety of research studies show significant effects on speed and ease of learning resulting from employing user interface alternatives such as these.

Last year, XYZ Company spent $8,000 per user on training. Presumably, this figure includes the time of users and trainers and other miscellaneous costs such as equipment, space, and materials. One thousand users (approximately one-half of the total number of users) were trained, and each spent 11 full weeks in the training course. Roughly 50% of this time was spent learning about the content and procedures of the job, and 50% was spent in learning the system itself.

A better user interface, realized through the capabilities of PCs mentioned earlier, could easily result in a training course of 10 weeks or less, rather than 11. A good user interface not only makes the system easier to learn, but the job content and procedures as well. Thus, this is probably a very conservative estimate of the potential benefit of decreased training time.

Presumably, a training course that takes 1/11 less time will cost 1/11 less. Thus, the benefit of decreased training time is calculated as $1/11 \times \$8,000$ per user.

Not every user is trained every year. However, according to XYZ Company staff, due to high turnover, roughly half the total work force is trained each year (i.e., 1000 as compared with 2000). Thus, a reasonable per-user, per-year benefit in decreased training costs can be calculated by taking half the per-user, per-training program figure. This gives a per-year benefit figure in the same terms as the calculation of the other two types of benefits—increased productivity and decreased errors—which can be combined with them to arrive at a total per-user, per-year benefit amount.

According to XYZ Company staff, the learning curve after training is currently believed to be roughly six months. That is, it takes six months of on-the-job use before users become maximally efficient and productive with the system. A better user interface could easily increase this learning curve as well. This potential benefit is not directly figured in to this analysis, but it should be pointed out that, even if the training program is not decreased by a full week, this faster on-the-job learning curve would most likely contribute equal or greater benefits in increased overall productivity, above and beyond those discussed in the following section.

2. Increased Productivity

Established Parameters:
800 screens processed per user per day
230 days worked per user per year
20 user fully loaded hourly wage

General Benefit Assumptions:
Processing time reduced by 1.5 second per screen due to easier to use user interface

Specific Benefit Calculation:
Hours saved = $[(800 \times 1.5 \times 230) / 60] / 60 = 77$
Dollars saved = $20 per hour $\times 77$ hours = $1,540

Total: $1,540 per user per year

The following statistics and estimates were provided by XYZ Company staff. Last year, 1,428,963 customer service transactions of type A were processed. This took a total of 35,083 user hours. 1,202,287 transactions of type B were also processed. This took a total of 70,167 user hours. Dividing the number of hours by the number of transactions reveals that each transaction takes about 2.4 minutes to process. XYZ Company staff estimated that a user accesses approximately four different system screens, on average, to process these transactions, which will be called simple transactions.

Other transaction types are more complex. XYZ Company staff estimate that these transactions take an average of six minutes to process and involve an average of 10 system screens. Let us call these complex transactions.

Combining these statistics and estimates with some other assumptions that have been made, we can arrive at an average number of screens processed per day, per user as follows.

Let us assume that a given user processes one-half complex transactions and one-half simple transactions each day. At 2.4 minutes per simple transaction, a user can process 200 of them in an eight-hour day. At four screens per transaction, this is 200×4 or 800 screens per day.

At six minutes per complex transaction, a user can process 80 in an eight-hour day. At 10 screens per transaction, this is 80×10 or 800 screens per day.

Multiplying 800 screens times one-half and adding this to 800 screens times one-half results in an estimate of an average figure of 800 screens processed per user per day. This is the figure used in the benefit calculation for increased productivity.

As laid out earlier, we shall assume that PC capabilities such as better response time, graphics, windowing, color, intelligent prompting, etc. will allow users to process any given screen 1.5 seconds faster on the average than a screen presenting the same basic information on a dumb terminal that does not allow these techniques for information display.

This is an extremely conservative assumption. Research suggests that per-screen productivity benefits realized through PC display techniques can be several times greater than this (see Chapter 2, Table 2.2). For the purposes of a convincing cost-benefit analysis, however, it is always a good idea to make very conservative claims of expected benefits.

Also keep in mind that we are considering only improvements realizable on PCs, above and beyond improvements realizable by redesigning for dumb terminals. The total decrease in screen time on user interfaces redeveloped for the PC might be closer to three to five seconds, but the improvement attributable directly to PC capabilities as compared with dumb terminal capabilities is estimated here at 1.5 seconds.

Given an estimated time savings of 1.5 seconds per screen, and assuming an average of 800 screens per day and 230 days per year, per user, we conclude that the PC would allow users to process the same number of transactions in 77 hours less per year as compared with dumb terminals. Multiplying this by a user hourly wage of $20 results in the yearly benefit of $1,540 per user.

One might ask whether or not users will actually take productive advantage of the ability to process a screen 1.5 seconds faster, such that they really are 77 hours more productive over a year. This seems like a reasonable expectation, for several reasons.

First, studies show (see Chapter 2, Tables 2.2 and 2.3) that users indeed do accomplish complex tasks (i.e., involving many screens) in less time overall when design alternatives allow them to perform faster on a screen-by-screen basis. That is, these studies suggest that users do indeed utilize small amounts of time saved per screen to get overall tasks done faster.

Second, XYZ Company users are driven by external pressures for speed and efficiency, including ringing phones and impatient customers. There are also organizational incentives for productivity. Users are probably paced by these pressures and constrained mainly by the limits that the software user interface places on their ability to respond efficiently. With improved user interfaces, the external pressures remain, but the system allows them to work more efficiently. Thus, it seems likely that users will indeed take advantage of a better user interface to be more productive overall.

Third, while we know from available statistics that users process requests in 2.4 minutes (simple transactions) or six minutes (complex transactions) *on the average,* we also know that only part of this time is spent processing screens. The rest is spent talking to a customer, procrastinating in various ways, taking breaks, etc. Since users already spend time doing these things and this is figured into the overall task time of 2.4 or six minutes, there is no particular reason to believe that they will use the 1.5 seconds freed up by better interface design to do these things.

Finally, anecdotal and personal experience strongly suggest that people do indeed take advantage of tools that allow them to be more efficient and do realize the overall productivity gains made possible by those tools. People with word processors are indeed more productive than people with typewriters. They do not spend the time saved by word processors talking to their colleagues and otherwise wasting time; they produce more documents. People with more powerful word processors that are easier to learn and use do indeed produce more documents in the same amount of time as compared with people with less powerful, less easy to learn and use word processors. There simply is no particular reason to believe that XYZ Company users will not work faster if they are provided with a tool that allows them to do so. Although they might not take consistent, thorough advantage of optimal per-screen improvements, part of the reason for making such a conservative estimate as 1.5 seconds is to take account of this fact. Perhaps design improvements would allow a maximally motivated user under ideal conditions to work three seconds faster per screen. Since not everyone is maximally motivated and conditions are not always ideal, 1.5 seconds seems a reasonable average to assume.

3. Decreased User Errors

Established Parameters:
800 screens processed per user per day

230 days worked per user per year
$20 user fully loaded hourly wage

General Benefit Assumptions:
Each error (making and recovering) takes 10 seconds
Error rate reduced by 3% or 24 screens (3% × 800 screens/errors)

Specific Benefit Calculation:
Hours saved = ((24 × 10 × 230) / 60) / 60 = 15
Dollars saved = $20 per hour × 15 hours = $300

Total: $300 per user per year

User errors on software systems vary in seriousness, ranging from a few seconds to many minutes in recovery time. Error rates vary from as little as 1% or 2% to as high as 50% across transactions. Error times and rates produced by alternative user interface designs are well documented in the human factors literature.

Certain kinds of user errors persist even for experienced, high-frequency users, due to interfaces that overtax human short-term memory and perceptual and motor skills. PC capabilities allow user interfaces that are more compatible with human cognitive, perceptual, and motor skills.

The modest assumptions of 10 seconds per error in execution and recovery time and a reduction by 3% in the number of errors made on PC screens, as compared with dumb terminal screens, for experienced, high-frequency users has been made for the purpose of this analysis. Assuming one error per screen, this means that if users process 800 screens per day, they will make an error on 24 fewer screens per day (3% × 800 screens/errors). At 230 days per year and 10 seconds saved on each of 24 screens per day, this results in a savings of 15 hours per year per user. At $20 per hour, this time is worth $300.

Summary

Summarizing the assumed benefits described, each user could save $364 in decreased training costs, $1,540 in increased productivity, and $300 in decreased errors per year. This adds up to a yearly benefit of $2,204 per user. Given that the cost of realizing this benefit is $5,000 (that is, one-half the cost of a PC plus one-half the cost of maintenance over five years because two users on two different shifts would share a single PC), the cost of buying a PC for a user would be paid back in about 2.27 years, and a return on investment of $2,204 per year would be realized after that time period. Given that there are 2000 users, that ROI adds up to $12,040,000 over a five-year period.

Of course, some of this ROI will be cancelled out by the cost of borrowing money to purchase the PCs and developing new systems to run on them that take advantage of their greater capabilities. However, tax deductions on the purchase of the PCs are not figured in, the benefits are most likely significantly underestimated, and these additional costs are unlikely to decrease the final ROI so much that the purchase of PCs is unjustified.

There are two ways to consider the per-user benefit. One is that the user work force could be decreased because fewer users could process the same amount of transactions in the same time. Thus, the purchase cost of PCs would be significantly offset over a five-year period by the savings realized from eliminating the annual salary of some employees. If overall costs go down but business volume (i.e., income) remains the same, then profit increases.

Another way to look at the benefit, however, is to consider that the number of transactions could be increased—that is, the business and its associated profits could grow—without any increase in staff and thus in employee costs. Assuming that each transaction contributes to profits, the analysis suggests that the cost of PCs would be offset considerably over a five-year period by an increase in income, resulting in an overall increase in profits.

Summarizing this overall cost-benefit analysis, a number of quite conservative assumptions have been made in estimating the ROI for the purchase of PCs. The estimated ROI is so high ($12,040,000) that, even if some of the assumptions are not borne out, it is virtually certain that the investment in PCs will be worthwhile in a bottom-line sense. And, this analysis does not take into account other important but less tangible benefits of better user interfaces: increased user satisfaction leading to lower turnover with its associated costs, higher-quality service to customers, and better image in the marketplace.

One final note is that in some cases, XYZ Company will be able to test out the assumptions of this analysis and estimate actual benefits and ROI after implementation of PC-based systems. For instance, XYZ Company keeps statistics on the number and duration of different kinds of transactions. After PC-based systems have been in production some time, these statistics can be directly compared to see if the increased productivity that the analysis assumed actually occurs. And, eventually XYZ Company will know whether the training program developed for PC-based systems is actually one week (or more) less than the current training program. Other benefits not considered in this analysis may also become apparent. Although these data will be available too late for the purposes of making this purchase decision, they may prove valuable for making future technology purchase decisions.

Chapter 9

Software Reuse: A Case Study on Cost-Benefit of Adopting a Common Software Development Tool

Nuray Aykin

AT&T Bell Laboratories
Holmdel, New Jersey

Introduction

With today's rapidly advancing technology, the race among software-development companies is escalating in various dimensions. Software companies are striving to produce higher-quality software in shorter development cycles. Delivering a product with one extra feature or one month earlier than the competitors' products can make a significant effect on the market share. According to Daly (1992), the following trends have stimulated this drive toward higher-quality software and shorter development cycle.

- Rapidly growing industry
- Increase in small entrepreneurial companies
- Focus on product features
- Invisibility of software

Other factors that contribute to the drive toward higher quality and reduced cycle time include:

- Availability of high technology at a reasonable price
- Rapid technological advancements
- Alliances among companies to share technology
- High customer expectations
- Improved software development tools

To be competitive in the market, the software companies are looking into ways of improving the quality of their software and reducing the software development cost and cycle time. Many agree that the object-oriented software development with reusable components is a significant element toward reaching their goal (Wasserman, 1992). The concept of reusable software components was first formulated by McIlroy (1968). He envisioned standard catalogs of routines classified by precision, robustness, time-space requirements, and binding time of parameters. Since then, research on reusability, object-oriented programming, and modularity has concentrated on developing reusable software components. Object-oriented programming and use of new languages, such as C++, allow development of code in a fast and efficient manner. These effects have resulted in shared libraries of software components and resources. The advantages of software reuse are widely acknowledged, and software reuse is being implemented even though the tools, methods, languages, hardware capabilities, computing environment, and overall understanding of software engineering are constantly changing (Biggerstaff and Richter, 1989).

The objective of this chapter is to discuss advantages of reusability and some of the issues raised against implementing reusability. A methodology to quantify and analyze costs and benefits of adopting a common software development tool and generating a shared library of reusable components is presented via a hypothetical example. This case study is an example of how the results can be used to argue for or against implementing reusability.

Endoso (1992a) reports that the Department of Defense (DOD) plans to implement a networked, multirepository software warehouse, expanding on the Army's Reusable Ada Products for the Information Systems Development (RAPID) Library. Each of the reusable software components consists of about 500 to 5,000 lines of code. These reusable components are expected to give the developers the flexibility to create applications that will deliver better service.

Danca (1992) reports that the Defense Advanced Research Center (DARPA) has awarded a $7.3 million contract for research into software reuse and technology transfer in the DOD and industry. Moore, chairman of Reuse Library Interoperability Group (RIG), points out several technological and human issues that must be resolved before RIG can achieve its vision of creating standards that would allow a user to dial one library and simultaneously have access to components housed in other reuse facilities (Endoso, 1992b). Moore says that the human side of the issues is related to "shifting from a preferred developed mentality of coding from scratch to reusing software component" (Endoso, 1992b). Similarly, the Army's RAPID Center Library (RCL) was developed by Softech, Inc. The Softech officials say that the RCL application is only about 30,000 lines of code itself but contains 823 reusable software components that stretch to 600,000 lines (Green, 1991). The RCL advocates have found that the key to cost and time savings through RCL is the reuse of documentation and test results. This is an incentive for encouraging and promoting the use of the library resources. They say only about 30% of systems costs are reduced by reusing code. Cost savings can go above 50% when ancillary products such as requirements, documentation, and testing are reused. Softech spent about two years assembling policies and procedures for reuse, officials said.

Computrol's Vice President Rutolo has said that 70% of applications have code appropriate for almost any other application and that generic items such as screens, searchers, menus, and database access fall into the category, and another 15% of an application requires development of totally new code unique for the application (Cashin, 1991). Goering (1992) reports from Ron Collett, an industry analyst, that the average product reuses 38% of circuitry from previous designs, and it is expected that the reuse can go up to 45% to 50% in the next two years.

However, the transition from a traditional software programming from scratch to adopting reusability into development is difficult, and the benefits are not immediately apparent. For example, the National Aeronautics and Space Administration (NASA) has mandated that systems that will support the space station must use Ada products. These systems require millions of lines of code (Wasserman, 1991). NASA found no improvement in the number and severity of coding errors or coding speed, and it saw much worse performance from operational Ada systems (Anthes, 1990). In terms of effective productivity, as a result of reusable software components, the FORTRAN systems were able to get on average 32% of their code from earlier systems (Selby, 1989), even though the systems had 60% to 80% overlapping functionality. However, the Ada applications showed a dramatic increase over time in the amounts of reusable codes that they could borrow from the earlier systems. The NASA engineers realize that the change will not happen overnight; they expect it will take about 10 years to replace FORTRAN in their division. Anthes argues that it requires changes, not only in the software development tools and the languages that the developers use, but also in the culture of the organization.

The Japanese government spent 25 billion yen on Sigma, a project designed to produce tools and hardware for software development and databases on which the reusable codes could be stored (Lamb, 1990). The project was unsuccessful and has been criticized for not producing enough reusable components, adopting out-of-date Unix standards, and spending too much money on centers to hold databases of code and information. Some observers believe that the project was overly ambitious, thus elevating its cost to potential users (Cashin, 1991). Based on this experience, follow-up projects have been revised.

Developing and documenting reusable software often costs more than developing software for one-time use. Therefore, developing reusable components needs extra investment. This is also one of the reasons why the benefits of reusability are not immediately apparent. Although many companies see the benefits of reusability, they sometimes are reluctant to adopt this method because it may not fit into their environment. Studies that describe how reuse can be effective often discuss why it has proven so difficult to implement in the software development environment (Krueger, 1992; Biggerstaff and Perlis, 1989a, 1989b; Freeman, 1987; Tracz, 1988). Some argue that object-oriented design can provide the solution for the successful implementation of reusability (Bourbaki, 1992; Cashin, 1991; Phillips, 1991). In today's software development environment, object-oriented design is very popular. Using object-oriented design, code can be written in encapsulated modular forms based on defined objects, which can then be reused in different applications without major code changes.

The following two sections describe the benefits associated with reusability and the issues that may be raised by the developers and/or managers when such a concept is being introduced.

Benefits of Software Reuse

Some of the benefits of incorporating reusability into the software development environment include:

(1) *Reduced development cost:* In the long run, the overall development costs would be lower due to reusable components, documentation, and testing. Adopting reusable components into an application reduces the amount of code that needs to be generated for that application. This re-

sults in costs savings because of the reduced resources required for the development.

(2) *Reduced software development time:* Reusing existing components reduces the time to introduce a product into the competitive market. This is significant because reducing the development time not only lowers the product development costs, but also may result in financial returns. Conklin (1991), for example, reports that speeding up the product introduction may increase revenues by 10% as a result of higher volume of sales and/or higher sales of more valued product that is marketed at a premium price. Conversely, delays in product delivery may result in lost profits. Conklin estimates that shipping products into market with one-quarter year delay may cost an organization as much as 50% of expected revenues. Karat (1992), for instance, reports from House and Price (1991) a loss of 33% of after-tax profit when the products are shipped six months later than their scheduled time.

(3) *Fewer software components:* With reusability, fewer software components need to be specified, designed, implemented, and validated. This affects not only the programmers' productivity, but also the efficiency of the systems engineers and the designers.

(4) *Increased system reliability:* The components that have been used and tested in working systems should be more reliable.

(5) *More precise cost estimates:* It is easier to estimate the cost of using a reusable component than to estimate the cost of developing and integrating the same component from scratch.

(6) *Effective use of specialists:* A pool of specialists serving several projects is more effective than working on separate projects.

(7) *Consistency across products:* When the reusable components are developed according to the organizational standards, they provide component-level consistency across different products. These standards can range from user interface standards to protocol conversion standards.

(8) *Reuse tends to become more mature:* Riehle (1992) reports that one of the benefits of reuse is that "it tends to become more mature." Its behavior becomes more predictable in time; the reusable components may eventually become independent of data.

Issues with Reusability

The following is a list of issues raised by the software developers and/or managers against the implementation of reusability:

(1) *Not invented here (NIH) syndrome:* Developers often believe that software from another source is not efficient or reliable as the software they write themselves.

(2) *Lack of fit of reusable component:* The developers complain that they may end up spending more time to fit the reusable component into their application than to write the code themselves.

(3) *Quality of reusable components:* The developers often believe that the quality of reusable components tends to be lower than code written for a particular project.

(4) *Maintenance of reusable components:* The developers and managers believe that the maintenance of reusable components is costly compared with each project managing their own code.

(5) *Purity of reusable components:* There is a chance to have a virus-infected reusable component. The possibility of viral infestation will be always a threat to software developers when they share a public software library of reusable components.

(6) *Inflexible and limited reusable components:* The reusable components are inflexible and limited and cannot be tailored to specific applications. They may serve very well in small-scale problems as they offer stereotypical approaches, but may not be suitable for complex applications.

(7) *Reusable components do not function integrated:* The reusable components are sometimes viewed as a library of disparate modules that do not function in an integrated manner (Cashin, 1991).

(8) *No time to invest in reusable software:* The developers argue that they are very busy with existing work, with no time to investigate and invest in object-oriented programming and reusable software.

(9) *Does not follow a waterfall model:* Object-oriented programming with reusable components can appear as disorder or confusion because it does not follow a traditional top-down waterfall design that gives the illusion of orderly development and a straight-line mode of thinking. However, in the object-oriented design many activities are proceeding in parallel, and some were already completed before the project started (Riehle, 1992).

(10) *Requires a longer design period:* Writing codes for reusable components tends to have a longer design period than a waterfall, top-down design project (Riehle, 1992). It is usually associated with the fact that the programmers take a longer time to begin coding.

(11) *Unrealistic and premature expectations:* There are usually high expectations about the benefits of reusable components. It takes time to build up the foundation. Therefore, the savings do not show in year 1 or 2. The expectation of "the program should have saved us significant sums of money by now" is unrealistic (Mosemann, 1992).

(12) *Initial capitalization is too high:* The initial cost of developing reusable software components is too high. Sommerville (1992) points out that, until reuse is demonstrated to be cost-effective, organizations are reluctant to invest in creating a component library. According to him, computer-assisted software engineering (CASE) tool sets do not fully support reusability, and our current techniques for classifying, cataloging, and retrieving software components are immature.

(13) *Reusable software components are not by-products of an application:* Extra effort is needed to generalize the system components to make them reusable. Software development with reuse needs a library of reusable components that can be understood by the developers.

(14) *Retraining of software developers is costly:* Using either self-training or classroom training, it is costly to retrain the software developers in developing reusable components, object-oriented technology, and common software development tools and platforms.

The cost/benefit analysis of adopting reusability can help determine the decision to be made on whether it is cost- and time-efficient to implement reusability for a given environment. As can be seen from the list, many of the issues raised against reusability have reasonable grounds if the decision does not match the company's needs. On the other hand, the benefits cited and the trend followed by the competitors may very well initiate such an effort and change the software development environment drastically.

To illustrate such a cost-benefit analysis, a hypothetical case study is presented. The following section summarizes the COCOMO cost estimation model to be used in estimating the effort and schedule needed for software development, followed by a numerical example.

COCOMO Cost-Estimation Model

A number of algorithms and techniques are available for estimating software development costs, each with its own advantages and disadvantages. There are software tools commercially available to apply some of these algorithms to a given set of project parameters (AT&T, 1993).

In the cost-benefit analysis described later in this chapter, COCOMO (COnstructive COst MOdel), a cost-estimating model, is used to estimate the cost of the project. The model was developed by Boehm (1981). The advantages of this model are: (1) it is used widely, (2) it provides detailed estimates for individual pieces of the project, and (3) it is a typical example of a micromodel based on numerical information and entails rules capturing all possible data on the parts of the project (Londeix, 1987).

Some underlying assumptions and definitions of terms used in COCOMO are:

(1) The primary cost driver is the number of delivered source instructions (DSI) developed for the project. DSI includes all program instructions created by the project personnel and processed into machine code by some compilers and assemblers. It includes job control language, format statements, and data declarations. It excludes comment cards, unmodified utility software, and nondelivered support software such as test drivers.

(2) The development period starts with the product design phase and ends at the end of integration and test phase.

(3) COCOMO cost estimates cover the following activities:

Management
System engineering
Programming
Test and evaluation
Data
Documentation
Implementation
Maintenance

The cost estimation includes the functions directly related to the project planning, administration, and controls. It excludes the business planning aspect of software development such as scheduling, funding, product ideas, and quality goals. It also excludes user training, installation planning, and conversion planning. The cost-benefit of usability testing is excluded to keep the focus of the study on the benefits of the reusable software components. Other chapters in this book provide excellent sources on cost-benefit analysis for usability testing.

(4) COCOMO cost estimates cover all direct-charged labor on the project. This includes project managers, developers, user interface de-

signers, system engineers, and software programmers. It excludes overhead costs such as computer-center personnel, higher management, support staff, personnel department personnel, etc.

(5) A COCOMO man-month[1] consists of 152 hours of working time.
This is consistent with the average monthly work time excluding holi-
days, vacation, and sick days. To convert a man-month estimate to other
units, the following multipliers are used:

$$\text{Man-hours} = 152 * \text{man-month}$$
$$\text{Man-days} = 19 * \text{man-month}$$
$$\text{Man-years} = \text{Man-month}/12$$

The components of the software development process include:

Plans and requirements
Product design
Programming
   Detailed design
   Code and unit test
Integration and test

Some of the principles emphasized by this model are:

- Careful definition and validation of the software requirements
  specified by a small number of system engineers prior to work
  on the full system design.
- Careful design and validation of the software system design
  down to the unit level by a small group of people prior to any
  significant work on detailed design and testing.
- Detailed design, coding, and unit test performed by a larger
  group of programmers in parallel, working with the firmly base-
  lined system design framework.
- Integration and test of each increment based on a significant
  amount of early test planning.
- Early preparation of much of the documentation effort, including users' manuals.

Versions of COCOMO

The COCOMO has three versions: Basic, intermediate, and detailed.
Basic COCOMO is applicable to the large majority of small-to-medium–

---

[1]In this case study, we are using the asymmetrical "man"-month out of tradition to keep
the terminology the same as the COCOMO model. The programmers are just as likely to
be women.

size software projects. The products are usually developed in a familiar in-house software development environment. The basic COCOMO is good in early and rough estimates of software costs. The intermediate COCOMO includes other factors such as differences in hardware constraints, personnel quality and experience, use of modern tools and techniques, and other project attributes. Detailed COCOMO includes the influence of these additional factors on individual project phases. To simplify the calculations involved, basic COCOMO is used in the case study presented later in this chapter. Similar methodology can be followed to estimate the effort and schedule with the other versions of COCOMO.

Modes of Software Development

There are three modes of COCOMO software estimation: organic, semidetached, and embedded. These different software development modes reflect the nature of the software development process in the steps used to calculate the effort and the schedule. Any of these modes can be used in any versions of COCOMO.

(1) *The organic mode:* There are relatively small software teams that develop software in a highly familiar, in-house development environment . Most people will have extensive experience in working with the related systems within the organization. The size of the project is medium, about 50,000 lines of code.

(2) *The semidetached mode:* This is an intermediate step between the organic mode and the embedded mode. First, all team members have an intermediate level of experience with related systems, or the team has a wide mixture of experienced and inexperienced people, or the team members have experience related to some aspects of the system under development.

(3) *The embedded mode:* The product must operate within a strongly coupled complex of hardware, software regulations, and operational procedures. The problem is unique, and the cost of changing the parts of this complex is very high.

In this study, the organic mode and the semidetached mode are used to estimate the cost of the software development. The organic mode is used to estimate the cost of software development where there is no need for training on a new software development tool and the developers are highly familiar with the system and the environment. This applies to estimating cost of development with the existing software development tools. The semidetached mode is used to estimate the cost of software development where a new software development tool is introduced for object-oriented programming and a new concept is introduced for reusability. In this case, the software developers are considered to be unfamiliar with the development environment. But, it is assumed that after a year or two of experience in the new environment, the organic mode can be used to estimate the cost of software development.

The Organic Mode

The basic effort equation for a software project in organic mode of COCOMO is

$$MM = 2.4(KDSI)^{1.05} \tag{1}$$

where MM is the number of man-months for the software development phase of the life cycle and KDSI is the number of thousands of delivered source instructions in the software product. Boehm classifies projects into four sizes: small (2 KDSI), intermediate (8 KDSI), medium (32 KDSI), and large (128 KDSI). In this study, 50-KDSI product size will be used for calculations.

The basic schedule equation is

$$TDEV = 2.5(MM)^{0.38} \tag{2}$$

where TDEV is the number of months estimated for software development.

The Semidetached Mode

The basic effort equation for a software project in semidetached mode is

$$MM = 3.0(KDSI)^{1.12} \tag{3}$$

The basic schedule equation is

$$TDEV = 2.5(MM)^{0.35} \tag{4}$$

Software Conversion Cost

COCOMO considers conversion as an instance of adaptation of existing software for a new application (Boehm, 1981). The effects of adapted reusable components are handled in COCOMO by calculating the equivalent number of delivered source instructions (EDSI). EDSI will be used to calculate the cost of adapting reusable components from the shared library.

The EDSI is estimated as

$$EDSI = (ADSI)\frac{AAF}{100} \tag{5}$$

where ADSI (adapted DSI) is the number of delivered source instructions adapted from existing software to form a new product, and AAF is the adaptation adjustment factor. The AAF is calculated using the following equation:

$$AAF = 0.40(DM) + 0.30(CM) + 0.30(IM) \tag{6}$$

where DM is the percentage of the adapted software's design that is modified in order to adapt it to new objectives and environment, CM is the percentage of the adapted software's code that is modified in order to adapt it to the new objectives and environment, and IM is the percentage of effort required to integrate the adapted software into an overall product, as compared with the normal amount of integration effort for software of comparable size.

Boehm (1981) introduces another rating-based cost increment, called the conversion planning increment (CPI), to cover the added cost of feasibility analysis, planning, inventory, and documentation. Ratings for the CPI are shown in Table 9.1.

The following equations are used to estimate EDSI when reusable components are adapted for a new application:

$$CAF = AAF + CPI \tag{7}$$

$$EDSI = (ADSI)\frac{CAF}{100} \tag{8}$$

where CAF is the conversion adjustment factor. The quantity EDSI is used to calculate effort and schedule using the appropriate basic COCOMO equations.

Table 9.1 CPI ratings

CPI	Level of Conversion Analysis and Planning
0	None
1	Simple conversion schedule, acceptance plan
2	Detailed conversion schedule, test, and acceptance plans
3	Add basic analysis of existing inventory of code and data
4	Add detailed inventory, basic documentation of existing system
5	Add detailed inventory, detailed documentation of existing system

Cost-Benefit Analysis of Adopting a Common Software Development Tool: A Case Study

The following is a hypothetical case study to show the cost and benefits of using a common software development tool and sharing reusable software code.

Problem Statement

The software development organization of the ABC Software Company, a hypothetical company, is considering adopting a common software development tool and establishing a reusable software library for maintaining reusable software components. Currently, they have five product managers. Each product manager oversees a development group that is responsible for developing and maintaining a different product. There are no existing codes to use for these products, but developers are well experienced in working with similar products. Minimal cooperation exists among the development groups, each developing its own code from scratch using a different software development tool. Upper-level management realizes the disadvantages of developing and maintaining five different products. They are planning to adopt a common software development tool that will eventually bring all development groups under one umbrella. They are planning to establish a common reusable software library that can be shared by the developers with the intention of reducing the development time, cost, and maintenance of the products. The upper-level management is interested in the cost of such an effort in comparison with retaining the existing tools and procedures, as well as the benefits associated with adopting a common software development tool and establishing a software library with reusable components.

Parameters

The parameters used for this case study are listed in Table 9.2. The dollar values are best guesses reflecting a reasonable market estimate. Other values are chosen to represent an average-size software development effort with a reasonable number of developers.

Cost of Software Development with the Existing System

The cost of developing five products with an average size of 50,000 DSI in the existing environment is calculated using basic COCOMO Eqs. (1) and (2) for organic mode. Thus, the effort needed is

Table 9.2 Parameter values used in the analysis

Number of products	5
Number of developers	100
Cost of developers	$10,640/month*
Cost of software development tool	$9,000 + $100/user
Cost of hardware for shared library	$20,000
Average software product size (DSI)	50,000

*Based on 152 man-hours working time per month (see COCOMO model assumptions) and $70 per hour loaded salary.

$$MM_{existing} = 2.4(50)^{1.05} = 145.93 \text{ man-months}$$

and the amount of time needed is

$$TDEV_{existing} = 2.5(145.92)^{0.38} = 16.61 \text{ months}$$

Then the cost of existing software development is

$$Cost_{existing} = MM_{existing} \times (\text{Developer cost/Month})$$
$$= 145.93 \times \$10,640 = \$1,552,695$$

The total cost of development for five products is estimated as

$$\text{Total cost}_{existing} = 5 \times \$1,552,695 = \$7,763,475$$

Cost of Software Development with the New Software Development Tool

Cost of Development in the First Year. The cost of developing applications in the first year with the new software development tool is calculated using the COCOMO Eqs. (3) and (4) for semidetached mode. Thus, the effort needed is

$$MM_{new(first\ year)} = 3.0(50)^{1.12} = 239.87 \text{ man-months}$$

and the amount of time needed is

$$TDEV_{new(first\ year)} = 2.5(239.87)^{0.35} = 17.02 \text{ months}$$

Thus, the cost development in the first year is given by

$$Cost_{new(first\ year)} = MM_{new\ (first\ year)} \times (\text{Developer cost/Month})$$
$$= 239.87 \times \$10,640 = \$2,552,217$$

The total cost of development for five products is estimated as

$$\text{Cost of five products}_{new(first\ year)} = 5 \times \$2,552,217 = \$12,761,085$$

Cost of Development in Subsequent Years. ABC Software Company estimates that the percentage of the code reused will be 10% in the second year and will increase 10% per year thereafter, leveling off at 50% after five years. To illustrate the cost-benefit evaluation, consider the fourth year. ABC Software Company estimates about 30% of the code (i.e., on average 15,000 lines of code of a 50,000 lines of code) will be taken from the shared library of reusable components. To calculate the cost of adapting 15,000 lines of code, the conversion cost estimate, Eq. (6), is used.

Let's assume that, on average, 15% of the adapted software's design is modified in order to adapt it to new objectives and environment. Similarly, 30% of the adapted software's code is modified and 15% of effort is required to integrate the adapted software into an overall product. Therefore, with DM = 15, CM = 30, and IM = 15 in Eq. (6), AAF is

$$AAF = 0.40(15) + 0.30(30) + 0.30(15) = 19.5$$

Assuming an average conversion planning increment, CPI = 3, and using Eqs. (7) and (8), CAF and EDSI are estimated as

$$CAF = 19.5 + 3 = 22.5$$

$$EDSI_{new(4th\ year)} = (15000)\frac{22.5}{100} = 3375$$

After the first years of adopting the software development tool, the organic mode can be used to calculate the cost of software development in a reusable environment. Then, the effort needed for development is

$$MM_{new} = 2.4[(KDSI(1 - Percent\ code\ reused))^{1.05} + EDSI_{new}^{1.05}] \quad (9)$$

$$MM_{new(4th\ year)} = 2.4(35^{1.05} + 3.375^{1.05}) = 108.95\ man\text{-}months$$

and the amount of time needed is

$$TDEV_{new(4th\ year)} = 2.5(108.95)^{0.38} = 14.86\ months$$

Thus, the cost of development is

$$Cost_{new(4th\ year)} = MM_{new(4th\ year)} \times (Developer\ cost/Month)$$
$$= 108.95 \times \$10,640 = \$1,159,228$$

and the total cost of development for five products is estimated as

$$Cost\ of\ five\ products_{new(4th\ year)} = 5 \times \$1,159,228 = \$5,796,140$$

Other Costs Associated with Adopting a New Software Development Tool

Additional costs of adopting a common software development tool and creating and maintaining a software reuse library include:

- Training
- User interface design and style guide
- Prototyping
- Maintaining shared library of resources
- Software development tool
- Hardware for the shared library

Training. According to Crabb (1991), the training cost may vary between $250 and $1,000 per day and may last three to four days depending on the language and the operating system. The existing software development tools and languages may not necessarily work with the object-oriented design. The developers may need new tools and training on them. In addition to the training cost, switching to object-oriented programming has hidden costs; developers' time is consumed with learning instead of developing.

Assuming $1000 training cost per developer on today's object-oriented programming software, the total cost for training 100 developers on a new software development tool is

Training cost = 100 × $1000/developer = $100,000

User Interface Design and Style Guide. It is vital to define the user interface specifications to be followed by the applications. The software development methods should integrate user interface design methods and techniques into their development phases. Not only does a good user interface design ensure customer satisfaction, but it also reduces the software development cycle by efficiently generating code specific to the user interface part of the application. The magnitude of this savings can be significant since the percentage of total code devoted to user interface can be as high as 48% (Myers and Rosson, 1992). Day and Boyce (1993) discuss the reduction of development through better identification of users' needs early in system development, iterative prototyping, and testing. One of the first steps toward a good user interface design is to define the user interface specifications applicable to the selected applications. Mayhew (1992) argues that no user interface design specification can be sufficient to ensure usability and that it does not eliminate the need for usability testing. In this case study, only the costs of defining user interface design specification, writing the style guide, and prototyping are included. The cost-benefit analysis of usability testing can be found in the other chapters of this book and elsewhere (Mantei and Teorey, 1988; Mayhew, 1990; Karat, 1990).

Assuming that developing user interface design specifications for five products may take about 10 man-months, the cost of user interface design excluding prototyping is

UI design and style guide cost = 10 man-months × \$10,640 = \$106,400

Prototyping. Assuming that it takes four man-months to prototype the user interfaces, the cost of prototyping is

Prototyping = 4 man-months × \$10,640 = \$42,560

Cost of Software Development Tool. The ABC Software Company did a survey on the existing tools that might fit their needs and has decided on one that they'll choose if they adopt a common software development tool. Assume that the cost of the software development tool is a \$9,000 one-time fee and \$100 licensing fee per user. Hence, the total cost for purchasing the new software development tool is

Cost of software development tool = \$9,000 + \$100/user
× 100 users = \$19,000

Cost of Hardware for Shared Library. In order to maintain a library of reusable software components, the ABC Software Company has to purchase hardware to store the reusable components and network it with the development teams. Assume the cost of all hardware necessary for the shared library is \$20,000.

Cost of Shared Library Maintenance. In addition to the maintenance of individual applications, there is a cost associated to maintain the shared library of resources. The basic COCOMO estimates the cost for annual software maintenance as the following:

$$MM_{AM} = 1.0(ACT)MM_D \qquad (9)$$

where MM_{AM} is the basic annual maintenance effort, ACT (annual change traffic) is the fraction of software product's source instructions that undergo change during a (typical) year either through addition or modification, and MM_D is the estimated development effort. The MM_D calculated for the organic mode is 108.95 man-months. For example, assume that 1,000 lines of software code are modified each year and 5,000 more lines are added to the existing code in the library; then ACT is

$$\text{ACT} = \frac{1000 + 5000}{50000} = 0.12$$

Then the total maintenance effort is

$$(\text{MM})_{\text{AM}} = 1.0(0.12)(108.95) = 13.07 \text{ man-months}$$

And the annual cost of maintenance of the reusable library is obtained as

$$\text{Cost of maintenance} = 13.07 \times \$10,640 = \$139,065$$

Total Cost of Adopting a Common Software Development Tool and Establishing a Reusable Library

Cost of Software Development in the First Year. Total cost of software development and other costs associated with adopting a common software development tool and establishing a reusable library in the first year is

$$\begin{aligned}\text{Total cost}_{\text{new(first year)}} = \ &\text{Cost of five products}_{\text{new(first year)}} + \text{Training cost} \\ &+ \text{Cost of UI design} + \text{Cost of prototyping} \\ &+ \text{Cost of the software tool} \\ &+ \text{Cost of hardware for shared library}\end{aligned}$$

Thus,

$$\begin{aligned}\text{Total cost}_{\text{first year}} = \ &30,625,320 + 48,000 + 26,600 + 17,500 \\ &+ 13,800 + 20,000 = \$30,751,220\end{aligned}$$

Cost of Software Development in Subsequent Years. Total cost of software development and the maintenance cost of the shared library in subsequent years is

$$\begin{aligned}\text{Total cost}_{\text{new(}n\text{th year)}} = \ &\text{Cost of five products}_{\text{new}} \\ &+ \text{Cost of shared library maintenance}\end{aligned}$$

In the fourth year, for example, the total cost is obtained as

$$\text{Total cost}_{\text{new(4th year)}} = 5,796,140 + 139,065 = \$5,935,205$$

The total software development costs for the first seven years are shown in Table 9.3.

Table 9.3   The total cost of adopting a common software tool and establishing a reusable library

Year	Reuse (%)	MM_{new}	$TDEV_{new}$	Total Cost*$_{new}$
1	0	293.87	17.02	$13,049,045
2	10	133.36	16.05	7,233,817
3	20	121.07	15.47	6,579,985
4	30	108.95	14.86	5,935,205
5	40	96.99	14.22	5,298,933
6	50	85.19	13.54	4,671,173
7	50	85.19	13.54	4,671,173

*Undiscounted.

Break-Even Point

As seen from the results, the first-year development will cost more with the new software development tool. But, the more that reusable components become available to the developers and the more that developers gain experience with the new environment and the library of reusable components, the greater the reduction in cost and time of development.

ABC Software Company expects that, in subsequent years, the percentage of software reuse will increase when more reusable components become available and the developers gain experience with the new tool and the environment. Assuming that the time value of money used by ABC Software Company in economic analysis is 8% and the factors ADSI, DM, CM, IM, and CPI remain the same over the years, the cost of development with the existing and the new systems for the first seven years can be shown. The cost values shown in Table 9.4 are the present values of the development costs given 8% time value of money.

As shown in Table 9.4, adopting a new software development tool and a shared library of reusable components has a high cost during the first few years, and it may take six to seven years before the break-even point is reached. However, the development time can be reduced significantly in the first two years. Thus, the speed and volume at which new products are introduced into the market can be improved significantly, resulting in increased profits.

Other Benefits of Adopting a Common Software Development Tool and Reusable Library

Some of the additional benefits of adopting a common software development tool and the software reuse library include reduced development

Table 9.4 Present value of the cost of development of the existing and the new systems

Year	Reuse (%)	Cost of Existing	Cost of New	Total Present Value Existing	Total Present Value New
1	0	$7,763,475	$13,049,045	$7,188,202	$12,082,111
2	10	7,763,475	7,233,817	13,844,605	18,283,662
3	20	7,763,475	6,579,985	20,007,251	23,506,854
4	30	7,763,475	5,935,205	25,713,406	27,869,230
5	40	7,763,475	5,298,933	30,997,227	31,475,684
6	50	7,763,475	4,671,173	35,889,769	34,419,457
7	50	7,763,475	4,671,173	40,419,756	37,145,086

cycle, sharing developers across products, and increased sales due to better user interface. The following sections describe these in detail.

Reduced Development Cycle. In addition to the cost savings in other areas due to adopting a common software development tool and reusable components, the estimated number of months (TDEV) for development is also reduced. For ABC Software Company, the estimates of the number of months needed for development in the existing system and in the new system in the first year are

$$TDEV_{existing} = 16.60 \text{ months}$$

$$TDEV_{first\ year} = 17.01 \text{ months}$$

As expected, in the first year, the development with the new tool takes longer than with the existing tool. This is due to the factors included in the COCOMO semidetached mode; the developers have experience with the products but not with the development tool. It can take several years for the developers to become experts on the new development tool and start utilizing the reusable components in an efficient manner. This is reflected in the schedule savings of about a month in the second year and thereafter (see Table 9.3). If more reusable components are developed, the percentage of components derived from the shared library will increase, affecting both the effort and the schedule of the development.

Sharing Developers across Products. Since the software developers will be using the same software development tool and the library, the flexibility in the development environment will be increased. Products can be phased out so that, when one is in the planning stage, the other one can be in the programming stage. Due to their knowledge of the reusable components, the developers can join a project even at an advanced stage and can move to the other projects when needed. The developers' expertise will not be limited to the application that they work on.

Increased Sales due to Better User Interface. Having consistent, easy-to-use products increases the sales. The ABC Software Company can define a user interface style guide that reflects the company's signature. The products developed by the company will look and feel the same. Since the same reusable components and the user interface style guide will be shared by all products, it will be easier to achieve the same look and feel. This will increase customer satisfaction.

Summary

This chapter provides a methodology to show monetary benefits of adopting a common software development tool and generating a shared library of reusable components. A hypothetical case study was presented that revealed that the initial cost of adopting a common software development tool and a library of reusable components is high and that it took a few years for the ABC Software Company to reach a break-even point. However, after a few years of implementation, the benefits of reusability become apparent in the effort and the schedule of software development. This case study is a good example of how the results can be used to argue for or against implementing reusability.

The results of the cost-benefit analysis performed for ABC Software Company can be summarized as follows:

• The initial cost of adopting a new software development tool and developing a shared library of resources is high. The projected costs are $7,763,475 per year when the existing system is retained, whereas it can cost $13,049,045 in the first year if a new software development tool is adopted.

• The cost in the subsequent years can be reduced drastically if the developers share a library of reusable components. For example, if 30% of the application code is adapted from the library, then it would cost $5,935,205 per year, about $2 million less compared with the existing system.

• It may take six to seven years before ABC Software Company reaches a break-even point.

- The development time is also reduced. The development time in the existing system is 16.61 months. If 30% of the code is adapted from the reusable library, then the development time can be reduced to 14.86 months.

If the ABC Software Company's initial goals are to reduce cost and schedule in one year and if they have no future plans for developing similar products, then it would not be justifiable to adopt reusability. If, on the other hand, ABC Software Company plans to continue to develop similar software products in the future, this is hardly the case. Many companies are aware that they have to invest on reusability before they really gain on software development effort and schedule.

If the ABC Software Company decides to adopt a common software development tool, it should investigate object-oriented design and programming that can generate well-defined reusable objects and ensure successful and efficient software reuse. Phillips (1991) suggests that, even if object-oriented programming is not used, one can apply its principles to traditional programming, for example, abstracting the program during design and hiding information and details in subroutines, keeping the integration to a function separate from the implementation, writing modular programs by grouping logically related items, and using hierarchies in data structures and subroutines.

Some companies may choose to build a library of reusable components via donations (i.e., components of reusable library that are donated by the developers as side-products of their applications). A log-in scheme can be a donation to the library. Some companies may choose a formal methodology of building a library of reusable components, forming groups of highly experienced developers to build components for reuse. There are other ways to add reusable components to the library, such as purchasing or leasing commercially available software libraries.

The planning of reusable programs includes managerial commitment and support, personnel responsibility, library system implementation, software personnel training, and continued measurement of results. It takes time to change the culture within the software development environment.

Discussion

The benefits of reusability include reduced development effort, fewer software components, increased system reliability, and consistency across products. But, there has been resistance to the idea because of the problems associated with the reusable components such as lack of fit and quality and high initial investment. One of the challenges is to quantify the costs and benefits of reusability and compare them with those of the traditional software development practices. Furthermore, benefits considered with reusability cannot be realized without a carefully planned and implemented organizationwide program. Incentives, royalties, reinforcement schedules, and market forces are only a fraction of the factors that may promote reusability (Constantine, 1992). To measure success of reusability, one has to measure the time that it takes to find a component and adapt it for an application and the number of times the developers consulted the library as compared with developing from scratch. If the library is successful, the developers will tend to use more components from the library and even contribute to the library with their pieces of code. Particular attention has to be paid to the following points in developing and implementing a library of reusable components (Comaford, 1992; Perry, 1992).

(1) *Intelligent prototyping:* Use joint application design and joint requirements planning techniques to gather user requirements efficiently before the initial prototype is developed.

(2) *User interface design standards:* Standards will expedite coding and ensure consistency among user interfaces. The standards will include a list of common words, specifications for symbols, dialog boxes, message boxes, commands, diagrams, etc.

(3) *Writing and distributing common code:* Identify reusable templates such as windows, dialog boxes, user message boxes, menus, reserved words, and icons. Use a tool equipped with a library manager or a repository, and assign a librarian to maintain the common components.

(4) *An enterprise-wide data model:* Development time will be reduced if programmers can grab entities from the repository without having to create them from scratch. However, setting up the enterprisewide data model is a time-consuming process in itself.

(5) *Using object-oriented programming tools:* Object-oriented programming tools can provide object classes that are reusable and maintainable. The use of well-capsulated and well-planned objects can reduce the development cycle and cost drastically.

(6) *Control of reuse repository:* Place only the well-defined modules, preferably small size for easy adaptation. The larger the module, the lower the probability that it will be reused.

(7) *Cataloging easy-to-use identifiers for the code in the repository.*

(8) *Providing search capability:* Provide an easy-to-use search tool that will help the developers in locating the modules and the related information they need.

(9) *Training:* In order to realize the full potential of a reusable library, the developers should be trained both on the use of the modules in the library and the search tool and the cataloging system used in the library.

(10) *Getting management commitment and involvement:* In order to assure wide acceptance and change in attitudes, there should be a corporate commitment to the reuse program, and a senior level person should be in charge of the program and manage that commitment. The management should establish reuse goals, develop and implement programs that will encourage employees to reuse code, and reward those who do. When the reuse program in place, the reusable components can be identified earlier; then the project manager can assign programmers to search for and test existing components. In some cases, it will be necessary to design and build your own components, but that should be a last resort.

Acknowledgments

I would like to thank my friends and colleagues who provided valuable comments on the drafts of this chapter: especially Turgut Aykin, Marie Dumbra, and Antoinette Habib, who worked very hard to help me meet my deadlines and provided detailed comments on the content and style. I would also like to thank Deborah Follett for her comments on the first outline, Mary Carol Day and Satish Desai for their reviews, and Randolph Bias and Deborah Mayhew for their valuable comments. My special thanks go to Jim Cunningham for his support and understanding during the preparation of this manuscript.

References

Anthes, G. H. (1990). For better or worse. *Computerworld* **24,** 31–32.
AT&T Bell Laboratories (1993). Best Current Practices: Software Cost Estimation Handbook. Select Code: 010-810-115. Indianapolis, Indiana.
Biggerstaff, T. J. and Perlis, A. J. (1989a). *Frontier Series: Software Reusability: Volume I—Concepts and Models.* ACM Press, New York.
Biggerstaff, T. J. and Perlis, A. J. (1989b). *Frontier Series: Software Reusability: Volume II—Applications and Experience.* ACM Press, New York.

Biggerstaff, T. J. and Richter, C. (1989). Reusability framework, assessment, and directions. In: (Biggerstaff, T. J. and Perlis, A. J., eds.) *Frontier Series: Software Reusability: Volume I—Concepts and Models.* ACM Press, New York.

Boehm, B. W. (1981). *Software Engineering Economics.* Prentice Hall, Englewood Cliffs, New Jersey.

Bourbaki, N. (1992). Reuse is not inheritance. *AI Expert* **7,** 19–24.

Cashin, J. (1991). To move beyond a metaphor, reusability needs to get real. *Software Magazine* **11,** 100.

Comaford, C. (1992) Tips for truly rapid application development (mission critical). *PC Week* **9,** 60.

Conklin, P. (1991). Bringing usability effectively into product development. Paper presented at the *Human–Computer Interface Design: Success Cases, Emerging Methods, and Real-World Context.* Boulder, CO.

Constantine, L. (1992). Rewards and reuse. *Computer Language* **19,** 104–108.

Crabb, D. (1991). Objects of curiosity: Object-oriented operating systems are the future, but they've already hit center stage. *InfoWorld* **13,** 53–55.

Daly, J. (1992). Bug-free code: The competitive edge: Automated software testing equipment uses advanced tools and technology to eliminate code error. *Computerworld* **26,** 55.

Danca, R. A. (1992). DARPA awards software reuse contract to Virginia consortium. *Federal Computer Week* **6,** 38.

Day, M. C. and Boyce, S. J. (1993). Human factors in human-computer system design. In: *Advances in Computers, Vol. 36* (Yovits, M., ed.). Academic Press, Boston, 333–430.

Endoso, J. (1992a). Strassman: Expect 6 new CIM tools in '92. *Government Computer News* **11,** 1.

Endoso, J. (1992b) Group wants common standards for reuse libraries. (Reuse Library Interoperability Group). *Computer News* **11,** 63.

Freeman, P. (1987). *Tutorial: Software Reusability.* IEEE Computer Society Press, Washington, D.C.

Goering, R. (1992). Synopsis tools pioneer design reuse. *Electronic Engineering Times* **709,** 4–6.

Green, R. (1991). RCL goes on line, will be key in DOD Ada policy. The US Army Reusable Ada Products for Information Systems Development Center Library, or RCL. *Government Computer News* **10,** 55.

House, C. H. and Price, R. L. (1991). The return map: Tracking product teams. *Harvard Business Review* 92–100.

Karat, C. M. (1990). Cost-benefit analysis of usability engineering techniques. *Proceedings of the Human Factors Society 34th Annual Meeting,* 839–843.

Karat, C. M. (1992). Cost-justifying human factors support on software development projects. *Human Factors Bulletin* **35,** 1–4.

Krueger, C. W. (1992). Software reuse. *ACM Computing Surveys* **24,** 131–183.

Lamb, J. (1990). Modern methods reach Japan's software. *Computer Weekly* **1210,** 22–24.

Londeix, B. (1987). *Cost Estimation for Software Development*. Addison-Wesley Publishing Company, Wokingham, England.

Mantei, M. and Teorey, T. J. (1988). Cost/benefit of incorporating human factors in the software lifecycle. *Communications of the ACM* **31**, 428–439.

Mayhew, D. J. (1990). Cost-justifying human factors support—a framework. *Proceedings of the Human Factors Society 34th Annual Meeting*, 834–838..

Mayhew, D. J. (1992). *Principles and Guidelines in Software User Interface Design*. Prentice Hall, Englewood Cliffs, New Jersey.

McIlroy, M. D. (1968). Mass-produced software components. In: *Software Engineering Concepts and Techniques*. 1968 NATO Conference Software Engineering, 88–98.

Mosemann L. K., II (1992). Interview: "Mr. Software" pioneers reuse. *Government Computer News* **11**, 16.

Myers, B. A., and Rosson, M. B. (1992). Survey on user interface programming. *Proceedings of CHI'92 Human Factors in Computing Systems*. ACM, New York, 195–202.

Perry, W. E. (1992). For DOD software reuse to succeed, it must be easy. *Department of Defense DP Issues* **11**, 22.

Phillips, D. (1991). OOP: Now It's Hot. *Computer Shopper* **11**, 734–736.

Riehle, R. (1992). Recyclable software? Some questions arise when considering reuse of software objects in OOP. *HP Professional* **6**, 66–69.

Selby, R. W. (1989). Quantitative studies of software reuse. In: *Frontier Series: Software Reusability—Volume II: Applications and Experience*. (Biggerstaff, T. J. and Perlis, A. J., eds.) ACM Press, New York.

Sommerville, I. (1992). *Software Engineering*. Addison-Wesley Publishing Company, Wokingham, England.

Tracz, W. (1988). *Tutorial: Software Reuse: Emerging Technology*. IEEE Computer Society Press, Los Alamitos, California.

Wasserman, A. I. (1991). Object-oriented software development: issues in reuse. *Journal of Object-Oriented Programming* **4**, 55–57.

Chapter 10

Design of a Human Factors Cost-Justification Tool

Mary C. Harrison, Richard L. Henneman, and Louis A. Blatt

AT&T Global Information Solutions
Technology and Development Division
Atlanta, Georgia

Introduction

Human factors practitioners are often asked to justify their involvement in a project or to explain what the payback will be for performing a specific method or piece of research. This chapter is about making the process of cost-justifying human factors support usable. The premise of this effort is that we must go beyond providing approaches, models, and methodologies for cost-justifying human factors support; we must provide tools to make these approaches useful and usable to the people who perform them. The chapter describes a user-centered approach to designing such a tool. The work is still in progress; in fact, our original thoughts regarding the content and form of the tool have been altered significantly as a result of interviews with primary potential users of the tool. Although research and issues in modeling cost justification are discussed, no substantially new techniques for modeling cost-justification data are presented. Rather, the intent is to focus on identifying requirements that users have for a tool that would support providing cost-justification data.

The chapter proceeds as follows. First, we describe the nature of cognitive engineering (human factors) at NCR Corporation. This background is necessary to give the reader some context for the user-centered approach that follows. Second, we discuss issues in building models for cost justification for human factors support. The discussion includes approaches taken within the human factors community, as well as approaches from other disciplines. Third, we discuss issues in developing a tool to support cost justification. A user-centered approach is taken here, with data generated from structured interviews with tool users (NCR cognitive engineering professionals) playing a key role in generating tool requirements. In this section, we describe characteristics of end users, the tasks they perform, and the environment of use. In the fourth section, we describe tool requirements. Finally, in the fifth section, we discuss some technologies relevant for implementation and describe future directions.

Cognitive Engineering at NCR

NCR Corporation is structured as a group of financially independent business units. Since 1991, NCR has been a subsidiary of AT&T. Cognitive engineers are scattered across the corporation with, in general, a single cognitive engineer providing human factors support to a plant or business unit. (In this chapter, the term "cognitive engineer" will be used to describe any person who has training and skills in developing and using tools and methods that support user-centered design. Other labels that could be used include human factors engineer, interface design specialist, user interface designer, or usability scientist.) In several cases, there is a small group of cognitive engineers that provides user-centered design services to both internal and external customers. The history of human factors at NCR has included several ups and downs, ranging from a large, centralized group of human factors professionals in the late 1960s, to the dispersion of human factors professionals in the mid-1970s, to a dearth of human factors support in business units by the late 1980s. In the last several years, there has been a resurgence of interest in human factors within the corporation. Since 1989, the number of cognitive engineering professionals in the corporation has increased from four to 25.

A group of cognitive engineers located at NCR's Human Interface Technology Center in Atlanta has corporate responsibility for developing and supporting an infrastructure of cognitive engineering professionals within the corporation. The group is a part of the NCR Design Center, working closely with both industrial designers and software developers to ensure the ease of use of NCR products. Thus, the group is concerned with justifying to NCR business units the benefits of integrating human factors support into their development processes by following a user-centered design approach. Beyond convincing business units of the efficacy of including human factors support, the corporate cognitive engineering group has its own services group. A second interest of the group, therefore, is to provide justification data on a project-by-project basis to potential clients. The work reported in this chapter, therefore, was undertaken to serve three purposes:

- To assist cognitive engineers in NCR business units and service groups in justifying their involvement in projects,
- To assist the corporate cognitive engineering group in justifying to NCR business units the addition of cognitive engineering professionals to their development staffs, and
- To assist cognitive engineers in planning user-centered design activities for specific projects.

Methodology

A user-centered approach was followed for developing requirements and a plan for a tool to support human factors cost justification. As such, the approach focused on understanding tool user characteristics, the tasks that users perform, and the environment of use. The information used as a basis for this project was derived from two main sources. First, secondary research consisting of a cross-disciplinary literature review was conducted using sources from numerous industries and covering such domains as marketing, finance, human factors, advertising, economics, management, engineering, quality assurance, customer service, and information technology. Industry analyst research and reports were also reviewed as a part of this effort. The topics reviewed for the secondary research portion of this project included general cost-benefit, specific cost justification of human factors, usability effects on user, company benefits realized due to customer satisfaction, ease-of-use effects on purchasing behavior, impact to development organizations, and consideration of intangibles. The purpose of this secondary research effort was to explore issues related to building models for cost justification.

Second, primary research was conducted to gain insight into demand and requirements for a cost-justification tool. Potential users of the tool were interviewed to allow for needs assessment for the cost-benefit model and to obtain information about both the users and the environment of use. Also, the interviews provided a way to derive design and feature ideas for the tool and to identify potential projects and preliminary data on those projects involving the design and testing phases of model development.

The method used for gathering data was a structured telephone interview that consisted of more than 60 open-ended questions. Participants included 13 cognitive and human factors engineers, all of whom were either employed by or under contract to NCR. Fifty-four percent of the interviewees were located at various NCR development facilities spanning three countries, while the remainder were centralized, either at NCR's Human Interface Technology Center in Atlanta, Georgia, or at NCR's World Headquarters in Dayton, Ohio.

Issues in Building Models for Cost Justification

Human Factors Approaches to Cost Justification

At least two major classes of argument can be made to justify human factors support during product development. The first argument involves showing that cognitive engineering involvement in projects results in productivity gains for end users. These efficiency savings can then be translated into financial savings. Demonstrating this to be true can be fairly straightforward: by decreasing user task time, it is possible to show gains in end-user productivity. A second argument that can be made is that developers can work more productively when following a user-centered development process. The argument is that user-centered design identifies user interface requirements early in development before changes are too expensive to implement.

Most cognitive engineering-related efforts at cost justification have focused on end-user productivity. For example, Mayhew (1990) provides a summary of research that has been performed to show the effects that various design alternatives have on user performance. Karat (1990) describes two studies that demonstrate productivity-related cost savings from two projects that underwent usability testing. It is reasonable that the focus of benefit quantification efforts have been aimed at user productivity. Not only is user productivity more easily measured than other areas of benefits, but it focuses on the very method that human factors professionals excel at, that is, observing and measuring human behavior.

This productivity argument appears to make sense for a product intended for internal use (although, as Sassone (1992) points out, overall office productivity improvements may be dependent on environmental factors such as the office staffing mix and intellectual specialization levels). The problem comes in translating those productivity gains to increased sales for products developed for external use. When a product sells well, it may be difficult to make the case that it is due to increased end-user productivity. If this case cannot be made, however, the veracity of the cost justification is questionable.

Other approaches have taken a more fine-grained approach to cost justification. Cost-benefit methods can be applied to analysis of specific human factors techniques for the purpose of improving efficiency and aiding management decision making for resource allocation (Karat, 1992). Specific user interface issues, such as whether or not to adopt a corporate standard, can also be subject to the cost-benefit analysis process (Rosenberg, 1989). Mantei and Teorey (1988) describe a comprehensive approach for performing cost-benefit analysis of human factors in which individual benefits are matched to specific human factors activities. This concept is an important one since any cost-benefit model must take into consideration which benefits apply in a particular case. For example, development cost savings that result from design changes occurring earlier in the product development cycle will be realized for those projects where prototyping and user testing are utilized. Mantei and Teorey also describe problems associated with quantifying the costs and benefits. As shown by the assumptions and equations they developed, determining the value of costs and tangible benefits can be straightforward and relatively easy. The intangible benefits, however, pose a far greater problem.

Identifying benefits is far easier than quantifying them. Given this fact, it is no wonder that many of the cost-benefit models proposed in the past have focused on the tangible benefits and merely mentioned the intangibles as if they were a bonus. It is these benefits, however, that are probably the largest and most important to the development organization.

Some attempts have been made at recognizing various benefits. Mayhew (1990) has segmented benefits into those realized by data processing companies and those appropriate for vendor companies, while Karat (1992) has divided benefits into classes for either internal or external products. These are important distinctions because the audience for the data that result from different cost-benefit analyses will pay more attention to the class of benefits that is most relevant to their needs. For example, when marketing a product based on its usability, it makes sense to focus on findings related to increased productivity. However, when trying to convince a development organization to use human factors techniques, the message will be most effective if it is focused on development cost savings.

Another reason for segmenting benefits by classes in terms of the beneficiaries is that, in the aggregate, one benefit may have multiple values. Take, for example, the effect that increased usability can have on training requirements. End users of a product benefit if they do not have to attend lengthy training sessions (that may result in greater job satisfaction). Their companies benefit if they realize lower training costs and decreased downtime due to training. Lastly, the development organization benefits because they do not have to provide training programs. Further, they may obtain an increase in market share if they have a competitive advantage in the area of training requirements.

Marketing and Financial Approaches to Cost Justification

Given the range of possible benefits and the intangible nature of many of the benefits that need to be estimated for any given cost-benefit analysis, it is useful to examine other approaches to benefit estimation. In particular, the field of marketing bears some interesting similarities to the discipline of human factors. For example, marketing departments have had difficulties measuring and estimating the effect of their activities upon sales, as has the field of human factors. Because it is a go-between or boundary function between other internal functions and external groups such as customers and end users, the complexity and the variables involved in measuring effectiveness are increased. Also, marketing practitioners have historically focused far more of their efforts on efficiency, as opposed to effectiveness (Bonoma and Clark, 1988). This appears to be true of the human factors discipline as well, given the wealth of research that has been done on areas such as how to best run a usability test or whether an expert walkthrough is better than a usability test at identifying interface problems. Relatively little focus has been placed upon relevant areas such as how usability effects customer satisfaction or how to increase the implementation levels of design change recommendations.

In light of the difficulty of estimating some of the benefits, it is useful to examine some quick and simple methods for calculating outcomes without knowing the value of the benefits. One approach is to calculate the likelihood of benefits occurring and assign a probability to each (Brownlie, 1991). The next step would be to determine the expected value of each benefit. Although this method does not provide a means for predicting the actual value of the benefits expected from something such as an increase in usability, it does dilute the risk of basing a decision on a particular assumption by considering the full range of possible outcomes and the likelihood of their occurrence. For example, if you can estimate and project that certain design changes have a 60% chance of increasing user productivity by 10%, an 80% chance of decreasing development costs by 15%, and a 30% chance of increasing a product's market share by five points, you may be able to get a quick idea of whether to proceed with the changes without having to spend the time and effort proving the exact level of user productivity before and after the design changes.

Another approach, sensitivity analysis, in which one determines a best case, worst case, and most likely outcome, is also aimed at diluting the risk associated with making assumptions. This approach is commonly used for financial analyses when either all the variables or the relationships between the variables have not been concretely established and therefore the outcome cannot be predicted with certainty. For example, a best-case scenario from a usability test on a product intended for internal use may result in 35 recommended design changes that can translate into a 20% increase in user productivity and training cost savings of $25,000. The worst-case scenario may be 10 design change recommendations that result in user productivity increases of 5% and a $10,000 savings in training costs. By assigning dollar values to the increases in productivity, adding this to the training cost savings, and comparing the total with the cost of running the usability test, it is possible to obtain the necessary information to make a quick decision about the value of performing the usability test.

Zeller (1988) proposes a model for determining the value of focus group input. Simply stated, the value of insight gained equals the increase in the expected profit by using focus group knowledge. This is equal to the expected profit when the product design takes into account the attitudes and opinions expressed in the focus groups minus the expected profit without this input. Given the outcome of this relationship, one can determine to use the focus group if the increase in expected profit is more than the expenses of the research. Using this model and example cases, Zeller concludes that if the payoff or expenditure is in the hundreds or thousands of dollars, the investment in research is unwarranted. However, when the payoff or expenditure is in the millions or billions of dollars, one should invest in obtaining information that will maximize the chances for success in the client's endeavor. Although this serves as a good rule of thumb, the problem of quantifying the expected outcome still remains. Zeller solves this problem by acknowledging that the expected profit and probability of obtaining that profit are highly subjective judgments. He advises that determining these values should be the responsibility of the client. At the very least, this approach may help to ensure that the audience for the cost justification data finds it valid.

Quantification of Benefits

Clearly, a number of studies have been performed that are relevant to justifying the involvement of human factors professionals in the development of new products. Tables 10.1, 10.2, and 10.3 summarize some results from these studies. These three tables differ based on the groups they benefit: end users, the users' organization, and the development organization. The benefits have been differentiated in this manner so as to eliminate the need for distinction between internal/external *products,* internal/external *projects,* and vendor companies vs. internal development organizations.

Table 10.1   User-centered design benefits: end users

Benefits to End Users	Related Research
Increased usability	• More than 20 American companies have in-house usability labs according to a survey conducted by Usability Sciences Corporation. These companies estimate that their product usability is increased by as much as 20% to 60% (Potter, 1989). • The average usability test results in 70–100 recommendations for usability improvement according to Jeff Schueler, president of Usability Sciences Corporation in Irving, TX (LaPlante, 1992). • A *Which Computer* (1992) study found that first-time purchasers ranked the advice of a colleague as the number-one source of information when selecting a software product and that whether a package met their needs and was easy to use were ranked as the first and second key purchase decision criteria, respectively.
Increased job satisfaction	Humantech, Inc. studied ergonomic office environments and productivity for 4000 managerial, technical, and clerical workers in a broad cross-section of North American industries. Surveys showed that video display terminal (VDT) workers had twice as many complaints of neck and shoulder discomfort, eye strain was reported three times as often, and there were higher rates of absenteeism, less job satisfaction, and increased (30%) turnover (Schneider, 1985).

Continued

Table 10.1 *Continued*

Benefits to End Users	Related Research
Decreased training time	A study by *Computer + Software News* (1986) found that *users* rated ease of use second at 6.8 out of 10, while ease of learning was rated fourth at 6.4 on a scale of important purchase factors.
Less time spent getting support and help	No relevant research was found for this specific benefit.
Increased implementation of time saving features	Mayhew (1990) summarizes research showing performance differences of various design alternatives.
Less documentation required	A study by *Computer + Software News* (1986) found that users' most common software problems were compatibility with other software (42%), clarity of manuals (32%), organization of manuals (32%), vendor tech support (25%), installation (15%), usefulness (11%), and ease of use (9%).
Easier to recover from errors	No relevant research was found for this specific benefit.
Consistency across applications	Temple, Barker, and Sloane (1990) found that a graphical user interface had several measurable advantages over a character-based user interface.
Performing basic functions is easier, less time consuming, and less frustrating	Temple, Barker, and Sloane (1990) found that a graphical user interface (GUI) had advantages over a character-based user interface (CUI): GUI users completed 35% more tasks; they correctly completed 91% of the tasks compared with a 74% completion rate for CUI users; GUI users accomplished 58% more correct work in the same time; after two days, GUI novices rated frustration levels at 2.7 out of 10 whereas CUI novices rated their frustration at 5.3; fatigue levels were rated at 4.3 for GUI users and 5.8 for CUI users; GUI novices were better able to self-teach and explore than CUI novices; and GUI novices attempted 23% more tasks than CUI novices.
Fewer errors	Temple, Barker, and Sloane (1990) found that GUI users correctly completed 91% of the

Continued

Table 10.1 *Continued*

Benefits to End Users	Related Research
	tasks compared with a 74% completion rate for CUI users. GUI users accomplished 58% more correct work in the same time.
Less fatigue	Temple, Barker, and Sloane (1990) found that fatigue levels were rated at 4.3 out of 10 for GUI users and 5.8 for CUI users.
Products better meet needs	• A Data Decisions Applications Software Survey (1985) showed that 40% of the time, when buyers seek alternative packages, they do so because their installed system does not meet their needs. • A *Which Computer* (1992) study found that, when first-time purchasers selected a software product, whether a package met their needs and was easy to use were ranked as the first and second key purchase decision criteria, respectively.
Learning new tasks is easier	Temple, Barker, and Sloane (1990) found that GUI novices were better able to self-teach and explore, and that CUI novices and GUI novices attempted 23% more tasks than CUI novices.
Less chance of injury	• Surveys showed that VDT workers had twice as many complaints of neck and shoulder discomfort, eye strain was reported three times as often, and there were higher rates of absenteeism, less job satisfaction, and increased (30%) turnover (Schneider, 1985). • Chapanis (1991) cites two independent studies that showed a 54% reduction in rear-end accidents with the use of human factors improvement: the centered high-mount brake light on autos.
Increase in effective work time	• Poppel (1982) reported on a study by Booz, Allen, and Hamilton that demonstrated office workers could save an average of 15% of their time with appropriate technology. • Management workers in one department of a major auto manufacturer used computer equipment less than 12% of the day until ergonomic equipment was installed and the

Continued

Table 10.1 *Continued*

Benefits to End Users	Related Research
	usage rates went up four times. The average manager had at least three more hours per week for work (Schneider, 1985).
Product supports both novice and experienced performance as the user's needs evolve	No relevant research was found for this specific benefit.
Can focus on the task objectives instead of the mechanics	Sassone (1992) claims that past attempts to measure the productivity impact of technology have failed to determine the value of technology because they have focused on the physical attributes as opposed to the intellectual content of the office worker's tasks.
Can use product on an infrequent basis	No relevant research was found for this specific benefit.
Increased work quality	• Temple, Barker, and Sloane (1990,) found that a graphical user interface (GUI) had the following advantages over a character-based user interface (CUI): GUI users completed 35% more tasks, than CUI users; they correctly completed 91% of the tasks compared with a 74% completion rate for CUI users; and GUI users accomplished 58% more correct work than CUI users in the same time. • A telemarketing group reported an increase from 10% to 80% on final closing of sales after ergonomically improving their office (Schneider, 1985).
Increased productivity of users	• Humantech, Inc. studied ergonomic office environments and productivity for 4000 managerial, technical, and clerical workers in a broad cross-section of North American industries. Surveys showed VDT workers had higher rates of absenteeism, less job satisfaction, and increased (30%) turnover. Subjective ratings that managers made of their own performance indicated that more than 70% felt effectiveness had improved "very much," and 90% rated the productivity of their employees as "much improved" (Schneider, 1985).

Table 10.2   User-centered design benefits: user's organization

Benefits to User's Organization	Related Research
	• Office workers' performance at Blue Cross/Blue Shield, Detroit, improved 4.4% when they moved to an ergonomically improved environment (Schneider, 1985). • Martin Dainoff, University of Miami, showed that the keystroke rates for data entry tasks increased 5% when workers were changed from ergonomically unacceptable environments to one that was ergonomically correct (Schneider, 1985).
Increased value	No relevant research was found for this specific benefit.
Increased usability	• The average usability test results in 70–100 recommendations for usability improvement, according to Jeff Schueler, president of Usability Sciences Corporation in Irving, TX (LaPlante, 1992). • More than 20 American companies have in-house usability labs, according to a survey conducted by Usability Sciences Corporation. These companies estimate that their product usability is increased by as much as 20%–60% (Potter, 1989).
Decreased errors	Humantech, Inc. studies showed a drop in absenteeism from 4% to slightly greater than 1% with an ergonomically designed office environment (Schneider, 1985).
Ability to hire and use lower-level staff	Sassone (1992) has important findings related to office staffing mix and productivity improvements resulting from implementation of technology.
Lower support costs	Chapanis (1991) explains that human factors improvements to a text editor manual resulted in more successful use of commands and fewer operational questions from users.

Continued

Table 10.2 *Continued*

Benefits to User's Organization	Related Research
Decreased turnover	No relevant research was found for this specific benefit.
Decreased training costs	• A study by *Computer + Software News* (1986) found that Information Systems (IS) managers rated ease of use fourth at 8.3 (out of 10) and ease of training seventh at 7 on the scale of important purchase factors. • Chapanis (1991) mentions an AT&T success story where human factors improvements resulted in training cost savings of $2.5 million.
Increased product quality	*Which Computer* (1990) found that 10% of their readers surveyed cited quality as the most important purchase consideration.
Can hire less staff	• Sassone (1992) has important findings related to office staffing mix and productivity improvements resulting from implementation of technology. • Chapanis (1991) describes a study concerning modifications to a software product where a decrease in user error rates allowed for a potential reduction in data entry operators by one-third.
Decreased maintenance costs	Purchase criteria varies by industry and product line. For example, a report from International Data Corporation (1990) showed that, in the minisupercomputer market, ease of use was not found to be a key purchase criteria and that items such as cost of ownership (which incorporates the effects of usability) was more important to the aerospace industry and less important to the defense industry.
Increased employee morale	No relevant research was found for this specific benefit.
Decreased absenteeism	Humantech, Inc. studies showed a drop in absenteeism from 4% to slightly greater than 1% with an ergonomically designed office environment (Schneider, 1985).

Continued

Table 10.2 *Continued*

Benefits to User's Organization	Related Research
Avoids cost of lawsuits	Chapanis (1991) cites examples of lawsuits resulting from user frustration and products not meeting users' needs.
Improved ROI on technology investment	Strassman (1986) claims that more than one-third of all producers' durable investments are spent on information technology.
Competitive advantage through technology	Bacon (1992) interviewed an Information Systems VP at New England Life who claims that they have realized a competitive advantage through effective information technology application.
Less system sabotage and false error reports	No relevant research was found for this specific benefit.
Increase in active work time	• Subjects reported that an ergonomically designed office environment resulted in an increase in time spent using computer equipment from 60% to 86% and an overall increase in active work time of more than 40% (Schneider, 1985). • Management workers in one department of a major auto manufacturer used computer equipment less than 12% of the day until ergonomic equipment was installed and the usage rates went up 4 times. The average manager had at least three more hours per week for work (Schneider, 1985).
Improved employee effectiveness	• A telemarketing group reported an increase from 10% to 80% on final closing of sales after ergonomically improving their office (Schneider, 1985). • Springer Associates Inc., St. Charles, IL, demonstrated that the performance of State Farm clerical workers improved 15% with ergonomically acceptable workstations and seating (Schneider, 1985).
Can standardize on one product for different user types	No relevant research was found for this specific benefit.

Table 10.3   User-centered design benefits: development organization

Benefits to Development Organization	Related Research
User data results in a product that better matches user needs	• A Data Decisions Applications Software Survey (1985) showed that buyers rated performance based on four factors, the second being ease of use, and that 40% of the time when buyers seek alternative packages, they do so because the installed system does not meet their needs. Fifty-two percent of the respondents cited *performance* and *ease of use* as the major factor upon which they base their buying decision. • A *Which Computer* (1992) study found that first-time purchasers ranked the advice of a colleague as the number-one source of information when selecting a software product and that whether a package met their needs and was easy to use were ranked as the first and second key purchase decision criteria, respectively.
Decreased development time and costs	• House and Price (1991) cite a McKinsey study that reports that, on average, companies lose 33% of after-tax profit when they ship products six months late as compared with losses of only 3.5% when they overspend by 50% on product development. • Smith and Reinertsen (1991) have shown that, in high-growth markets with product life cycles of five years, a 50% development cost overrun cut lifetime profits by only 3.5%, but the impact on profits was as much as one-third from a six-month delay in shipping. • American Airlines has found that catching a usability problem early in the design can reduce the cost of fixing it by 60% to 90% (LaPlante, 1992).

Continued

Table 10.3 *Continued*

Benefits to Development Organization	Related Research
	• Rubey, Browning, and Roberts (1989), claim that 40% of development resources are used for specifying requirements and creating design, while 20% of the resources are used for coding and 40% of the resources are used for testing. They also state that software error correction cost is a function of the interval between when the error was made and when the error is discovered and corrected. Studies that have attempted to quantify costs associated with this interval show, at an extreme, a 100:1 ratio, so that it can cost up to 100 times as much to correct a requirements error discovered late in the test phase as it would to correct it during the requirements definition phase.
	• The first 10% of the design process is when key system design decisions are made that can determine 90% of a product's cost and performance (Smith and Reinersten, 1991).
	• Data from studies shows that about two-thirds of the errors made are requirements and design errors and that the earlier an error is made in the life cycle, the later it is likely to be discovered. For improving the reliability of the product, doing perfect coding is the most desirable approach, but, for reducing costs, having perfect requirements is the most desirable. A model shows that, if quality assurance (QA) can increase the number of errors detected at the initial phase of software development from 20% to 50%, the amount of software development costs spent to correct errors can be cut in half, so QA can be justified by comparing QA costs to savings (Rubey, Browning, and Roberts, 1989).

Continued

Table 10.3 *Continued*

Benefits to Development Organization	Related Research
Identifies and refines product ideas	The time span from identification of need to the beginning of the official design process is 50% of the actual development time, and the cost of delaying the design and development can range from 500 to 5000 times the cost of starting when market needs and/or the product ideas are still "fuzzy" (Smith and Reinersten, 1991).
Simplified/cheaper documentation and help	• A study by *Computer + Software News* (1986) found that users' most common software problems were compatibility with other software (42%), clarity of manuals (32%), organization of manuals (32%), vendor tech support (25%), installation (15%), usefulness (11%), and ease of use (9%). • *Which Computer* (1990) found that 71% of their readers surveyed found fault with documentation.
Increased product quality	• Gartner Group (1992) has stated that the "hold a joint application development and prototype" approach with an iterative development methodology will increase productivity by 25% and increase quality by 30%. • Most organizations can save $10 currently lost to internal failures and $100 lost to external failures for every additional $1 invested in prevention (Bohan and Horney, 1991).
Increased customer satisfaction	• Gartner Group (1992) has stated that there is an 80% probability that the "code and repair" methodology will result in a 40% error rate in user requirements, a 30% reduction on the structure of the resulting code, and a 25% decrease in testing costs. The "hold a joint application development and prototype" approach with a rigorous requirements analysis and design process will result in overall improvement in user satisfaction by 40%. The probability of this being true is 80%.

Continued

Table 10.3 *Continued*

Benefits to Development Organization	Related Research
	• Muller (1991) mentions several examples of findings that relate customer satisfaction to an increase in purchases: (1) According to market analyses conducted by a German frozen-foods delivery company, 100 satisfied customers generate 30 new customers which reduces costs and increases inventory turnover. (2) Ford reported a 23% difference in actual repurchase loyalty between those customers who were very satisfied with dealership service and those who were very dissatisfied. (3) Volkswagon has found that if a dealer receives a satisfaction index of 85 (max = 100) on average, 96% of their customers come back to buy a new car. (4) Studies in the consumer products industry have shown that customers with problems who do not complain have repurchase intentions of less than 10%. If a customer complains and then is completely satisfied, the likelihood of remaining loyal rises to 20%. • In terms of marketing budget, retaining loyal customers is five to eight times less expensive than attracting new customers (Muller, 1991).
Facilitates decision making	Nunamaker and Chen (1989) state that personnel and the ability to function as a team is the second most significant factor in software cost, while lines of code was the most important factor.
Decreased cost of providing training	A study by *Computer + Software News* (1986) found that IS managers rated ease of use fourth at 8.3 (out of 10) and ease of training seventh at 7 on the scale of important purchase factors.
Lower support costs and decreased maintenance	One study of banking operations and data processing executives found that the top reason for purchase of a system was to improve efficiency and that maintenance and service was the greatest purchase influence (Caradonna, 1986).

Continued

Table 10.3 *Continued*

Benefits to Development Organization	Related Research
Increased productivity of developers	Identification of incorrect requirements early in the development cycle reduces the amount of rework required and identifies useless code that is discarded. This has a ripple effect on integration, testing, and maintenance (Balda and Gustafson, 1990).
Increased market share	• Davis (1985) has shown that, given the same functionality, users will adopt the less complex software package. • Early product introduction can increase market share since the first product out will have 100% share and it is easier to keep share, especially in computer-related areas where it is more difficult for a customer to switch brands once a standard is chosen (Smith and Reinertsen, 1991). • Most of the research on advertising effectiveness shows that changes in attitude precede rather than follow purchase and that intentions to buy are related to usage and not the other way around as most models assume (Murray, 1986).
Increased sales volume and profits	• A Data Decisions Applications Software Survey (1985) showed that buyers rated performance based on four factors, the second being ease of use, and that 40% of the time when buyers seek alternative packages they do so because the installed system does not meet their needs. Fifty-two percent of the respondents cited *performance* and *ease of use* as the major factor upon which they base their buying decision. • Smith and Reinertsen (1991) have shown that in high-growth markets with product life cycles of five years, a 50% development cost overrun cut lifetime profits by only 3.5% but the impact on profits was as much as one-third from a six-month delay in shipping.

Continued

Table 10.3 *Continued*

Benefits to Development Organization	Related Research
	• House and Price (1991) cite a McKinsey study that reports that, on average, companies lose 33% of after-tax profit when they ship products six months late as compared with losses of only 3.5% when they overspend by 50% on product development.
Decreased test time	Identification of incorrect requirements early in the development cycle reduces the amount of rework required and identifies useless code that is discarded. This has a ripple effect on integration, testing, and maintenance (Balda and Gustafson, 1990).
Identifies product problems	• Data from studies show that the cost of correcting errors is approximately 25% of the total software development cost for programs 10,000 source instructions in length or smaller and increasing to 30% for programs 100,000 source instructions in length (Rubey, Browning, and Roberts, 1989). • The average usability test results in 70–100 recommendations for usability improvement according to Jeff Schueler, president of Usability Sciences Corporation in Irving, TX (LaPlante, 1992).
Allows for shared interface code	• The reuse of work products very early in the development process can provide benefits far greater than the development cost of those items. Models should accommodate "ripple effects" from reuse occurring at different stages in the development cycle (Bollinger and Pfleeger, 1990). • It is in the analysis and design phases, not coding, that most software development project efforts are expended, so reuse of analysis and design knowledge is considered more important than the reuse of code (Nunamaker and Chen, 1989).

Continued

Table 10.3 *Continued*

Benefits to Development Organization	Related Research
	• Studies have shown different types of software to have various reuse rates: application programs have the highest reuse rates ranging from 40% in non-MIS programs to 60% in business programs and as high as 85% in some cases; utility programs have a reuse rate of 32%; and systems software has a reuse rate of 10%–25% (Balda and Gustafson, 1990).
Allows for product differentiation	Recent research conducted by NCR (1992) shows that resources spent on design yield broad results and play a key role in differentiating products and human factors improvements. This research also showed that usability and human factors were the number-one determinant of design excellence.

Summary

Taken as a whole, findings reported in this section suggest that the benefits of user-centered design are a multivariate function of end-user productivity improvements, customer or company benefits, and developer productivity increases. Although the impact of an improved user interface on user productivity is certainly measurable, the task of cost justification is considerably more complex than simply measuring human performance in using the device. The least concrete (yet most important) link, the relationship between usability, customer satisfaction, and sales volume, is particularly elusive. In order to develop an automated tool that is generic enough to apply to a breadth of product lines and variety of markets, this link must be understood. It is, however, still possible to apply a cost-benefit analysis to any given project using only those variables that are identifiable and measurable. But, in order to gain broad acceptance as a tool within the cognitive engineering community, the tool will have to be quick and, of course, easy to use. The lack of available data, however, should not stop us from understanding the requirements and demand for, as well as the alternatives to, a human factors cost justification tool.

Issues in Cost-Justification Tool Development

Interviews conducted with NCR cognitive and human factors engineers provided a mechanism for understanding users' needs for cost benefit information and assessed the demand for a cost-justification tool within the NCR development organization. Most of the tables appearing in this section that list percentages are the result of multiple responses from each interviewee and therefore will be greater than 100 percent. The number refers to the percentage of participants who provided that response.

Cost-Justification Tool Users

As originally conceived, this tool would be used by a varied group, including cognitive and human factors engineers, development managers, project managers, and product managers. Following the initial interviews with the cognitive engineers and human factors engineers, the scope of the user population was considerably reduced: All interviewees reported that they would be the primary tool users. Two-thirds of the respondents thought that managers could be a secondary user group.

The primary user group, cognitive and human factors engineers, intended to use the tool to justify their overall involvement on a project and also to justify individual methods or proposed changes. Ninety-two percent of the interviewees were currently practicing user-centered design for NCR products, including both products for internal use and those being developed for resale. One-third of them were working on external projects (e.g., NCR customer and third-party vendor products) as well. Product lines covered by their projects included the financial, retail, system administration, system development, and office automation markets. Sixty-two percent of the respondents had cognitive or human factors experience prior to joining NCR.

The secondary user group consisted of managers, including directors of engineering and executive-level management at external clients. Some of the NCR human factors engineers that were currently performing cost-benefit analyses were providing their models directly to their external clients when information deemed confidential was required as input to the model. This enabled the customers to realize the advantages of the cost-benefit analysis and to perform "what-if" calculations without divulging proprietary information.

Twenty-three percent of the interview participants thought that product or project managers would also use the tool. This user group most likely would use the cost benefit analysis to justify human factors activities and design changes for their particular project. Other potential users of the model mentioned include financial analysts, clients, marketing types, customer service personnel, and developers. It was mentioned that customer service could use cost-justification data to provide credible information to developers about customer problems and suggestions for design changes.

Tasks

NCR cognitive and human factors engineers practice a variety of user-centered design methods. Methods mentioned by the respondents (listed in order of decreasing frequency) include: usability testing, needs finding analysis, rapid prototyping, design, expert evaluation, market research/focus groups, competitive product testing, task analysis, storyboarding, walkthrough analysis, design reviews, menu and icon testing, menu and icon generation, education, and customer model development. Any tool developed will need to take into account the specific costs and benefits of this entire range.

Tools Used. Although 85% of the cognitive and human factors engineers interviewed knew of cost-benefit tools and methods, only 38% had used any of these methods. Many of this group were not satisfied with the tools that they used because they were either too complex and time consuming or the underlying models did not address an important class of benefits, such as those experienced by the end user's company. Forty-five percent of those who knew of tools and methods learned of them through human factors journal articles and papers and courses that they had attended at conferences, while 36% knew about cost-benefit methods through previous work experience. The 62% of the respondents who had not used any cost-benefit tools or methods said that they never had the need to do so.

Slightly less then half (46%) of the respondents said that they used project planning software, such as Microsoft Project. Although standard development processes exist within the company, development groups are free to adapt processes to their specific situation. This approach allows individual business units to have a great deal of freedom to match their approach to the needs of their product line and the business strategies of the group. Thus, any tool developed for cost justification of human factors activities will have to remain flexible to address a range of changing and evolving planning methods.

Project Involvement. When used in the project planning stages, the cost-benefit analysis tool will justify cognitive and human factors engineers' overall involvement on a project. For this reason and in order to derive information about the process, the interview participants were questioned about the way that they typically get involved in a project. Forty-two percent of the interviewees mentioned that they are usually involved at an early stage in the product development cycle. Ninety-one percent of this group was located at NCR development sites.

Seventy-one percent of those located in the business units proactively sought out involvement in projects. Other than proactive involvement, other key initiators for user-centered design services were project, product, and development managers, developers and documentation specialists, and marketing or sales people.

The top reason for seeking human factors services is the instigator's belief that the application needs help. Reasons for initiating user-centered design typically varies based on who does the soliciting. For example, cognitive engineers, developers, and documentation writers tend to get involved in user-centered design because the product needs help, while sales and marketing people initiate involvement to ensure compliance with standards. Other reasons mentioned by respondents include management mandate and prior experience.

The process and patterns of initiating user-centered design become important considerations for the cost-benefit tool. Not only will this information allow for proper planning in terms of the target audience for the cost-justification data, but the information on the reasons that involvement is typically initiated will enable the output messages concerning human factors involvement to highlight appropriate benefits in terms of the specific audience's criteria.

Education and Promotion. Considering that one of the primary objectives of the cost-justification tool is to provide data for the promotion of human factors activities and education about the benefits of user-centered design, the NCR human factors and cognitive engineers were questioned about other tasks that they currently perform in the areas of promotion and education. All of the interviewees who were practicing user-centered design were performing educational tasks in some format. Education included information discussions, presentations, circulation of literature, courses, and adding user-centered design methods to the project schedule. Audiences for this information ranged from project management to peers to upper management.

The presentations typically consisted of an overview of user-centered design, which described the process, methods, examples, and application to the client's specific project. Also, some of the cognitive engineering groups offered a service that documented the human factors methods and got developers to participate in the user-centered design process. Management was educated through literature, discussions, and examples. In some instances, a course series had been offered to developers covering issues such as screen design, task analysis, usability testing, and prototyping.

The variety and quantity of educational and promotional tasks that were taking place indicate the importance of the function. Data derived from the cost-justification tool can be used to either replace or supplement and enhance these educational and promotional efforts.

Environment

The environment of use for the cost-justification tool is a major consideration. Not only will the environment determine some of the tool's requirements, but, given that the tool will be used in the initial stages of a project, its output will serve to influence and set clients' expectations of the user-centered design process. This becomes even more important when one considers that clients' perceptions about user-centered design are formed based upon their expectations and experiences. For this reason, NCR cognitive and human factors engineers were queried about their clients' perceptions and expectations. It should be noted that follow-up interviews are being conducted since the clients themselves should be interviewed as well in order to confirm these findings.

Project Team Awareness and Attitudes about User-Centered Design.
Thirty-eight percent of the interviewees said that *developers'* expectations varied based upon a number of factors including project schedule, maturity of the development team, user interface design experience, job level, and background and skill sets of the developers. Thirty-one percent of the participants made positive comments about developer expectations, while 46% made negative comments. Negative responses included developers feeling slighted, not believing in cognitive engineering or thinking that it is unnecessary, not taking it seriously, being biased to the

machine, not caring. Positive comments included developers understanding the difficulty of user interface design, being impressed, appreciating the customer reaction, thinking that cognitive engineers have a "Midas touch," and taking their word on interface design issues as "gospel." Constructive comments include developers expecting a design solution, being familiarized by exposure to quality programs, wanting to use human factors' rules, and wanting ideas, answers, and suggestions as well as a graphical user interface like their competitors'.

On the other hand, 23% of the interviewees said that *management's* expectation varied based on project schedule and previous exposure to user-centered design. Thirty-eight percent had positive comments including management appreciating the benefits, being open to involvement, having an awareness of the process, and considering user-centered design to be strategically important. Sixty-nine percent thought management expectations were more on the negative side, with comments such as: management will sacrifice design for the schedule; their interest is self-serving; they expect miracles, do not understand, want to postpone changes, think cognitive engineers' skills are merely common sense, and are unrealistic about time frames.

In addition to questions about clients' expectations, the NCR cognitive and human factors engineers were also questioned about clients' awareness and understanding of user-centered design. None of the cognitive and human factors engineers thought that user-centered design was understood by the project team. Thirty-eight percent of the interviewees said that there was some level of understanding and familiarity with user-centered design processes and concepts. No one thought there was enough awareness of the benefits, although sixty-two percent said that there was some level of awareness and thirty-eight percent said there was no awareness of the benefits.

When asked about concerns with negative side effects of human factors activities, all interviewees mentioned that there were concerns, including schedule impacts (mentioned by two-thirds of the respondents), costs, developers' feelings/communication issues, and design changes. Significantly, none of the respondents mentioned resource requirements as a concern.

When asked if the opinion of the project team changed throughout the product development cycle, all respondents answered "yes" and gave the following reasons for the change in opinion: experience/education/ exposure, seeing the deliverable, success stories, management support, impartiality of the cognitive engineer, minimal impacts on schedule, and customer reaction.

Table 10.4 What convinces people of the value of user-centered design

What Convinces People	Response (%)
Testimonials/case stories/demonstrated results	62
Support from customers/management/outside companies	23
Cost-benefit information	15
Experience	8

Demand for Cost-Benefit Information. Respondents were also asked what would convince people that user-centered design is beneficial and legitimate. Answers are categorized in Table 10.4.

As depicted in Table 10.4, only 15% of the interviewees thought that cost-benefit information could convince people of the merits of their services. Also 54% of the cognitive and human factors engineers reported that they have never been asked for cost-benefit information, although they believed that if they offered it, 75% of their clients would want it. Of the 46% who have been asked for cost-benefit data, the request occurs on average on 38% of their projects.

Although a cost-benefit model was not seen as the primary way to influence people of the value of user-centered design, the interview participants did think that their clients would want the information and that it would make their job easier. This conclusion should be verified by researching the opinions of development managers and others who are the audience for the cost-benefit information since it is possible that the cognitive and human factors engineers did not accurately represent manager's needs. Also see Chapters 3 and 11 in this volume for further evidence in support of the value of cost-benefit analysis.

Although cost-justification data was not thought of as a primary influence, it was seen as an important component of large external projects that may be strategic business opportunities. Also, cognitive engineers should be prepared to supply quantified cost-benefit information to higher-level management, since they were mentioned as a group that was likely to request the information. In any case, the findings have pinpointed the relevance of employing additional methods of promoting user-centered design either as an alternative or complement to cost-justification data.

Tool Requirements

The NCR human factors and cognitive engineers were questioned about requirements for the tool, usage patterns, and ways to implement the tool.

Tool Usage Patterns

Forty-six percent of the participants thought that the model would be used once on each project, while another 46% thought that it would be used once or twice. Only one participant thought that it would be used more than twice on a project. Interviewees were asked at what stage(s) of the product development cycle they would use the tool. Seventy-seven percent of the respondents indicated that the model would likely be used at the beginning of a project, and 23% thought that it would also be used when there were major changes or updates. Fifteen percent of the interviewees mentioned that the model may also be used at the end of the project, while another 30% said that it would used during the project to verify each method or to justify a specific and strategic method. Reasons subjects gave for how the tool would be used are summarized in Table 10.5. Percentages indicate the frequency of response for that particular item.

Functionality

Domain. In general, almost all the respondents had ideas about what type of tool they would like to use. Interviewees asked for a Microsoft Windows-based product that did not require the use of specific methods but would identify the needs based on each project. Users wanted to be able to plug their numbers into an English form, then have a number pop up, with the benefits broken out over the next five years. Requests for the ability to show how to improve productivity or save the customer

Table 10.5 Intended uses for the cost-justification tool

How the Tool Will Be Used	Response (%)
As a sales tool to justify involvement on the project	62
To justify individual changes or methods proposed	31
To show the benefits of user-centered design	31
To show cost estimates	23
To compare products	23
To determine the focus of cognitive engineering efforts	15
Planning and scheduling	8
Education	8
To verify the results of each method	8
To support decision making	8
To predict the product's impact	8

a specific amount were common. Potential users wanted the model to calculate, given the specific environmental variables and organizational characteristics, numbers that depicted the cost of both performing and not performing user-centered design in order to calculate the potential savings to the development organization.

It was made clear that the tool should not require the user to have any special skills in order to use it and that it should call on relevant case examples specific to the project to illustrate the points made by the results of the analysis.

Features. All interview respondents had ideas about features for the cost-benefit tool, with the top requirements being validity and accuracy, flexibility, and ease of use. Other ideas mentioned were that the model should provide estimates for soft accounting issues and comparisons between products that use and do not use user-centered design, should show what user-centered design can do for the company's bottom line, and should motivate people and get them to act on the data. A wide range of features was mentioned; they are ranked in order of the frequency of mention in Table 10.6. The number following each feature indicates how many times that particular feature was mentioned.

Model Input. Some of the potential users had a good understanding of what the model would require as input and expected the model to ask questions about the vertical market, internal vs. external product, number of screens, number of end users, current training costs, documentation, ease-of-use importance to the target user population, and competitive products. When it came to gathering input for the model, however, 85% of the interviewees thought that there would be some data they couldn't get due to unavailability or confidentiality issues, especially if the project was an external one. The Appendix contains a project data form that was compiled as an example of the type of information that is needed for input to the model.

Output. In addition to showing quantified benefits and cost savings, interview participants wanted the model to prepare budgets and schedules and provide a simple, one-page presentation illustrating the key findings of the analysis. There were requests for the ability to produce plans that included phases, goals, steps with an objective, procedures and deliverables for each step, and a budget that is broken down by phase/step with totals for each phase (fees plus expenses) and time for each step. Table

Table 10.6   Cost-justification tool features

Features and Number of Respondents Mentioning Each Feature

What-if capability (4)
Flexibility for different project types/size (4)
Flexibility for methods used (2)
Ease of use (2)
Weighted customer data (1)
Support management decision making (1)
Show costs of *not* using user centered design (1)
Should provide a schedule (1)
Should *not* require user performance measurement (1)
Result of analysis should be a number (1)
Quick to use (1)
Quantify social and environmental aspects (1)
Provide disclaimer with data (1)
Optimize for a given budget (1)
Notify the cognitive engineer when tool is used by client (1)
Mimic proposal process (bartering) (1)
Graphical output with supporting data (1)
Focus on cost first, not productivity (1)
Flexibility for different types of users (1)
Explanation of methods (1)
Define costs (1)
Compatible with Windows, DOS, and other tools (1)
Compare sales projections with competitors (1)
Behavioral performance model (1)
Provide overview of model upon request (1)

10.7 represents the range of responses, with the number following each item indicating the number of times that response was mentioned.

Roll Out and Implementation

As the data reported in the previous sections indicate, the cost-benefit model was not seen by the cognitive and human factors engineers as the primary way to convince people of the value of user-centered design. There are indications, however, that they thought it could be a useful and important tool. As previously mentioned, this conclusion should be verified by researching the opinions of those who are the audience for the cost-benefit information.

Table 10.7   Cost-benefit tool output

Output Features and Number of Respondents Mentioning Each Type of Output

Quantified benefits (5)
Estimates on cost savings for both customers and management (5)
Budgets (4)
Schedules (3)
One-page, simple presentation (3)
ROI projections (2)
Visual output (1)
Use NCR's current buzzwords (1)
Training performance estimates (1)
Plan (1)
Case studies (1)
Back-up data should be available (1)

Interview participants were questioned about validity of the model since this was seen as an important requirement. All the participants thought that a cost-benefit analysis of user-centered design could be modeled, but in order to believe in it, 54% wanted to have in-depth information about how the model worked and the assumptions and data that it used. Forty-six percent also wanted to see demonstrated case examples so that they could accept the model. Twenty-three percent claimed that it didn't matter how good the model was anyway because it wouldn't necessarily be the correct tool to convince people of the need for user-centered design. A listing of response excerpts appears in Table 10.8.

Many ideas and suggestions were made about how to make the tool available. Twenty-three percent of the respondents stated that the model should be rolled out with some type of personal follow up; another 23% said that it should be distributed through the cognitive and human factors engineering groups, while another 23 percent said that it could be sold.

The group reported that the model would make their jobs easier by providing more credibility, improving the ability to get funding for research, making management expectations more reasonable, supporting the development process and timelines, allowing the cognitive engineer to focus more on practicing user-centered design, helping to allocate resources, and helping the education process.

Table 10.8   What would make the model believable

What Is Needed to Make the Model Believable
Support for different product lines and verticals
Showing the algorithms
Quantify soft accounting issues
An educational approach
Not marketing materials
A credible source
Experiencing the benefits personally
Good historical data
Demonstrated case examples
Quantify soft accounting issues
Tests done in controlled environment
Should make intuitive sense
Demonstration of before and after using vignettes and videos
Case stories
Doesn't matter if they don't want to believe

Clearly, the NCR cognitive and human factors engineers would appreciate the benefits offered by a cost-justification tool; however, it will be a wasted effort if the tool is not implemented correctly because the demand for cost-benefit data, per se, may not be at a sufficient level to require that the user-centered design practitioners employ the cost-justification tool.

Two major issues must be resolved in order to provide a high-quality cost-justification tool: ensuring the success of the cognitive engineer in the data collection process and overcoming the lack of quantifiable benefit information. Also, when considering the ultimate goal of the tool, the promotion of user-centered design, it makes sense to incorporate the tool as a strategic component in an overall plan containing a number of other vehicles designed to enhance and complement the cost-justification efforts. These efforts could consist, in the short term, of education and promotional programs, while in the long term, there are a number of technologies available that can enable the cost-justification tool to exist as part of an advanced user-centered design system.

Future Directions

As the preceding analyses have indicated, potential users of a cost-justification tool see its primary benefit in justifying their involvement in development projects. Such a tool could be used by cognitive engineers in staff positions, as well as by groups selling services. It is likely, of course, that as user-centered design activities become more prevalent, there will be increased need for tools to support resource allocation. Users reported that, contrary to initial expectations, examples, testimonials, and case studies would be the most useful form of cost-justification data.

These results suggest that the most immediately useful tool would be one with capabilities of retrieving example cases with attributes similar to the project at hand. Examples are most useful when they appear to be similar to the current situation. Case-based reasoning technology offers a viable means of storing, searching, and retrieving similar cases. Case-based reasoning can adapt old solutions to meet new demands and use old cases to explain new situations, critique new solutions, or reason from precedents to interpret a new situation or create an equitable solution to a new problem. A case-based approach relies on describing examples through a number of attributes. A major difficulty in developing such a tool is obtaining a sufficient number of examples that lead to making a credible sales story. The appendix contains an example form for collecting project data that could form a basis for a case-based reasoning approach to supporting cost justification.

As mentioned previously, a second use of cost-justification information is for resource management: What user-centered design activities should be performed during development of Product X and who should perform them? Such questions become increasingly complex as the development of user interfaces becomes more complex. Graphics, video, animation, sound, artificial intelligence, and other technologies, although having the potential of creating user interfaces that are much easier to use, also force development strategies that are much more involved. Thus, project management issues are much more involved. Accordingly, the needs of a cost-justification tool to support resource management issues become considerably more complex.

Blatt and Zacherl (1993) have described a user interface design guidance system (UIDGS). This proposed system provides an integrated suite of automated tools and methods to support the design and implementation of easy-to-use user interfaces. The primary purpose of the UIDGS is to provide developers and designers access to human-factors–related information and methods. In addition, the UIDGS can provide tools to support the proposal and planning functions associated with user-centered design. Key to the proposal generation function are examples of cost-justification data for other similar projects. Key to the project-planning function are cost models or examples on a much more detailed level. Besides providing design advice, therefore, the UIDGS will assist developers, project management, and cognitive engineers in making necessary project management trade-offs.

The research summarized and presented in this chapter provides the necessary groundwork for building an automated cost-justification modeling tool. We have discussed approaches to quantifying user-centered design benefits. Given the lack of research and the intangible nature of many of these benefits (especially concerning the important links between benefits derived by end users, their organizations, and user-centered design), there is much work to be done if a solid and comprehensive cost-benefit model is to be built. Sassone and Schaffer (1978) claim that, because cost-benefit models and studies are usually intended to be decision aids, they must be analytically sound, credible to both the user and to his or her audience, and they must be tractable. They describe the challenge and the art of cost-benefit analysis as developing models that meet all three of these criteria.

There are two important tasks remaining in support of the goal of developing a comprehensive model for cost-benefit analysis of user-centered design. The first step is to continue gathering information on research that proves the link between user-centered design and benefits to users, their organizations, and development organizations. The next step is to investigate further the findings about cognitive engineers' perceived need for a cost-benefit tool. Early indications from our ongoing research in this area show a high level of interest from product managers in a cost-benefit tool. Assuming that these findings can be verified and given the potential for applying advanced technologies, we are confident that we understand the requirements and process for developing an automated cost-justification tool for user-centered design.

Appendix: Detailed Project Data

Contact

Contact name: _____
Phone number: _____   Organization: _____

Project

Project name: _____

Ship date: _____   Price/unit: _____

Platform: _____   Upgrade?   Y   N

Platform change?   Y   N

Development Effort

Planned time frame: _____   Actual time frame: _____

Number of developers: _____   Number of man-months: _____

KLOC: _____   Other development effort

estimates: _____

Market Data

No. of potential customers: _____   No. of competitors: _____

Market share projected: _____   Actual: _____

Product uniqueness/Scale of differentiation:

Highly unique   Somewhat unique   Common

Usability Scale of Importance

No. of end users: _____   Users: Internal/external

User type: Nontechnical/technical

Usage patterns: Uses per day: _____   Uses per week: _____

Time between uses: Task complexity:

High   Medium   Low

_____

Legal implications: Y   N   Health and Safety

Implications: Y   N

Costs

Projected development costs: _____   Actual development costs: _____

Cost of goods: _____

Revenues

Projected: _____   Actual: _____

Unit Shipments

Projected: _____   Actual: _____

User-Centered Design Cost Data

UCD Methods	People	Equipment	Outside Resources	Overhead
Needs finding analysis				
Usability testing				
Competitive products testing				
Prototyping				
Storyboarding				
Walkthrough analysis				
Design reviews				
Menu and icon testing				
Menu and icon generation				
Expert evaluation				
Task analysis				
Other				
Other				

Benefits Derived from User-Centered Design

Level of UCD Implementation: High   Medium   Low

Increases in usability/productivity:

_____

_____

_____

Decreases in cost:

_____

_____

_____

Increased customer satisfaction/market effects:

_____

_____

_____

References

Bacon, S. E. (1992). What's the use? *Best's Review (Life/Health)* **93**(4), 88–92.

Balda, D. M. and Gustafson, D. A. (1990). Cost estimation models for the reuse and prototype software development life-cycle. *ACM SIGSOFT Software Engineering Notes* **15**(3), 42–50.

Blatt, L. A. and Zacherl, A. (1993). User interface requirements for the representation of examples in a user interface design guidance system. *INTERCHI '93 Adjunct Proceedings.* Amsterdam, The Netherlands, April 24–29, 31–32.

Bohan, G. P. and Horney, N. F. (1991). Pinpointing the real cost of quality in a service company. *National Productivity Review* **10**(3) 309–317.

Bollinger, T. B. and Pfleeger, S. L. (1990). The economics of reuse: Issues and alternatives. *Proceedings of the Eighth Annual National Conference on ADA Technology.* Atlanta, Georgia, March 5–8, 436–447.

Bonoma, T. V. and Clark, B. H. (1988). *Marketing Performance Assessment.* Harvard Business School Press, Boston, Massachusetts.

Brownlie, D. T. (1991). A case analysis of the cost and value of marketing information. *Marketing Intelligence and Planning* **9**(1), 11–18.

Caradonna, L. (1986). Maintenance is top factor for 69 percent of software buyers. *Bank Systems and Equipment* **23**(8), 40–42.

Chapanis, A. (1991). The business case for human factors in informatics. in: *Human Factors for Informatics Usability.* (Shackel and Richardson, eds.) Cambridge University Press, 39–71.

Computer + Software News (May 19, 1986). Vendors, IS managers, users differ on desirable factors. **4**(20), 16.

Data Decisions (May 1, 1985). The applications software survey. *Datamation* **39**(9), 118–138.

Davis, F. D. (1985). A technology acceptance model for empirically testing new end-user information systems: Theory and results. Ph.D. Dissertation. Sloan School of Management, MIT, Cambridge, Massachusetts.

Gartner Group (July 16, 1992). Selecting and implementing a systems development methodology. Stamford, Connecticut.

House, C. H. and Price, R. L. (January–February 1991). The return map: tracking product teams. *Harvard Business Review* 92–100

International Data Corporation (April 1990). Competing beyond technology: user satisfaction and buying criteria among minisupercomputer users. Framingham, Massachusetts.

Karat, C. M. (1990). Cost-benefit analysis of usability engineering techniques. In: *Proceedings of the Human Factors Society 34th Annual Meeting—1990.* Human Factors Society, Santa Monica, California, 839–843.

Karat, C. M. (1992). Cost-justifying human factors support on software development projects. *Human Factors Society Bulletin* **35**(11), 1–4.

LaPlante, A. (July 27, 1992). Put to the test. *Computerworld* **27**, 75.

Loveman, G. W. (July 1988). An assessment of the productivity impact of information technologies. *Working Paper—Management in the 1990s.* MIT, Cambridge, Massachusetts.

Mayhew, D. J. (1990). Cost-justifying human factors support—a framework. In: *Proceedings of the Human Factors Society 34th Annual Meeting—1990.* Human Factors Society, Santa Monica, California, 834–838.

Mantei, M. M. and Teorey, T. J. (April 1988). Cost/benefit analysis for incorporating human factors in the software lifecycle. *Communications of the ACM* **31**(4), 428–439.

Muller, W. (1991). Gaining competitive advantage through customer satisfaction. *European Management Journal* **9**(2), 201–211.

Murray, H. (1986). Advertising's effect on sales—proven or just assumed? *International Journal of Advertising* **5**(1), 15–36.

NCR. (July 1992). The search for design excellence. Dayton, Ohio.

Nunamaker, J., Jr. and Chen, M. (1989). Software productivity: A framework of study and an approach to reusable components. *Proceedings of the Twenty-Second Annual Hawaii International Conference on System Sciences. Vol. II: Software Track,* 959–968.

Poppel, H. L. (Nov.–Dec. 1982). Who needs the office of the future? *Harvard Business Review* 146–155.

Potter, P. (1989). Usability labs make a difference. *Insurance Software Review* **14**(6), 15–17.

Rosenberg, D. (1989). A cost benefit analysis for corporate user interface standards: What price to pay for a consistent "look and feel"? In: *Coordinating User Interfaces for Consistency* (Nielsen, J., ed.). Academic Press, San Diego, California, 21–34.

Rubey, R. J., Browning, L. A, Roberts, A. R. (1989). Cost effectiveness of software quality assurance. *Proceedings of the IEEE 1989 National Aerospace and Electronics Conference NAECON 1989.* May 22–26, Dayton, Ohio. **4**, 1614–1620.

Sassone, P. G. (Spring 1992). Survey finds low office productivity linked to staffing imbalances. *National Productivity Review.* 147–157.

Sassone, P. G. and Schaffer, W. (1978). *Cost Benefit Analysis: A Handbook.* Academic Press, Boston.

Schneider, M. F. (1985). Why ergonomics can no longer be ignored. *Office Administration and Automation* **46**(7), 26–29.

Smith, P. G. and Reinertsen, D. G. (1991). *Developing Products in Half the Time.* Van Nostrand Reinhold, New York.

Strassman, P. A. (1986). Improving information worker productivity: White House conference on productivity. *Information Management Review* 1(4), 55–60.

Temple, Barker & Sloane, Inc. (Spring 1990). The benefits of the graphical user interface. Lexington, Massachusetts.

Which Computer? (May 1990). Software quality. 139–141.

Which Computer? (February 1992). 15(2), 107.

Zeller, R. A. (Aug. 29, 1988). How to calculate the value of focus group research. *Marketing News*, 45.

Part IV

Special Issues

Chapter 11

Guerrilla HCI: Using Discount Usability Engineering to Penetrate the Intimidation Barrier

Jakob Nielsen

SunSoft, Inc.
Mountain View, California

One of the oldest jokes in computer science goes as follows:

Q: How many programmers does it take to change a light bulb?
A: None; it is a hardware problem!

When asking how many usability specialists it takes to change a light bulb, the answer might well be four: two to conduct a field study and task analysis to determine whether people really need light, one to observe the user who actually screws in the light bulb, and one to control the video camera filming the event. It is certainly true that one should study user needs before implementing supposed solutions to those problems. Even so, the perception that anybody touching usability will come down with a bad case of budget overruns keeps many software projects from achieving the level of usability that their users deserve.

The Intimidation Barrier

It is well known that people rarely use the recommended usability engineering methods (Nielsen, 1993; Whiteside *et al.*, 1988) on software development projects in real life. This includes even such basic usability engineering techniques as early focus on the user, empirical measurement, and iterative design, which are used by very few companies. Gould and Lewis (1985) found that only 16% of developers mentioned all three principles when asked what one should do when developing and evaluating a new computer system for end users. Twenty-six percent of developers did not mention even one of these extremely basic principles. A more recent study found that only 21% of Danish software developers knew about the thinking-aloud method and that only 6% actually used it (Milsted *et al.*, 1989). More advanced usability methods were not used at all.

One important reason that usability engineering is not used in practice is the cost of using the techniques. Or rather, the reason is the *perceived* cost of using these techniques, as this chapter will show that many usability techniques can be used quite cheaply. It should be no surprise, however, that practitioners view usability methods as expensive considering, for example, that a paper in the widely read and very respected journal *Communications of the ACM* estimated that the "costs required to add human factors elements to the development of software" were $128,330 (Mantei and Teorey, 1988). This sum is several times the total budget for usability in most smaller companies, and one interface evangelist has actually found it necessary to warn such small companies against believing this estimate (Tognazzini, 1990). Otherwise, the result could easily be that a project manager would discard any attempt at usability engineering in the belief that the project's budget could not bear the cost. Table 11.1 shows the result of adjusting a usability budget according to the discount usability engineering method discussed in this chapter. The numbers in Table 11.1 are for a medium-scale software project (about 32,000 lines of code). For small projects, even cheaper methods can be used. Really large projects might consider additional funds to usability and the full-blown traditional methodology, though even large projects can benefit considerably from using discount usability engineering.

British studies (Bellotti, 1988) indicate that many developers don't use usability engineering because HCI (human–computer interaction) methods are seen as too time consuming and expensive and because the techniques are often intimidating in their complexity. The "discount usability engineering" approach is intended to address these two issues. Further reasons given by Bellotti were that there were sometimes no perceived need for HCI and a lack of awareness about appropriate techniques. These two other problems must be addressed by education (Perlman,

Table 11.1 Cost savings in a medium-scale software project by using the discount usability engineering method instead of the more thorough usability methods sometimes recommended

Original usability cost estimate by Mantei and Teorey (1988)	$128,330
Scenario developed as paper mock-up instead of on videotape	−2,160
Prototyping done with free hypertext package	−16,000
All user testing done with three subjects instead of five	−11,520
Thinking-aloud studies analyzed by taking notes instead of by video taping	−5,520
Special video laboratory not needed	−17,600
Only two focus groups instead of three for market research	−2,000
Only one focus group instead of three for accept analysis	−4,000
Questionnaires only used in feedback phase, not after prototype testing	−7,200
Usability expert brought in for heuristic evaluation	+3,000
Cost for "discount usability engineering" project	$65,330

1988, 1990; Nielsen and Molich, 1989) and propaganda (Nielsen, 1990a), but even for that purpose, simpler usability methods should help. Also, time itself is on the side of increasing the perceived need for HCI since the software market seems to be shifting away from the "features war" of earlier years (Telles, 1990). Now, most software products have more features than users will ever need or learn, and Telles (1990) states that the "interface has become an important element in garnering good reviews" of software in the trade press.

As an example of "intimidating complexity," consider the paper by Karwowski *et al.* (1989) on extending the GOMS model (Card *et al.*, 1983) with fuzzy logic. Note that I am not complaining that doing so is bad research. On the contrary, I find it very exciting to develop methods to extend models like GOMS to deal better with real-world circumstances like uncertainty and user errors. Unfortunately, the fuzzy logic GOMS and similar work can easily lead to intimidation when software people without in-depth knowledge of the HCI field read the papers. These readers may well believe that such methods represent *the* way to do usability engineering even though usability specialists would know that the research represents exploratory probes to extend the field and should only serve as, say, the fifth or so method one would use on a project. There are many simpler methods that one should use first (Nielsen, 1992a, 1993).

I certainly can be guilty of intimidating behavior too. For example, together with Marco Bergman, I recently completed a research project on iterative design where we employed a total of 99 subjects to test various versions of a user interface at a total estimated cost of $62,786. People reading papers reporting on this and similar studies might be excused if they think that iterative design and user testing are expensive and overly elaborate procedures. In fact, of course, it is possible to use considerably fewer subjects and get by with much cheaper methods, and we took care to say so explicitly in our paper. A basic problem is that, with a few exceptions, published descriptions of usability work normally describe cases where considerable extra efforts were expended on deriving publication-quality results, even though most development needs can be met in much simpler ways.

As one example, consider the issue of statistical significance. I recently had a meeting to discuss usability engineering with the head of computer science for one of the world's most famous laboratories, and when discussing the needed number of subjects for various tests, he immediately referred to the need for test results to be statistically significant to be worth collecting. Certainly, for much research, you need to have a high degree of confidence that your claimed findings are not just due to chance. For the development of usable interfaces, however, one can often be satisfied by less rigorous tests.

Statistical significance is basically an indication of the probability that one is not making the wrong conclusion (e.g., a claim that a certain result is significant at the $p < 0.05$ level indicates that there is a 5% probability that it is false). Consider the problem of choosing between two alternative interface designs (Landauer, 1988). If *no* information is available, you might as well choose by tossing a coin, and you will have a 50% probability of choosing the best interface. If a small amount of user testing has been done, you may find that interface A is better than interface B at the 20% level of significance. Even though 20% is considered "not significant," your tests have actually improved your chance of choosing the best interface from 50/50 to 4-to-1, meaning that you would be foolish not to take the data into account when choosing. Furthermore, even though there remains a 20% probability that interface A is not better than interface B, it is very unlikely that it would be *much* worse than interface B. Most of the 20% accounts for cases where the two interfaces are equal or where B is slightly better than A, meaning that it would almost never be a *really* bad decision to choose interface A. In other words, even tests that are not statistically significant are well worth doing since they will improve the quality of decisions substantially.

The Discount Usability Engineering Approach

Usability specialists will often propose using the best possible methodology. Indeed, this is what they have been trained to do in most universities. Unfortunately, it seems that *"le mieux est l'ennemi du bien"* (the best is the enemy of the good) (Voltaire, 1764) to the extent that insisting on using only the best methods may result in having no methods used at all. Therefore, I will focus on achieving "the good" with respect to having some usability engineering work performed, even though the methods needed to achieve this result are definitely not "the best" method and will not give perfect results.

It will be easy for the knowledgable reader to put down the methods proposed here with various well-known counterexamples showing important usability aspects that will be missed under certain circumstances. Some of these counterexamples are no doubt true, and I do agree that better results can be achieved by applying more careful methodologies. But remember that such more careful methods are also more expensive—often in terms of money, and always in terms of required expertise (leading to the intimidation factor). Therefore, the simpler methods stand a much better chance of actually being used in practical design situations, and they should therefore be viewed as a way of serving the user community.

The "discount usability engineering" (Nielsen, 1989b, 1990a, 1993) method is based on the use of the following three techniques: scenarios, simplified thinking aloud, and heuristic evaluation. Additionally, the basic principle of early focus on users should, of course, be followed. It can be achieved in various ways, including simple visits to customer locations.

Scenarios

Scenarios are a special kind of prototyping, as shown in Figure 11.1. The entire idea behind prototyping is to cut down on the complexity of implementation by eliminating parts of the full system. Horizontal prototypes reduce the level of functionality and result in a user interface surface layer, while vertical prototypes reduce the number of features and implement the full functionality of those chosen (i.e., we get to play with a part of the system).

Scenarios take prototyping to the extreme by reducing both the level of functionality and the number of features. By reducing the part of in-

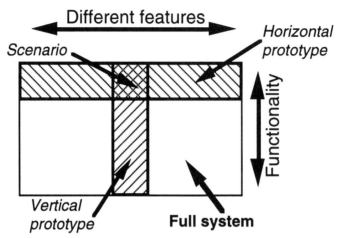

Figure 11.1 The concept of scenario compared to vertical and horizontal prototypes as ways to make rapid prototyping simpler.

terface being considered to the minimum, a scenario can be very cheap to design and implement, but it is only able to simulate the user interface as long as a test user follows a previously planned path.

Since the scenario is small, we can afford to change it frequently, and, if we use cheap, small thinking aloud studies, we can also afford to test each of the versions. Therefore, scenarios are a way of getting quick and frequent feedback from users.

Scenarios can be implemented as paper mock-ups (Nielsen, 1990b) or in simple prototyping environments (Nielsen, 1989a) that may be easier to learn than more advanced programing environments (Nielsen *et al.*, 1991). This is an additional savings compared with more complex prototypes requiring the use of advanced software tools.

Simplified Thinking Aloud

Traditionally, thinking-aloud studies are conducted with psychologists or user interface experts as experimenters who videotape the subjects and perform detailed protocol analysis. This kind of method certainly may seem intimidating for ordinary developers. However, it is possible to run user tests without sophisticated labs, simply by bringing in some real users, giving them some typical test tasks, and asking them to think out loud while they perform the tasks. Those developers who have used the thinking-aloud method are happy about it (Jørgensen, 1989; Monk *et al.*, 1993), and my studies (Nielsen, 1992b) show that computer scientists are indeed able to apply the thinking-aloud method effectively to evaluate user interfaces with a minimum of training and that even fairly methodologically primitive experiments will succeed in finding many usability problems.

I have long claimed that one learns the most from the first few test users, based on several case studies. In earlier papers, I have usually recommended using between three and five test users per test as a way of simplifying user testing while gaining almost the same benefits as one would get from more elaborate tests with large numbers of subjects. Recently, Tom Landauer and I developed a mathematical model of the number of usability problems (Nielsen and Landauer, 1993), and when plugging in typical budget figures from different kinds of user testing, we derived curves like the ones shown in Figure 11.2 for the ratio between the benefits of user testing and the cost of the test for medium-sized development projects. The curves basically show that the benefits from user testing are much larger than the costs, no matter how many subjects are used. The maximum benefit-cost ratio is achieved when using between three and five subjects, confirming my earlier experience.

Besides reducing the number of subjects, another major difference between simplified and traditional thinking aloud is that data analysis can be done on the basis of the notes taken by the experimenter instead of by videotapes. Recording, watching, and analyzing the videotapes is expensive and takes a lot of time which is better spent on running more subjects and on testing more iterations of redesigned user interfaces. Video taping should only be done in those cases (such as research studies) where absolute certainty is needed. In discount usability engineering, we don't aim at perfection anyway, we just want to find most of the usability problems, and a survey of 11 software engineers (Perlman, 1988) found that they rated simple tests of prototypes as almost twice as useful as video protocols.

Heuristic Evaluation

Current user interface standards and collections of usability guidelines typically have on the order of one thousand rules to follow and are therefore seen as intimidating by developers.[1] For the discount method, I

---

[1]Table 1 in Thovtrup and Nielsen (1991) shows that the average length of popular user interface standards and guidelines documents is 324 pages, which corresponds to between about 500 and 2,000 rules. The trend is towards ever-larger documents. For example, one set of guidelines increased from 166 small pages in the first edition to 384 large pages in the second edition five years later (Apple Computer, 1987, 1992).

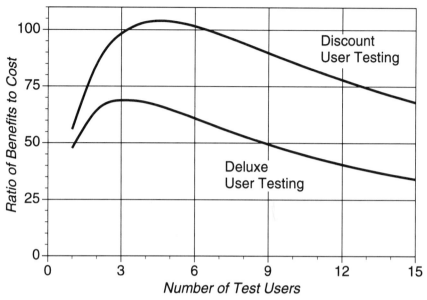

Figure 11.2 Cost-benefit trade-off curve for a "typical" project, varying the number of test users, using the model and average parameters described by Nielsen and Landauer (1993). The curve shows the ratio of benefits to costs, that is, how many times the benefits are larger than the costs. For example, a benefit-to-cost ratio of 50 might correspond to costs of $10,000 and benefits of $500,000.

advocate cutting the complexity by two orders of magnitudes and instead relying on a small set of heuristics such as the ten basic usability principles listed in Table 11.2.

These principles can be presented in a single lecture and can be used to explain a very large proportion of the problems that one observes in user interface designs. Unfortunately, it does require some experience with the principles to apply them sufficiently thoroughly (Nielsen, 1992c), so it might be necessary to spend some money on getting outside usability consultants to help with a heuristic evaluation. On the other hand, even nonexperts can find many usability problems by heuristic evaluation, and many of the remaining problems would be revealed by the simplified thinking-aloud test. It can also be recommended to let several different people perform a heuristic evaluation as different people locate different usability problems (Nielsen and Molich, 1990). This is another reason why even discount usability engineers might consider setting aside a part of their budget for outside usability consultants.

Table 11.2 These ten usability principles (the "heuristics" in heuristic evaluation) should be followed by all user interfaces. This list was developed by Molich and Nielsen (1990) but it is similar in nature to other usability guidelines. These principles are discussed in further detail in Chapter 5 of Nielsen (1993).

1. *Simple and natural dialogue:* Dialogues should not contain information that is irrelevant or rarely needed. Every extra unit of information in a dialogue competes with the relevant units of information and diminishes their relative visibility. All information should appear in a natural and logical order.

2. *Speak the users' language:* The dialogue should be expressed clearly in words, phrases, and concepts familiar to the user, rather than in system-oriented terms.

3. *Minimize the users' memory load:* The user should not have to remember information from one part of the dialogue to another. Instructions for use of the system should be visible or easily retrievable whenever appropriate.

4. *Consistency:* Users should not have to wonder whether different words, situations, or actions mean the same thing.

5. *Provide feedback:* The system should always keep users informed about what is going on through appropriate feedback within reasonable time.

6. *Provide clearly marked exits:* Users often choose system functions by mistake and will need a clearly marked "emergency unit" to leave the unwanted state without having to go through an extended dialogue.

7. *Provide shortcuts:* Accelerators—unseen by the novice user—may often speed up the interaction for the expert user such that the system caters to both inexperienced and experienced users.

8. *Good error messages:* They should be expressed in plain language (no codes), precisely indicate the problem, and constructively suggest a solution.

9. *Prevent errors:* Even better than good error messages is a careful design that prevents a problem from occurring in the first place.

10. *Help and documentation:* Even though it is better if the system can be used without documentation, it may be necessary to provide help and documentation. Any such information should be easy to search, focused on the users' task, list concrete steps to be carried out, and not be too large.

Table 11.3 Result of Experiment 1: a double-blind test ($N=152$) comparing the original and the revised version of a bank account statement. The values measured are: How many of the subjects could correctly answer each of four questions about the contents of the statement (and the combined average for those four questions), the average time needed by subjects to review the statement and answer the questions, and the subjects' average subjective rating (scale: 1 [bad] to 5 [good]). The rightmost column indicates whether the difference between the two account statements is statistically significant according to a t-test.

	Original Design	Revised Design	p
Size of deposit (%)	79	95	<0.01
Commission (%)	34	53	<0.05
Interest rates (%)	20	58	<0.01
Credit limit (%)	93	99	<0.05
Average correct (%)	56	76	<0.01
Task time (sec)	315	303	n.s. (0.58)
Subjective satisfaction (1–5)	2.8	3.0	n.s. (0.14)

n.s. = not significant.

Validating Discount Usability Engineering

In one case, I used the discount usability engineering method to redesign a set of account statements (Nielsen, 1989b). I tested eight different versions (the original design plus seven redesigns) before I was satisfied. Even so, the entire project required only about 90 hours, including designing seven versions of twelve different kinds of statements (not all the forms were changed in each iteration, however) and testing them in simplified thinking-aloud experiments. Most versions were tested with just a single user. To validate the redesign, a further experiment was done using traditional statistical measurement methods. It should be stressed that this validation was a research exercise and not part of the discount usability engineering method itself. The usability engineering work ended with the development of the improved account statements, but, as a check of the usability engineering methods used, it was decided to conduct a usability measurement of one of the new designs compared with the original design.

Experiment 1: Double-Blind Test Taking Usability Measurements

The validation was done using a double-blind test: 38 experimenters each ran four subjects (for a total of 152 subjects) in a between-subjects design. Neither the experimenters nor the subjects knew which was the original account statement and which was the new. The results reported in Table 11.3 show clear and highly statistically significant improvements in measurement values for the new statement with respect to the understandability of the information in the statement as measured by the average number of correct answers to four questions concerning the contents of the statement. The value had indeed been the usability parameter that had been monitored as a goal during the iterative design. Two other usability parameters that had not been considered goals in the iterative design process (efficiency of use and subjective satisfaction) were also measured in the final test, and the two versions of the statement got practically identical scores on those.

This study supports the use of discount usability engineering techniques and shows that they can indeed cause measurable improvements in usability. However, the results also indicate that one should be cautious in setting the goals for usability engineering work. Those usability parameters that have no goals set for improvement risk being left behind as the attention of the usability engineer is concentrated on the official goals. In this study, no negative effects in the form of actual degradation in measured usability parameters were observed but one can not always count on being so lucky.

Experiment 2: Recommendations from People without Usability Expertise

Two groups of evaluators were shown the two versions of the account statement (without being told which one was the revised version) and asked which one they would recommend management to use. All the evaluators were computer science students who had signed up for a user interface design course but who had not yet been taught anything in the course. This meant that they did not know the usability heuristics from Table 11.2 which they might otherwise have used to evaluate the two versions.

Table 11.4 Result of Experiment 2: asking two group of evaluators to recommend one of the two versions of an account statement. In Group A, each person had first run an empirical test with four subjects, whereas the evaluators in Group B had no basis for their recommendation except their own subjective evaluation. The difference between the two groups is statistically different at the $p <$ 0.05 level.

	Group A (%) $N = 38$	Group B (%) $N = 21$
Recommends original	16	48
Recommends revised	68	48
No recommendation	16	5

Group A consisted of the experimenters from Experiment 1 who had run two short experiments with each version of the account statement, while the evaluators in Group B had to make their recommendation on the basis of their own personal evaluation of the two versions. The results are reported in Table 11.4 and show a significant difference in the recommendations: Evaluators in Group A preferred the revised version four to one while evaluators in Group B were split equally between the two versions. This latter result is probably a reflection of the fact that the two versions are almost equally subjectively satisfying according to the measurement results reported in Table 11.3.

If we accept the statistical measurement results in Table 11.3 as defining the revised version as the "best," we see that Group A was dramatically better at making the correct recommendation than was Group B. This was in spite of the fact that each of the individuals in Group A had knowledge only of the experimental results from two subjects for each of the designs (the aggregate statistics were not calculated until after the recommendations had been made, so each evaluator knew only the results from the four subjects run by that individual).

So we can conclude that running even a small, cheap empirical study can help non-human-factors people significantly in their evaluation of user interfaces. If we count the evaluators who did not make a recommendation as having a 50/50 chance of picking the right interface, this experiment shows that running just two subjects for each version in a small test improved the probability for recommending the best of two versions from 50% to 76%.

Cost-Benefit Analysis of Heuristic Evaluation: A Case Study

A cost-benefit analysis of heuristic evaluation includes two main elements: first, estimating the costs in terms of time spent performing the evaluation and second, estimating the benefits in terms of increased usability (less the development costs for the redesign). Since these estimates involve some uncertainties, they will be converted into dollar amounts by using round numbers. Any given company will, of course, have slightly different conversion factors, depending on its exact financial circumstances.

The following case study regards a prototype user interface for a system for internal telephone company use which will be called the Integrating System in this chapter. The Integrating System is fairly complicated, and understanding its details requires extensive knowledge of telephone company concepts, procedures, and databases. Since a detailed explanation is not necessary to understand the generally applicable lessons from the study, the Integrating System will only be outlined here.

Briefly, the Integrating System provides a graphical user interface to access information from several systems running on various remote computers in a uniform manner despite the differences between the back-end systems. The Integrating System can be used to resolve certain problems when data inconsistencies require manual intervention by a technician because the computer systems cannot determine which information is correct. The traditional method for resolving these problems involves having the technician compare information across several of these databases by accessing them through a number of traditional alphanumeric terminal sessions. The databases reside on different computers and have different data formats and user interface designs, so this traditional method is somewhat awkward and requires the technicians to learn a large number of inconsistent user interfaces.

Performing this task involves a large amount of highly domain-specific knowledge about the way the telephone system is constructed and the structure of the different databases. Technicians need to know where to look for what data and how the different kinds of data are related. Also, the individual data items themselves are extremely obscure for people without detailed domain knowledge.

As a result of the heuristic evaluation of this interface with 11 evaluators (described in further detail in Nielsen (1994b), 44 usability problems were found. Forty of these problems are denoted "core" usability problems and were found in the part of the interface that was subjected to intensive evaluation, whereas the remaining four problems were discovered in parts of the interface that we had not planned to study as part of the heuristic evaluation.

Time Expenditure

As usual in usability engineering, the cost estimates are the easiest to get right. Table 11.5 accounts for the total time spent on the heuristic evaluation project in terms of person-hours. No attempt has been made to distinguish between different categories of professional staff. Practically all the person-hours listed in Table 11.5 were spent by usability specialists. The only exception is a small number of hours spent by development specialists in getting the prototype ready for the evaluation and in attending the debriefing session.

Note that the time given for the preparation of the scenario covers only the effort of writing up the scenario in a form that would be usable by the evaluators during the evaluation. Considerable additional effort was needed to specify the scenario in the first place, but that effort was part of the general task analysis and design activities performed before the evaluation. Scenario-based design is a well-known method for user interface design (Carroll and Rosson, 1990; Clarke, 1991), so one will often be able to draw upon interaction scenarios that have been developed in previous stages of the usability life cycle. Even so, we were probably lucky that the scenario developed for the present system could be used for the evaluation with such a small amount of additional effort.

The evaluation sessions were videotaped, and approximately eight hours were spent on mundane tasks like getting videotapes, learning to operate the video equipment in the specific usability laboratory used for the evaluation sessions, setting up and closing down the video equipment on each of the two days of the study, rewinding tapes, etc. This videotaping was not part of the heuristic evaluation as such, and the tapes were not reviewed for the purpose of arriving at the list of usability problems. The observers' notes were sufficient for that purpose. The videotapes were used to some extent in this research analysis of the study where an additional eight hours were spent reviewing details of some evaluation sessions, but since this use was not part of the practical application of the heuristic evaluation method, the time spent on the videotapes has not been included in Table 11.5.

Table 11.5 Estimate of the total number of person-hours spent on the heuristic evaluation study described in this article. The estimate of "time to prepare the prototype" does not include the time needed for the initial task analysis, user interface design, or implementation of the prototype since these actvities had already been undertaken independently of the heuristic evaluation.

Assessing appropriate ways to use heuristic evaluation, 4 people @ 2 hours	8
Having outside evaluation expert learn about the domain and scenario	8
Finding and scheduling evaluators, 1.8 hours + 0.2 hours per evaluator	4
Preparing the briefing	3
Preparing scenario for the evaluators	2
Briefing, 1 system expert, 1 evaluation expert, 11 evaluators @ 1.5 hours	19.5
Preparing the prototype (software and its hardware platform) for the evaluation	5
Actual evaluation, 11 evaluators @ 1 hour	11
Observing the evaluation sessions, 2 observers @ 11 hours	22
Debriefing, 3 evaluators, 3 developers, 1 evaluation expert @ 1 hour	7
Writing list of usability problems based on notes from evaluation sessions	2
Writing problem descriptions for use in severity-rating questionnaire	6
Severity rating, 11 evaluators @ 0.5 hours	5.5
Analyzing severity ratings	2
Total	105

It follows from Table 11.5 that the total number of person-hours spent on the evaluation can be determined by the formula

$$\text{time}(i) = 47.8 + 5.2i \tag{1}$$

where i is the number of evaluators. This formula is not exact for large numbers of i, since some of the effort devoted to room scheduling and to the analysis of the severity ratings is partly dependent on the number of evaluators and would change with large is.

The cost estimate in Equation (1) is probably larger than necessary for future heuristic evaluations. Major reductions in both the fixed and variable costs could be achieved by reducing the team of two observers to a single observer. This observer should be the person who is familiar with the application such that the observer can answer questions from the evaluators during the evaluation. Also, even though the observer should have a certain level of usability knowledge in order to understand the comments made by the evaluators, the observer need not be a highly skilled expert specializing in usability. A major difference between heuristic evaluation and traditional user testing is that an observer of a heuristic evaluation session is mostly freed from having to interpret user actions since the evaluators are assuming the task of explicitly identifying the usability problems. In contrast, the experimenter in a traditional user test would need a higher level of usability expertise in order to translate the subject's actions and difficulties into interface-related usability problems.[2]

This single change would result in the following, revised formula

$$\text{time}(i) = 37.3 + 4.2i \tag{2}$$

Transforming the time estimates in Equations (1) or (2) to money estimates can be done fairly simply by multiplying the number of hours by an estimate of the loaded hourly cost of professional staff. Note that the salary and benefits costs of the professional staff are not sufficient, since additional costs are incurred in the form of the computer equipment and laboratory space used for the test. To use round numbers, an estimated hourly loaded cost for professional staff of $100 translates into a total cost for the heuristic evaluation of $10,500 for the 105 hours that were actually spent.

Benefit Estimation

The only way to get an exact measure of the benefits of the heuristic evaluation would be to fully implement two versions of the user interface; one without any changes and one with the changes implied by the evaluation results. These two versions should then be used by a large number of real users to perform real tasks for a sufficiently long time that the steady-state level of expert performance is reached in both cases (Gray *et al.*, 1992). This process would provide exact measures for the differences in learning time and expert performance. Unfortunately, the version of the interface that was evaluated only exists in a prototype form with which one cannot do any real work, and it would be unrealistic to expect significant development resources to be invested in transforming this prototype to a final product with an identical user interface now that a large number of usability problems have been documented.

---

[2]Indeed, Nielsen (1992b) found a positive correlation between the methodological skills of experimenters and the number of usability problems discovered when they ran user tests.

Alternatively, one could build a detailed economic work-study model of the different steps involved in the users' workday in order to assess the frequency and duration of each subtask. One could then further use formal models of user interaction times to estimate the duration of performing each step with each of a set of alternative user interface designs (Gray *et al.*, 1992). Such an approach would provide fairly detailed estimates but would not necessarily be accurate because of unknown durations of the operations in the model. It would also be very time consuming to carry out.

It is thus necessary to rely on estimates of the benefits rather than hard measurement data. To get such estimates, the 11 evaluators were asked to estimate the improvements in usability from fixing all the 44 usability problems identified by the heuristic evaluation. Usability improvements were estimated with respect to two usability parameters:

(1) *Reduction of learning time.* How much less time would the users need to spend learn ing to use the system? Learning time considered as a usability parameter represents a one-time loss of productive time for each new user to learn the system, so any savings would be realized only once.

(2) *Speedup in expert performance.* Once the users have reached a steady state of expert performance, how much faster would they be able to perform their work when using a system with all the usability problems fixed than when using a system with all the problems still in place? Expert performance considered as a usability parameter represents a continued advantage for the use of the improved interface, so any savings would be realized throughout the lifetime of the system.

Other usability parameters of interest include frequency of user errors and the users' subjective satisfaction, but these parameters were not estimated. Since several of the usability problems that we found were related to error-prone circumstances, it is likely that the number of user errors would go down.

Ten of the 11 evaluators provided learning time estimates, and all 11 provided expert speedup estimates. Histograms of the distribution of these estimates are shown in Figure 11.3. Nielsen and Phillips (1993) found that estimates of changes in user performance made by usability specialists were highly variable, as also seen in Figure 11.3, but that mean values of at least three independent estimates were reasonably close to the values measured by controlled experiments.

Given that the benefit estimates are based purely on subjective judgments of experts rather than on empirical evidence, it would seem pru-

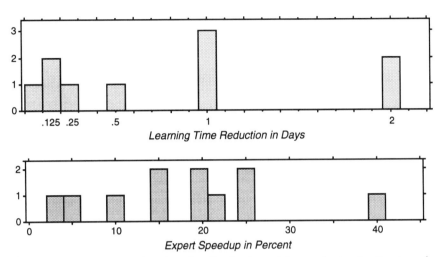

Figure 11.3 Histograms showing the distribution of the evaluators' estimates of savings in learning time (top) and expert performance speedup (bottom) for an interface fixing all the usability problems found in the heuristic evaluation. One evaluator did not provide a learning time estimate.

dent to be conservative in translating the evaluators' estimates into projected monetary savings. The mean values are 0.8 days for learning time reduction and 18% for expert speedup when all evaluators are considered, and 0.5 days and 16%, respectively, when excluding the perhaps overly optimistic outliers at two days and 40%. In order to be conservative, we will choose 0.5 days as our learning time reduction estimate and 10% as our expert speedup estimate.[3]

The 10% expert speedup obviously only applies to time spent using the interface. Studies of the users indicate that they will spend about one-third of their time doing other tasks, one-third of their time performing the task without operating the user interface, and one-third of their time actually operating the interface. The 10% expert speedup thus corresponds to 3.3% of total work time.

Translating these estimates into overall savings can be done under the following assumptions. We assume that 2,000 people will be using the system (this is somewhat conservative given that about 3,000 people cur-

---

[3]We should note that 10% is not at all an unrealistic improvement in a user interface. For example, Nielsen and Levy (1994) found a 25% median difference in measured user performance for 153 pairwise comparisons of alternative designs reported in the user interface literature. Even though some of this difference is due to chance (one of the two interfaces will *always* be better when you compare two designs), the mean difference corrected for chance is 20%, which is still twice what we are assuming here.

rently perform this job). Having 2,000 people each save 0.5 days in learning to use the system corresponds to a total of 1,000 user-days saved as a one-time saving. Furthermore, having 2,000 users perform their work 3.3% faster after having reached expert performance corresponds to 67 user-years saved each year that the system is in use. Again, to be conservative, we will only consider the savings for the first year, even though computer systems of the magnitude we are talking about here are normally used for more than one year. Sixty-seven user-years correspond roughly to 13,000 user-days saved. The total number of user-days saved the first year is thus about 14,000.

To value the total savings in monetary terms, we will assume that the cost of one user-day is $100, and, to be conservative, we will assume that only half of the usability problems can actually be fixed, so that only half of the potential savings are actually realized.[4] Furthermore, we need to take into account the fact that the savings in user time are not realized until the system is introduced and thus have a smaller net present value than their absolute value.[5] Again, to use round numbers, we will discount the value of the saved learning time by 20% and the value of the expert speedup in the first year by 30%. Learning time can be discounted by a smaller percentage as this saving is realized on day 1 after the introduction of the system. Using these conservative assumptions, we find one-year savings of $540,000.

Of course, the savings are not realized just by wishing for half of the usability problems to be fixed, so we have to reduce the savings estimate with an estimate of the cost of the additional software engineering effort needed to redesign the interface rather than just implementing the interface from the existing prototype. Assuming that the amount of software engineering time needed for this additional work is 400 hours, and again assuming that the loaded cost of a professional is $100 per hour, we find that the savings estimate needs to be reduced by $40,000. This expense is incurred here and now and thus cannot be discounted. Our final estimate of the net present value of improving the user interface is thus $500,000.

---

[4]By taking advantage of the prioritized list of usability problems, it might be possible to achieve more than half of the savings even if only half of the problems can be fixed; one could concentrate on fixing the most severe problems. However, to continue to be conservative, we will assume that fixing half of the problems results in half the savings.

[5]Saving $1 next year is not worth as much as saving $1 today due to the time value of money: If I have $1 today, I can invest it to make it worth maybe $1.10 in one year and $1.21 in two years.

Still being conservative, we have not taken into account the value of the saved software engineering costs from not having to modify the system after its release. Assuming that the original user interface were to be fully implemented and released, is it very likely that the users would demand substantial changes in the second release, and it is well known that making software engineering changes to a released system is *much* more expensive than making changes at a prototype stage of the software life cycle.[6]

The $500,000 benefit of improving the interface should be compared with the cost of the heuristic evaluation project, estimated at $10,500. We thus see that the benefit-cost ratio is 48. This number involves significant uncertainties but is big enough that we do not hesitate to conclude that the heuristic evaluation paid off.

As a final comment on the cost-benefit analysis, we should note that the benefits do not translate to an actual cash flow. Instead, they represent the avoidance of the penalty represented by the extra time the users would have had to spend if the prototype interface had been implemented and released without further changes. It is an interesting and an important management problem to find ways to represent such savings properly in the funding of software development.

Cost-Benefit Analysis of User Testing

After the heuristic evaluation exercise, additional user testing was performed on the same interface, running four test users. A major reason for using so many more heuristic evaluators than test users was that the users of this particular application were highly specialized technicians and difficult to get into the lab, whereas it was reasonably easy to get a large number of usability specialists to participate in the heuristic evaluation session. Four new usability problems were found by the user testing which also confirmed 17 of the problems that had already been found by heuristic evaluation.

One can discuss whether the 23 core problems that were not observed in the user test are in fact problems given that they could not be seen to bother the real users. As argued elsewhere (Nielsen, 1992b), such problems can indeed be very real, but their impact may just have too short a duration to be observable in a standard user test. Problems that have the effect of slowing users down for 0.1 second or so simply cannot be observed unless data from a very large number of users are subjected to

---

[6]According to common estimates, it is about 40–100 times more expensive to fix problems in the maintenance phrase of a program than in the design phase (Boehm, 1981).

statistical analysis, but they can be very real and costly problems nevertheless. Also, some problems may occur too infrequently to have been observed with the small number of users tested here.

The main cost of the user test activity was having two professionals spend seven hours each on the running of the test and the briefing and debriefing of the test users. No time was needed for the traditionally time-consuming activity of defining the test tasks since the same scenario was used as that developed for the previous usability work. Additionally, half an hour was spent finding and scheduling the users for the test[7] and two hours were spent on implementing a small training interface on which the users could learn to use a mouse and standard graphical interaction techniques like pull-down windows. These activities sum to a total of 16.5 person-hours of professional staff or a cost of $1,650.

Furthermore, the four users and their manager spent essentially a full day on the test when their travel time is taken into account. Again assuming that the cost of one user-day is $100, and furthermore assuming that the cost of one manager-day is $200, the total cost of user involvement is $600. Adding the cost of the professionals and the users gives a total estimate of $2,250 as the cost of user testing.

The $2,250 spent on user testing could potentially have been spent on additional heuristic evaluation efforts instead. According to Equation (1), this sum corresponds to using 4.3 additional evaluators. Nielsen and Landauer (1993) showed that the finding of usability problems by i evaluators can be modelled by the prediction formula

$$\text{Problems found}(i) = N(1 - (1-\lambda)^i) \qquad (3)$$

For the core usability problems in the present study, the best-fit values for the parameters in this equation are $N = 40$ and $\lambda = 0.26$. Increasing the number of heuristic evaluators, n, from 11 to 15.3 can thus be expected to result in the finding of about 1.1 additional usability problems. This estimate shows that the available additional resources do indeed seem to have been spent better on running a user test and finding four problems than on potentially extending the heuristic evaluation further.

We have no systematic method to estimate the benefits of having found the four additional problems that were discovered by user testing. However, one easy way to arrive at a rough estimate is to assume that the average severity of the four new problems is the same as the average severity of the 17 problems that had already been found by heuristic eval-

---

[7]Often, it will take longer to make contact with users, but we again took advantage of the early task analysis efforts in this project which had resulted in field contacts that could be used in invite a few test users.

uation. As part of the heuristic evaluation study, severity was measured on a rating scale, with each usability problem being assigned a severity score from zero to four, with higher scores denoting more serious problems. The sum of the severity scores for the original 44 usability problems was 98.41, and the sum of the severity scores for the 17 problems that were seen both in the user test and in the heuristic evaluation was 41.56. We can thus estimate the relative severity of the additional four problems as compared with the original problems as $4/17 \cdot 41.56/98.41 = 0.099$.

Knowing about the additional problems found by user testing would thus add 9.9% to the total potential for improving the interface. Furthermore, we might assume that the proportion of the new problems that can be fixed, the impact of fixing them, and the cost of fixing them are all the same as the estimates for the problems found by heuristic evaluation.[8] Under these assumptions, the benefit of having found the additional four usability problems can be valued at $500,000 \cdot 0.099 = \$49,500$.

Using these estimates, the benefit/cost ratio of adding the user test after the heuristic evaluation is 22. Of course, the benefits of user testing would have been larger if we had credited it with finding the problems that were observed during the user test but had already been found by the heuristic evaluation. We should note, though, that the cost of planning the user test would have been higher if the heuristic evaluation had not been performed, confirming the value of the usage scenario. Also, there is no guarantee that all the observed problems would in fact have been found if there had been no prior heuristic evaluation. Now, we knew what to look for, but we might not have noticed as many problems if the user test had been our first usability evaluation activity for this interface.

If the user test were to be credited with all 17 duplicate problems as well as the four new ones, taking the higher-than-average severity of the seventeen problems into account, the benefit of the user test would be valued at $260,500. Of course, this amount would be the benefit from the user test only if no prior heuristic evaluation had been performed. Therefore, it would seem reasonable to charge this hypothetical analysis of the user test with some of the costs that were in fact spent preparing for the heuristic evaluation. Specifically, referring to Table 11.5, we will add the costs of assessing the appropriate way to use the method, having

---

[8]The estimate assumes that the financial benefit of fixing a usability problem is proportional to its severity rating. Unfortunately, the true relation between the two measures is not known. It could easily be nonlinear.

the outside evaluation expert learn about the domain and scenario, preparing the scenario and the software, as well as half the time spent writing the problem descriptions (since about half as many problems were found). These activities sum to 24 hours, or an additional cost of $2,400, for a total estimated cost of $4,650 for running the user test without prior heuristic evaluation. This translates into a benefit-cost ratio of 56.

To provide a fair comparison, it should be noted that the benefit-cost ratio of performing the heuristic evaluation with only four evaluators would have been 53. This number is larger than the benefit-cost ratio for the full evaluation since more previously unfound usability problems are identified by the first evaluators than by the last, as shown by Equation 3. Furthermore, the heuristic evaluation provided severity estimates that can be used to prioritize the fixing of the usability problems in the further development process, and the availability of these data probably adds to the actual value of the method as measured by delivered usability. If the time spent on the debriefing and severity ratings is deducted from the time spent on the heuristic evaluation, the benefit-cost ratio for the full 11 evaluators becomes 59 and the ratio for four evaluators becomes 71.

Thus, within the uncertainty of these estimates, it appears that user testing and heuristic evaluation have comparable cost-benefit ratios and that doing some of each may have additional value.

The Evolution of Usability Engineering in Organizations

Two of the fundamental slogans of discount usability engineering are that "any data are data" and "anything is better than nothing" when it comes to usability. Therefore, I often advocate an approach to usability that focuses on starting to use a minimum of usability methods. Even so, there are many projects that would benefit from employing more than the minimum amount of discount usability methods. I used the term "guerrilla HCI" in the title of this chapter because I believe that simplified usability methods can be a way for a company to build up its reliance on systematic usability methods gradually, starting with the bare minimum and progressing to a more refined life cycle approach.

Based on observing multiple companies and projects over the years, I have arrived at the following series of steps in the increased use of usability engineering in software development.

(1) Usability does not matter. The main focus is to wring every last bit of performance from the iron. This is the attitude leading to the world-famous error message, "beep."

(2) Usability is important, but good interfaces can surely be designed by the regular development staff as part of their general system design. This attitude is symbolized by the famous statement made by King Frederik VI of Denmark on February 26, 1835: "We alone know what serves the true welfare and benefit of the State and People." At this stage, no attempt is made at user testing or at acquiring staff with usability expertise.

(3) The desire to have the interface blessed by the magic wand of a usability engineer often occurs at this point. Developers recognize that they may not know everything about usability, so they call in a usability specialist to look over their design and comment on it. The involvement of the usability specialist is often too late to do much good in the project, and the usability specialist often has to provide advice on the interface without the benefit of access to real users.

(4) GUI panic strikes, causing a sudden desire to learn about user interface issues. Currently, many companies are in this stage as they are moving from character-based user interfaces to graphical user interfaces and realize the need to bring in usability specialists to advise on graphical user interfaces from the start. Some usability specialists resent this attitude and maintain that it is more important to provide an appropriate interface for the task than to go blindly with a graphical interface without prior task analysis. Even so, GUI panic is an opportunity for usability specialists to get involved in interface design at an earlier stage than the traditional last-minute blessing of a design that cannot be changed much.

(5) Discount usability engineering is used sporadically on some projects. Typically, some projects use a few discount usability methods (like user testing or heuristic evaluation), though the methods are often used too late in the development life cycle to do maximum good. Projects that do use usability methods often differ from others in having managers who have experienced the benefit of usability methods on earlier projects. Thus, usability acts as a kind of "good" virus, infecting progressively more projects as more people experience its benefits.

(6) Discount usability engineering is used systematically in some project stages. At some point in time, most projects involve some simple usability methods, and some projects even use usability methods in the early stages of system development. Scenarios and cheap prototyping

techniques seem to be very effective weapons for guerrilla HCI in this stage.

(7) A usability group and/or usability lab is founded. Many companies decide to expand to a deluxe usability approach after having experienced the benefits of discount usability engineering. Currently, the building of usability laboratories (Nielsen, 1994a) is quite popular, as is the formation of dedicated groups of usability specialists.

(8) Usability permeates the life cycle. The final stage is rarely reached since even companies with usability groups and usability labs normally do not have enough usability resources to employ all the methods one could wish for at all the stages of the development life cycle. However, there are some, often important, projects that have usability plans defined as part of their early project planning and where usability methods are used throughout the development life cycle.

This model is fairly similar to the series of organizational acceptance stages outlined by Ehrlich and Rohn but was developed independently. Stages 1–2 in this list correspond to Ehrlich and Rohn's *skepticism* stage, stages 3–4 correspond to their *curiosity* stage, stages 5–6 correspond to their *acceptance* stage, and stages 7–8 correspond to their *partnership* stage.

Many teachers of usability engineering have described the almost religious effect it seems to have the first time students try running a user test and see with their own eyes the difficulties that perfectly normal people can have using supposedly "easy" software. Unfortunately, organizations are more difficult to convert, so they have to be conquered mostly from within by the use of guerrilla methods like discount usability engineering that gradually show more and more people that usability methods work and improve products. It is too optimistic to assume that one can move a development organization from stage 1 or 2 in this model to stage 7 or 8 in a single, sweeping change. In reality, almost all usability methods are extremely cheap to use compared with the benefits they provide in form of better and easier-to-use products, but often we have to start with the cheapest possible methods to overcome the intimidation barrier gradually.

Acknowledgments

The author would like to thank Randolph Bias, Tom Landauer, and Janice Rohn for helpful comments on an earlier version of the manuscript.

References

Apple Computer (1987). *Human Interface Guidelines: The Apple Desktop Interface.* Addison Wesley, Reading, Massachusetts.

Apple Computer (1992). *Macintosh Human Interface Guidelines.* Addison Wesley, Reading, Massachusetts.

Bellotti, V. (1988). Implications of current design practice for the use of HCI techniques. In: *People and Computers IV* (Jones, D. M. and Winder, R. eds.). Cambridge University Press, Cambridge, England, 13–34.

Boehm, B. W. (1981). *Software Engineering Economics.* Prentice-Hall, Englewood Cliffs, New Jersey.

Card, S. K., Moran, T. P., and Newell, A. (1983). *The Psychology of Human–Computer Interaction.* Lawrence Erlbaum Associates, Hillsdale, New Jersey.

Carroll, J. M., and Rosson, M. B. (1990). Human–computer interaction scenarios as a design representation. *Proc. HICSS-23: Hawaii International Conference on System Science.* IEEE Computer Society Press, 555–561.

Clarke, L. (1991). The use of scenarios by user interface designers. In: *Peoples and Computers VI* (Diaper, D. and Hammond, N., eds.). Cambridge University Press, Cambridge, England, 103–115.

Ehrlich, K. and Rohn, J. (1994). Cost justification of usability engineering: A vendor's perspective. In: *Cost-Justifying Usability* (Bias, R. G. and Mayhew, D. J., eds.). Academic Press, Boston, 73–100.

Gould, J. D. and Lewis, C. H. (1985). Designing for usability: Key principles and what designers think. *Communications of the ACM* **28**(3), 300–311.

Gray, W. D., John, B. E., and Atwood, M. E. (1992). The precis of project Grace, or, an overview of a validation of GOMS. *Proc. ACM CHI'92.* Monterey, California, May 3–7, pp. 307–312.

Jørgensen, A. H. (1989). Using the thinking-aloud method in system development. In: *Designing and Using Human–Computer Interfaces and Knowledge Based Systems* (Salvendy, G. and Smith, M. J., eds.). Elsevier Science Publishers, Amsterdam, 743–750.

Karwowski, W., Kosiba, E., Benabdallah, S., and Salvendy, G. (1989). Fuzzy data and communication in human-computer interaction: For bad or for good. In: *Designing and Using Human–Computer Interfaces and Knowledge Based Systems* (Salvendy, G. and Smith, M. J., eds.). Elsevier Science Publishers, Amsterdam, 402–409.

Landauer, T. K. (1988). Research methods in human–computer interaction. In: *Handbook of Human–Computer Interaction* (Helander, M., ed.). North-Holland, Amsterdam, The Netherlands, 543–568.

Mantei, M. M. and Teorey, T. J. (1988). Cost-benefit analysis for incorporating human factors in the software lifecycle. *Communications of the ACM* **31**(4), 428–439.

Milsted, U., Varnild, A., and Jørgensen, A. H. (1989). Hvordan sikres kvaliteten af brugergraensefladen i systemudviklingen. (Assuring the quality of user interfaces in system development, in Danish). *Proceedings NordDATA '89 Joint*

Scandinavian Computer Conference. Copenhagen, Denmark, June 19–22, pp. 479–484.

Molich, R. and Nielsen, J. (1990). Improving a human-computer dialogue. *Communications of the ACM* **33**(3), 338–348.

Monk, A., Wright, P., Haber, J., and Davenport, L. (1993). *Improving Your Human–Computer Interface: A Practical Technique.* Prentice Hall International, Hemel Hempstead, United Kingdom.

Nielsen, J. (1989a). Prototyping user interfaces using an object-oriented hypertext programming system. *Proceedings NordDATA '89 Joint Scandinavian Computer Conference.* Copenhagen, Denmark, June 19–22, 485–490.

Nielsen, J. (1989b). Usability engineering at a discount. In: *Designing and Using Human–Computer Interfaces and Knowledge Based Systems* (Salvendy, G. and Smith, M. J. eds.). Elsevier Science Publishers, Amsterdam, 394–401.

Nielsen, J. (1990a). Big paybacks from "discount" usability engineering. *IEEE Software* **7**(3), 107–108.

Nielsen, J. (1990b). Paper versus computer implementations as mockup scenarios for heuristic evaluation. *Proc. INTERACT'90 3rd IFIP Conf. Human–Computer Interaction.* Cambridge, United Kingdom, August 27–31, pp. 315–320.

Nielsen, J. (1992a). The usability engineering life cycle. *IEEE Computer* **25**(3), 12–22.

Nielsen, J. (1992b). Evaluating the thinking aloud technique for use by computer scientists. In: *Advances in Human–Computer Interaction, Vol. 3* (Hartson, H. R. and Hix, D. eds.). Ablex, Norwood, New Jersey, 75–88.

Nielsen, J. (1992c). Finding usability problems through heuristic evaluation. *Proc. ACM CHI'92.* Monterey, California, May 3–7, pp. 373–380.

Nielsen, J. (1993). *Usability Engineering.* Academic Press, Boston.

Nielsen, J. (1994a). Usability laboratories. *Behaviour and Information Technology* **13**, 1.

Nielsen, J. (1994b). Heuristic evaluation. In: *Usability Inspection Methods* (Nielsen, J. and Mack, R. L., eds.). John Wiley & Sons, New York, 25–64.

Nielsen, J. and Landauer, T. K. (1993). A mathematical model of the finding of usability problems. *Proc. ACM INTERCHI'93 Conf.* Amsterdam, The Netherlands, April 24–29, pp. 206–213.

Nielsen, J. and Levy, J. (1994). Subjective user preferences versus objective interface performance measures. *Communications of the ACM*, in press.

Nielsen, J. and Molich, R. (1989). Teaching user interface design based on usability engineering. *ACM SIGCHI Bulletin* **21**(1), 45–48.

Nielsen, J. and Molich, R. (1990). Heuristic evaluation of user interfaces. *Proc. ACM CHI'90.* Seattle, Washington, April 1–5, pp. 249–256.

Nielsen, J. and Phillips, V. L. (1993). Estimating the relative usability of two interfaces: Heuristic, formal, and empirical methods compared. *Proc. ACM INTERCHI'93 Conf.* Amsterdam, The Netherlands, April 24–29, pp. 214–221.

Nielsen, J., Frehr, R., and Nymand, H. O. (1991). The learnability of HyperCard as an object-oriented programming system. *Behaviour and Information Technology* **10**(2), 111–120.

Perlman, G. (1988). Teaching user interface development to software engineers. *Proceedings of the Human Factors Society 32nd Annual Meeting*, 391–394.

Perlman, G. (1990). Teaching user-interface development. *IEEE Software* 7(6), 85–86.

Telles, M. (1990). Updating an older interface. *Proc. ACM CHI'90* Seattle, Washington, April 1–5, pp. 243–247.

Thovtrup, H. and Nielsen, J. (1991). Assessing the usability of a user interface standard. *Proc. ACM CHI'91*. New Orleans, Louisiana, April 28–May 2, pp. 335–341.

Tognazzini, B. (1990). User testing on the cheap. *Apple Direct* 2(6), 21–27. Reprinted as Chapter 14 in *TOG on Interface*. Addison-Wesley, Reading, Massachusetts.

Voltaire, F. M. A. (1764). *Dictionnaire Philosophique*.

Whiteside, J., Bennett, J., and Holtzblatt, K. (1988). Usability engineering: Our experience and evolution. In: *Handbook of Human–Computer Interaction* (Helander, M., ed.). North-Holland, Amsterdam, 791–817.

Chapter 12

Justifying Prepaid Human Factors for User Interfaces

Ruven Brooks

Schlumberger Laboratory for Computer Science
Austin, Texas

Introduction

One approach to promoting human factors activities, such as usability studies, has been to view expenditures on them as investments and to compute the return on these investments. To do this, the improvements in products produced by the activities are measured and a financial value is attached. The return can then be computed by dividing the increase in product value by the costs of carrying out the human factors activities.

While such numbers may have value as part of an overall case for supporting human factors activities, by themselve they are unlikely to make much of an impact on decision makers. Managers implicitly believe that all of the activities under their control provide a positive return on investment, either directly or indirectly; otherwise, they would apply the resources elsewhere. In order to decide that investment should be made in human factors activities, managers must be convinced that this would be a better investment than other, competing alternatives. In particular, usability studies must frequently compete for investment with decreasing time to market and with enhancing product capabilities.

The problem that this presents is that accurate, predictive information on issues like the benefits of improved time to market or on the sales impact of improved capabilities is rarely available. Whether three months either way on market release date for a product makes a difference in sales may depend on what competitors are doing or on overall market trends, neither of which can be assessed accurately. Without accurate data on the return from these other resource investments, managers have no basis for comparative evaluation. If they have a bias in favor of one of them over human factors activities, they may even view what would objectively be an excellent return for human factors investment as inferior to the imagined return from this other activity.

In these kinds of situations, the path to convincing managers to incorporate human factors activities into their product development is demonstrating to them that these activities can contribute to product success in unique ways that cannot be interchanged with combinations of other types of activities. If the main benefit of human factors work is to improve the design of a graphical user interface that still fails to get around problems with the underlying data retrieval system, then managers may legitimately argue that an even greater improvement probably would have been obtained had equivalent resources been spent on improving the data retrieval system. On the other hand, if the outcome of human factors work is to suggest a new user interface design that makes the existing data retrieval system appear more powerful than the competition's, then the manager is more likely to conclude that the project must absolutely have some human factors input.

As this example illustrates, not every technically successful application of human factors techniques or knowledge will provide a good justification for further human factors activities. The human factors activities that offer the best research opportunities or are easiest to carry out, or for which the largest body of established research exists may not necessarily be those activities that make the most distinctive contribution when viewed from the product manager's standpoint. Instead, to be perceived as a cost-effective investment, human factors specialists must choose or create situations for applying human factors knowledge that are most likely to result in a unique contribution to product success, even if these situations do not result in as clear a focus on research issues or do not permit use of a large established base of human factors knowledge. Creating these situations will involve solving two kinds of problems:

(1) Human factors methods, such as usability techniques, are often developed in particular environments or contexts that are not universally present. Before those methods can be useful in product development, the human factors specialist must adapt and customize them to the particular characteristics of the environment or context in which product development is taking place. To make these adaptations, the human factors spe-

cialist must be highly knowledgeable about the product under development and the business areas to which it belongs.

(2) Human factors specialists can be located in a variety of different organizational structures. For example, in some cases, they are part of a human factors department; in others, they are part of a development team. The human factors specialist must select delivery techniques for human factors knowledge and methods that are appropriate to the structure of the organization supporting the human factors work.

Schlumberger Experience

About four years ago, a human factors activity focusing on software user interfaces was established at the Schlumberger Laboratory for Computer Science. This activity is funded as a percentage of the revenues of business units, so that they are not charged for the specific amount of services that they receive. Effectively, the service is prepaid. Although there is no need to bill for or cost-justify the time spent, the business units must still be convinced that human factors work is a worthwhile way for the laboratory to spend their contributions.

Schlumberger, Ltd., is a major international corporation with approximately 50,000 employees worldwide. It is organized as two major business areas: Oilfield Services provides services to the petroleum industry, such as well logging and interpretation, seismic acquisition and processing, measurement while drilling, well cementing, and fracturing and contract drilling. Measurement and Systems develops and manufactures electric, water, and gas meters, parking meters, "smart card" transaction systems, electronic test equipment, and CAD and electronic equipment test support software. The Oilfield Services business areas, in particular, offer considerable opportunities for human factors work on graphical user interfaces.

Successfully carrying out the human factors activity has required a substantial effort to solve the two problems mentioned previously: adapting human factors knowledge and techniques to particular product areas and developing appropriate organizational delivery vehicles.

Characteristics of Users and User Interfaces in Oilfield Services

Many of the usability techniques cited in the literature were developed with a focus on office automation tasks, such as word processing, or on corporate information systems tasks, such as data entry. Applications are often carefully designed to be simple and learnable in a brief period of time, and the typical users are frequently clerical personnel with little training. In contrast, Oilfield Services applications tend to have the following characteristics:

Inherently Complex Applications. Processing seismic data or running a well logging truck is as complex as statistical data analysis, practicing medicine, or flying a commercial aircraft. The complexity grows out of both the formal knowledge in areas such as physics, electronics, and geology, and the practical knowledge about how measurements are actually made, stored, and processed. These applications cannot be understood, much less learned, in a few weeks or months.

Computing systems to support these tasks reflect this complexity. Most of the software is written for internal use and is tailored to the particular equipment and operating practices of the company. Many of these systems are built as a base architecture and a number of applications modules that run within it. Each application is likely to have a large number of parameters and options that are needed to take into account different operating environments, geological conditions, and equipment combinations. Some commonly used modules have equivalent numbers of parameters to the number of options and preferences in a popular word processor on the order of several hundred.

More than a hundred modules may be available for some of these systems, and accomplishing a particular task may involve combining up to a dozen of these modules. Parameter settings for one module may have to take into account the other modules that will be used. As a user moves from job to job, different combinations of modules with different parameters will be needed, so that a user may eventually need to know about several thousand parameters and options.

Highly Trained Users. The users of these systems typically have a college degree in physics, electrical engineering, or geology. They receive additional formal training in the applications as well as learning from on-the-job experiences. For example, a seismic processor may start with a degree in geology, go through a six-month training course, and then spend two or three years as an apprentice before being trusted to process a complete job alone. The need for this training grows out of the complexities of the application, not the user interfaces. Seismic processors need training to learn about the complexities of sound propagation through the earth, not to learn the commands of the processing programs. Again, there is similarity here to medical and aerospace applications.

High-Status, High-Salary Users. In businesses such as the financial and telecommunication industries, there are large numbers of computer users who perform routine, clerical tasks. The chances are extremely low that individuals in these positions will rise in the management structure. In contrast, much of the upper management in the Oilfield Services businesses are former field engineers, and current field engineers are considered to be possible candidates for future management positions. Field engineers work alone or with one or two others at a job site. They are given a high degree of individual control over how they accomplish their work, and they are rewarded for doing whatever is necessary to get the job done. Pay rates for these users are the same as or higher than those for software developers. (Some classes of users of legal and medical systems may have similar characteristics.)

Application complexity, high user education levels, the high status and salary levels of users, and user independence combine to give a very different environment for system development and for human factors activities than is typical for many other user interface application areas. The highly technical nature of the applications means that there is a substantial gap between the typical backgrounds of software developers and the specific application knowledge required to develop effective user interfaces. Bridging this gap is not simply a matter of allowing developers to talk to users. Because of the high value of user time, economics dictate that developers should learn as much as possible on their own and keep their interactions with users to the minimum necessary. This learning needs to be accomplished at the same time that they are performing system development and updating their own professional skills. Under these conditions, developers tend to defer the learning, or, in some cases, seek other employment in industries that do not have this burden.

Since developers do not always have adequate application domain knowledge, and since domain expertise is a scarce resource, it is easier for some system requirements to be omitted or overlooked than in other industries. For a newly introduced system, the most critical user interface problems are more likely to be in the area of functions or information that are not available in the interface than in misleading menu labels, excessive effort to perform frequent operations, or designs that place excessive memory loads on users.

Another impact of the high status of the user community is that users have more control over the introduction of new systems. In some organizations, decisions about whether a new system is of sufficiently high quality to be introduced are essentially made by the development organization; the approval of the user organization or community is nominal at best. In contrast, in many of the Oilfield Services business areas, effective control over the introduction of new systems lies on the user side, and the development organization frequently has to undertake a considerable sales effort to convince the user organization that the new system is ready for use.

Other impacts of highly valued users are more positive. Users tend to be very vocal about their needs, and the development organizations take user requests very seriously. It is relatively easy to argue for spending resources to save user time or make things more convenient for users.

Because of the sheer size of the systems in question, the production and updating both of the base system and of individual modules is usually spaced out over a relatively long period of time and occurs as a succession of releases. This means that projects are frequently racing against changes in the technological environment. Just when the last of the application modules has been converted to the new graphical user interface system, a major new release of the system appears, and all of the applications have to be updated. Developers are constantly faced with the danger of allocating too much time to an individual module at the risk of delaying work on all of the others.

Since users typically get extensive experience in operating computing systems almost as a by-product of their training in the application area, ease of learning is a relatively minor issue in the design of user interfaces. Instead, the primary focus is on efficiency and flexibility for routine, trained users.

Adapting Human Factors Techniques for this Environment

The importance of good user interfaces, particularly those for graphical display of data, is well understood and appreciated in the organization. All systems currently under development have graphical user interfaces, frequently using multiple display screens. Anywhere from a quarter to a half of the code in million-line systems is devoted to the user interface, and many of the developers have considerable experience in graphical user interface development. Not surprisingly, user interface issues produce a disproportionate amount of comment from the user community.

In this environment, development managers tend to look favorably on any speciality or technology that offers the potential for improving interface quality. While this environment is fundamentally favorable for adoption of human factors evaluation and modeling techniques, achieving successful use of these techniques is still difficult for two reasons:

- The human factors specialist must devote substantial amounts of time and effort to learn about the applications.
- Many user interface usability techniques developed in other environments require considerable modification and adaptation before they can be applied to oilfield applications.

The need for the human factors specialist to have substantial knowledge about the application area grows in part out of the expectation of developers and their management that the contribution of human factors will be improvements in the design, not in the design process. Typical questions might be "what can be done to improve this interface?" or "what would be a better way to lay out these menus?" or "what's the best way to show that a file has already been read?". In a few rare instances, it may be possible to provide answers just on the basis of general human factors guidelines about user interfaces, but the far more common situation is that good advice depends, first, on understanding the application and, second, on gathering information directly from the users.

The need to understand the application, as separate from understanding the users, is a distinguishing characteristic of human factors work in this area. As described earlier, applications in this domain can be very difficult to understand, and many developers may not have a good grasp on the function that their system is performing. Lack of understanding of the application and of the user's task on the part of developers is a significant source of user interface design problems. For example, if developers do not understand the steps involved in analyzing well log data, they will have difficulty in deciding how to present the data or how to structure the system menus.

The human factors consultant must be in a position to determine whether an issue arises out of inherent properties of the application or whether it is an artifact of the design and implementation of the user interface. This may imply that the human factors consultant must know as much or more about the application than the application developers.

The second major problem in performing human factors work in this environment arises when the answers to questions about interface designs require gathering information about user needs or user behavior. As the preceding section illustrates, user interface development in Oilfield Services takes place in a very different context from that in which many of the existing usability techniques were developed. Many of the techniques that work well in these other contexts are not as suitable here.

The following two examples illustrate some of the problems that occur when applying approaches developed elsewhere.

Many approaches to usability engineering involve improving a design by cycles of design and evaluation that occur before the product is released for usage (Gould and Lewis, 1985). The evaluation is typically done in the development environment in a usability laboratory with tasks specified by the developers. In oilfield services, this approach fails for several reasons. First, since understanding the tasks performed by users is a major challenge for developers, chances of their selecting an appropriate and realistic set for testing are low. The end result may be that the design is iteratively improved for a set of tasks and situations never encountered in actual use.

Second, because of the sequential-release model of software development, there is a constant backlog of new features and capabilities to be added to the system. Lengthening the release interval to allow time for iteration within one development cycle means that more requested changes must be deferred to later releases. Given a choice between crude, even poorly designed functionality now and a longer wait for a better design, users exert pressure to get things out the door as soon as possible.

Several modifications to published usability engineering approaches have been needed to introduce techniques for gathering information from users in this environment. Instead of having the usability studies run by the developers, one change has been to have the evaluation set up and run by representatives from the user community who are able to select and pose realistic tasks. Instead of trying to conduct usability studies in time to revise the current release, usability work is done on the actual software for one release with the goal of providing requirements for the next release. Not only does this avoid having usability work be a cause of release delay, but it permits the usability work to be done in the user's normal work context which increases the face validity of the tests.

A second example of difficulties with conventional usability techniques is in the use of techniques that involve meetings with groups of users to review designs or to gather requirements. For many of the oilfield applications, the users are widely dispersed geographically. For example, a base office for well logging engineers may have as many as fifteen engineers assigned to the base, but rarely will more than two or three be at the base at a time. Having a larger number present would be financially prohibitive since it would require losing the revenue that these engineers could be obtaining.

This problem of accessibility to users has been more difficult to address. The obvious approach of having systems developers visit job sites has several problems: First, travel is costly both financially and in developer time. Second, field engineers are typically quite busy at the job site or during their shifts and may not be willing to participate during their free time. Finally, visiting users individually does not produce the interactions among the users themselves that frequently contribute to developer's understanding of the task (Bias, Lanzetta, and Scanlon, 1993).

A partial substitute for group meetings with current users has been meetings arranged with former users. These are typically former field engineers who have moved to training, coordination, or engineering positions. Although they are still a source of valuable information, their experience is usually with much earlier versions of systems, and it may be only a matter of months before their familiarity with field operations fades.

Organizational Strategies for Delivering Human Factors Expertise

A second major problem to be solved in carrying out human factors activities is the selection of appropriate techniques for delivering human factors expertise. Which techniques are most effective is likely to depend on the organizational position of the human factors specialists; approaches that work for a specialist who is a member of a design team may not work for one who is associated with a central research facility. We have utilized the following four techniques.

Long-Term Collaborations between Human Factors Specialists and Engineering Groups. Typically, these collaborations last about one year and cover about one release version of a product. In these projects, the human factors specialist assists in collecting and analyzing requirements, reviews and critiques designs, performs design evaluation activities such as usability studies, and on occasion actually designs part of the interface.

Our experience has been that for these collaborations to succeed, the human factors specialist must acquire two types of knowledge: First, the specialist must learn substantial amounts about the application area. Just presenting general principles of behavior analysis or user interface design is ineffective; developers rarely have the skills needed to apply textbook principles to their situation. Instead, the specialist must know enough to participate in or lead task analysis activities and to provide substantive, specific advice about design alternatives based on understanding the task that the user is performing.

Activities to achieve this level of knowledge have included studying textbooks in the application, the human factors specialist attending internal user training courses, and visiting job sites. These activities may consume as much as half of the time allotted to the project. Our experience has been that these activities have a beneficial side effect. For the reasons given earlier, software developers frequently have not received adequate training in the application; in particular, visits to job sites are often deferred indefinitely under the pressure of release schedules. Accompanying the human factors specialist on visits to job sites has often provided the opportunity for the developers themselves to make the visits.

The second type of knowledge that the human factors specialist must acquire is about the implementation environment. Abstractly, the specialist ought to just describe what the users need and leave it up to the developers to figure out how to implement it. In practice, there are usually many alternative ways to achieve the same effect. As Mulligan, Altom, and Simkin (1991) point out, the human factors specialist's suggestions are much more likely to gain acceptance if they are couched in terms of the capabilities of the application software and hardware platform.

In our case, we have found it worthwhile actually to develop some interfaces using one of the most widely used development environments and to assist in training efforts for developers on use of this environment. For the developers, this means "one-stop shopping"; there is a single source for expertise on both the design of the interface and on implementation of the design.

Despite the high learning overhead for these collaborations, they have proven to be one of the most effective ways of supplying human factors expertise when judged in terms of impact on the development organization and the final product. Managers in development organizations spontaneously comment on the value of the assistance, and there are always several choices available for the next organization willing to participate in these collaborations.

Surprisingly, this impact is not necessarily due to being able to influence the product at an early stage; in some of the collaborations, the product had already been in use for a considerable length of time before the collaboration began. Rather, the opportunity to learn both about the application and the development environment in depth has meant that it is possible to give advice and information that is more closely tailored to the needs of the development organization. In turn, this increases the likelihood that the advice and information will be absorbed and acted on.

Internal Training Courses. These take the form of a three- or four-day course on human interface evaluation and design. The goal of the course is to provide an initial exposure to the disciplines and knowledge required for successful user interface design. It begins with an overview of basic cognitive and perceptual psychology organized around the "model human processor" (Card, Moran, and Newell, 1983). It then moves into engineering techniques for modeling and evaluating interface designs. The final part of the course is oriented towards software process issues and covers topics such as task analysis and usability assessment techniques. Recently, the course has been expanded to include a day spent reviewing and critiquing the interface of an existing product or one that is currently under development.

Although enrollment continues to be high in these courses and the student evaluations are positive, the longer-term impact has been more difficult to assess. At best, a three- or four-day course can only touch on the highlights of a discipline that normally requires several years of university study. For the course to have a significant influence on interface design, students would have to go substantially beyond the material presented in the course, both in terms of learning more of the formal content of the field and in adapting what they learn to their own projects. The developers who take the course, though, rarely have the time to engage in the necessary self-study or the several semesters of university courses. Because of the lack of the necessary follow-up learning, the course does not appear to contribute noticeably to developers' ability to design good interfaces.

The course does appear to have a different kind of value that justifies continuing to offer it. Many software developers, particularly those who received their formal education more than five years ago, are unaware of the value or role of behavioral science in interface design. Even if the four-day course does not provide them with enough knowledge to use this science on their own, it does make them realize that this type of knowledge exists and that specialists in this area can make useful contributions to their projects. This leads to later in-depth collaborations and begins to create a community of user interface developers.

Human Interface Design Guides. The typical introductory course textbook on human factors or on interface design has two disadvantages for software developers in Schlumberger. First, it is structured so that the chapters at the end of the book assume knowledge of the chapters at the beginning of the book. For developers with tight deadlines, the need to read through 254 pages of text so that they can understand the material on page 255 means that the necessary material simply won't get read.

Second, most texts do an inadequate job of covering some aspects of interface design that are particularly important to the petroleum industry; the graphical display of quantitative information is a prime example.

For these two reasons, we have developed a series of short guides to various aspects of user interface design. Each guide is intended to be read as a stand-alone document, even if this requires repeating some of the material found in other guides.

The guides are distributed throughout the company, with a distribution list targeted at developers and managers of projects with a substantial user interface component. These guides have been relatively successful. Requests for guides first distributed three years ago are still being received; the guides have been cited in requirements documents, and there have been requests for clarifications and amplification of material covered in the guides.

"Flash" Consultations. These are one- to three-day activities consisting of a visit to the engineering group to review a product, often followed by a written report. They resemble the type of interaction that occurs with an outside consultant on an initial visit. Although demand for these consultations is high, it is probably the least successful method for delivering expertise. They have two problems. First, they rarely give the human factors specialist time to learn enough about the application area to make useful comments on the human interface. Second, in a prefunded context, the consultations create the expectation that the specialist is available for deeper future involvement, such as the long-term collaborations described earlier, without providing the necessary signals that the involvement has to be negotiated organizationally. For projects that request this type of interaction, we are currently offering to assist them in finding an outside consultant.

Conclusion

Justifying human factors activities by showing the financial return on investment requires that a similar analysis be carried out for other competing technology investments. In many cases, such an analysis is not possible, and presenting human factors cost information in isolation runs the risk of unfavorable comparison with unrealistic estimates of the cost-benefits of other technologies. In such situations, a more workable approach to obtaining ongoing support for human factors activities is to ensure that they make a unique contribution to product development and to create an awareness of this contribution.

In accomplishing these goals, two types of problems need to be solved.

• Human factors methods and techniques must be adapted and customized to the particular characteristics of the environment or context in which product development is taking place.
• The human factors specialist must select delivery techniques for human factors knowledge and methods that are appropriate to the structure of the organization in which the human factors work takes place.

For the human factors activity at the Schlumberger Laboratory for Computer Science, a key aspect of addressing both of these problems has been the investment of considerable effort to learn and adapt to both the application areas and the development environment. This has enabled us to assist in improvements in user interfaces that could not be produced with equivalent investments in other technologies or tools. The appreciation of the unique nature of these improvements has provided a justification for continuing investment in human factors activities.

References

Bias, R. G., Lanzetta, T. M., and Scanlon, J. (1993). Concensus requirements: Low- and high-tech methods for discerning systems requirements from groups of users. *Proceedings IEEE Systems, Man and Cybernetics International Conference.* IEEE, New York.

Card, S. K., Moran, T. P., and Newell, A. (1983). The psychology of human–computer interaction. Lawrence Erlbaum Associates, Hillsdale, New Jersey.

Gould, J. and Lewis, C. (1985). Designing for usability: Key principles and what designers think. *Communications of the ACM* **30**(9), 758–759.

Mulligan, R. M., Altom, M W., and Simkin, D. K. (1991) User interface design in the trenches: Some tips on shooting from the hip. In: *Proceedings 1991 Conference on Human Factors in Computing Systems.* (Robertson, S., Olson, G. M., and Olson, J. S., eds.) Association for Computing Machinery, New York, 232–236.

Chapter 13

Organizational Inhibitors and Facilitators

Deborah J. Mayhew

Deborah J. Mayhew & Associates
West Tisbury, Massachusetts

Randolph G. Bias

IBM Corporation
Austin, Texas

Usability engineering is still a new concept to many software development organizations. Introducing usability engineering techniques into a development organization involves effecting organizational change—never an easy thing to accomplish and the subject of much research and study.

Anyone, usability engineer or not, who is trying to introduce usability engineering techniques and practices into an organization for the first time has to view him or herself first and foremost as an organizational change agent, not as a usability specialist, engineer, technical writer, product manager, marketer or whatever else they might be. Failing to take this view of one's role will most likely result (and indeed often *has* resulted) in a failure to introduce usability engineering into the software engineering methodology of a given organization in a lasting, integrated way. All the technical skills, good intentions, and sound logic in the world will not necessarily cause organizational change. Understanding what motivates and causes organizations to change is key.

In any organization, there are inherent inhibitors to change. They may differ from organization to organization in their exact nature, but they are always there. Anyone who aspires to be a change agent must recognize this basic fact, identify the particular and unique inhibitors that exist in the organization, and address them directly and specifically. Failing to do so will usually result in failure to effect the desired results. One must understand the sources of resistance in order to overcome them.

It is also true that there are usually factors, approaches, techniques, tactics and strategies that can serve as facilitators in effecting change. Facilitators can be divided into two types: *motivators* and *success factors.* Sometimes motivators are present outside of the change agent's influence and can simply be advantageous. Sometimes the change agent must create or at least draw attention to a potential motivator.

Once a motivator is present and recognized by the organization, then an opportunity exists, but the change agent's ability to effect change is still dependent on strategic application of pertinent success factors. It is entirely possible to fail in effecting change, even when a strong motivation for change is present, if the appropriate success factors are not applied.

First, we discuss typical existing inhibitors to the introduction of usability engineering techniques into software development organization. Then, specific motivators and success factors for introducing usability engineering are introduced and discussed.

Inhibitors to Change

It is important that anyone attempting to facilitate organizational change understand the forces at work in the organization that maintain the status quo. In the case of a usability pioneer attempting to introduce usability methods and practices into a software development organization, these forces fall into several categories, including:

- Myths, beliefs, and attitudes
- Organizational incentives
- Organizational practices
- Organizational structures
- Positioning of the usability engineering resource

Each is discussed in turn in the following sections, followed by a summary.

Myths, Beliefs, and Attitudes

The commonly held myths, beliefs, and attitudes of the software development culture regarding usability account in part for the resistance to change. Myths, beliefs, and attitudes are revealed in the following typical statements:

- "The quality of the user interface doesn't really matter."
- "As long as designers are familiar with interface guidelines and principles, good user interfaces will be designed."
- "User interface design tasks don't arise until the detailed design phase of a software project."
- "Usability is subjective and cannot be measured or 'engineered.'"
- "User interface design can be done right the first time, in the design phase."
- "User interface design is an implicit part of software design and development and need not be explicitly planned and budgeted."

"The Quality of the User Interface Doesn't Really Matter." Back in the 1970s and early 1980s, it was common to hear managers and developers actually make this statement. And, to a certain extent, it was true. Before usability became an aspect of competitive edge, it really didn't matter, at least to vendors and developers, in a bottom-line sense. In the 1990s, usability *is* an aspect of competitive edge, and it is rare to hear anyone express this belief openly. However, the true measure of what people believe is not what they *say*, but what they *do*. And if behavior is the measure, then it is clear that this is still a common belief. For how many development organizations really commit significant time, money, and resources to usability? In spite of lip service and the best intentions, when push comes to shove (and it always does on software development projects!) and budgets and schedules get tight, usability plans and resources (if they were formally allocated in the first place) are often the first to get cut from the project plan.

The point of this whole book is that the quality of user interfaces *does* matter and in fact influences the bottom line in a direct way. Until managers and developers are convinced of this, however, their beliefs to the contrary will present a source of resistance to change.

"As Long as Designers are Familiar with Interface Guidelines and Principles, Good User Interfaces Will Be Designed." Another common myth or belief among software managers and developers is that, as long as there is a "guru" or two around in the organization, his or her expertise and knowledge will somehow find its way into the design of products. Nothing could be farther from the truth.

Just like software engineering in general, interface design in particular is a process that must be managed. No software engineer believes, in this day of structured development methodologies, that if you simply locked a group of expert architects and programmers in a room for six months, a product would emerge. It is generally accepted that a process for development must be planned and managed. For some reason, however, engineers still believe that usability requires only available expertise and not planning and management.

Successful user interface design requires not only available expertise and fluency in usability principles and guidelines, but also effective management strategies and techniques, and design, testing, and evaluation methods. A lack of understanding of this fact accounts for some of the resistance to change that usability specialists encounter in software development organizations.

"User Interface Design Tasks Don't Arise until the Detailed Design Phase of a Software Project." Many software engineers still believe that interface design is a simple matter of screen design and therefore does not really arise as an issue until the point at which individual screens are designed, usually in the detailed design phase. Thus, they see no reason to introduce new techniques and methods at earlier stages—or later stages—in the overall development methodology.

Ideally, however, user interface tasks should begin when the project begins. User profiling, task analysis, and usability goal setting are usability tasks that should and can begin in the earliest stages of a project, along with the traditional tasks of scoping, planning, and functional and architectural specification (Mayhew, 1992, Chapter 18). They provide crucial data that should drive design of all aspects of the interface; not just screen design, but also conceptual design, choice of dialog styles and input devices, and organization of functionality (Mayhew, 1992). Until development managers and engineers understand this, they are resistant to radical changes—or even minor modifications—to their established development methodologies and project plans.

"Usability is Subjective and Cannot Be Measured or 'Engineered'." This myth is perhaps most responsible for resistance to organizational change. Because developers do not believe that user interface design is any more than a matter of common sense, and usability any more than aesthetics and subjective opinion, they cannot see how it lends itself to an engineering approach, and they therefore cannot see how their engineering process should be altered to accommodate it.

Usability can, of course, be "engineered," through structured information gathering , objective goal setting, and testing. But again, a lack of belief in this possibility is a source of resistance to organizational change.

"User Interface Design Can Be Done Right the First Time, in the Design Phase." Partly because software engineers believe that usability is subjective and user interface design is a matter of common sense, and partly because they are unaware of the available techniques from experimental psychology for objectively measuring human performance, they see the process of interface design as a simple one of making decisions based on common sense, rather than as an engineering process requiring the familiar phases of goal setting and iterative testing and redesign. They also tend to believe that a design that seems sensible to them will also seem sensible to users, so again, the possibility of and need for objective testing are not at all apparent to them. Here simple ignorance of available techniques and tools is in part responsible for resistance to organizational change.

While it is widely understood and accepted that no programmer, no matter how expert, can be expected to design code on paper and never need to test or "debug" it, it is still widely believed that user interface designers can or should be able to simply design good interfaces, without any need for testing or debugging. In truth, however, the need for usability testing is even more crucial than the need for software testing, because human beings are inherently more complex and unpredictable than computers, and because the field of usability is still quite immature relative to the field of software engineering.

"User Interface Design Is an Implicit Part of Software Design and Development and Need Not Be Explicitly Planned and Budgeted." User interface design has, for at least 20 years, been a part of many software development projects and yet has rarely before been made an explicit, formal part of any software development methodology. It has almost always been treated as an implicit part of the design process. People are always hard pressed to see why they should change a way of doing things that has seemed to work for such a long period of time. Every interactive system that has ever been built has had an interface designed, but usually without any explicit planning and budgeting for this to happen. So why should it be necessary to radically alter an accepted and established development methodology? Until developers accept the importance of the goal of improved usability, they will be resistant to the idea of change to their development process that requires new tasks which must be planned and budgeted.

Organizational Incentives

Most of the rest of this book offers techniques for performing cost-benefit analyses of usability activities, that is, techniques for establishing the bottom-line value of usability techniques and methods. However, even the most convincing cost-benefit analysis can fall on deaf ears if crucial organizational incentives are not in place.

For example, software managers are typically held accountable for staying within planned budgets and schedules and for providing agreed-upon functionality. Their incentives—performance reviews, salaries and promotions—are tied to these deliverables. Software managers are *not* typically held accountable for such things as user productivity (in an internal development organization) or sales (in a vendor company). Other organizations (user groups and sales and marketing staff, respectively) are held accountable for these things, in spite of the fact that it is the user interface to the software that largely determines these outcomes.

For example, interface design often seems to be driven by the need for ease of implementation (that is, by what is a easiest to implement from a technical point of view and easiest to manage from an organizational point of view) rather than by an analysis of user tasks and requirements. This is because ease of implementation helps a project to stay within budget and schedule constraints.

For instance, many office automation systems are divided into separate applications, such as word processing, graphics, spreadsheet, and electronic mail. Data from each application can sometimes be cut from a parent object and pasted into another object of a different type, but usually editing capabilities are then sacrificed.

In fact, users do not think in terms of *applications* or *data types.* They think in terms of *tasks,* such as sending a document to a colleague or generating a report which might include text and graphics based on data. The way that office automation systems are organized by application may be logical and efficient from a technical implementation point of view, but it does not support the tasks of users as well as it might. Nevertheless, a clean separation of applications allows easier implementation from both an organizational and a technical point of view, and the budget and schedule of a development project is more easily managed with such an architecture. And, the development manager *is* held accountable for budget and schedule goals and is *not* held accountable for usability.

The cost-benefit analyses described in this book entail a set of costs and a set of benefits. But they also assume that the costs can be directly compared to the benefits, so that an overall benefit to the organization as a whole can be calculated. If, however, as in many organizations, development groups and user or marketing groups are organized as separate profit centers with separate budgets, it is easy to see how a case for introducing usability techniques based on a cost-benefit analysis might fail to attract attention. Such an analysis assigns most of the costs to the development organization and most of the benefits to the user or marketing organization. And why should the manager of one profit center (development) be expected to incur costs, when it is the manager of another profit center (users, marketing) who will realize all the benefits?

The problem here is not one of failing to understand the value of usability engineering, but of inappropriate incentives in the organization. Certainly, a company as a whole would be inspired to spend money in order to save money, but organizations and individual managers within the company—if they are set up as separate profit centers with unique goals—cannot be expected to be focused on companywide goals if they are neither held accountable for them nor rewarded for contributing to them.

The problem here is an organizational one, and, until it is addressed, one cannot expect development managers to be swayed by even the most compelling cost-benefit case for usability. In order for such an analysis to be effective, different organizational incentives must be in place. Development managers need to be held accountable for the potential benefits of usability, such as user productivity, training costs, sales, and customer support costs, as well as for development budgets, schedules, and functionality. Fortunately, this could be easily accomplished, since these benefits are, as described in other chapters in this book, easily quantified and measured.

For example, concrete, measurable goals and benchmarks for user performance or sales could be established in the early stages of a development project. Responsibility and authority for achieving these goals could be clearly assigned to the development manager, with objective data gathering established to determine if these acceptance criteria have been met. Any development manager who knows up front that his or her performance will be evaluated against the achievement of these goals—as well as against budget, schedule and functionality goals—will be most interested in a cost-benefit analysis that indicates the overall value of usability methods.

Unfortunately, most usability specialists are not in a position to make high-level organizational changes such as redesigning the incentive systems for development managers. However, it is useful to the usability specialist to understand the organizational incentives in place. There is no point in wasting one's energy lobbying to a development manager, even with the most convincing cost-benefit analysis, if that manager has no accountability for usability. One must find the right audience in the organization for the analysis. This needs to be someone sufficiently high up in the organization to be responsible for corporate goals that include performance of both development and user or marketing groups. While this person may not choose to make fundamental changes in the organizational structure and incentive system, he or she might nevertheless be inspired by a convincing cost-benefit analysis to mandate the introduction of usability methods within development groups.

It should be pointed out here that, by following this advice, there is the real potential of alienating the development manager, who may feel an "end run" has been used to abrogate his or her power. Here, as in any business dealings, one should be aware of the accepted business practices and take care not to lose support along the way. The best approach may be to alert the development manager and/or other appropriate parties as to the results of the cost-benefit analysis and attempt to engage them in co-owning the results and presenting them higher up the management chain. The main point is that unless the party who is being asked to incur the costs of usability is the same party realizing the benefits, the whole premise of a cost-benefit analysis is lost. The *audience* for the analysis thus must be chosen carefully.

Other goals and incentives in development organizations besides (but often related to) budgets and schedules, which may directly conflict with the goal of better user interface design, also present obstacles and inhibitors to introducing better interface design ideas and methodologies. These include (Grudin, 1991a, 1991b):

Technical Goals, such as

1. Ease of specification and documentation of design
2. Minimization of computer memory and processor use and maximization of system response time
3. Modularizing code, which may discourage smooth integration of functionality

Cognitive Processes and Individual Goals, such as

4. The inability on the part of designers with high-level technical skills to put themselves in the shoes of naive users
5. The desire to conquer and maintain organizational "turf"
6. The desire to apply new technologies (such as color, voice technology, windowing), simply in order to keep skills current

Social, Group, and Team Goals, such as

7. The need to reward programmer effort (designs that prominently feature novel, difficult-to-implement functions may not present those features in their most usable form)
8. Ease of communication of design ideas (a design that lends itself well to specification and documentation may not be usable when implemented in interactive form)
9. Desire for cooperation, which often leads to design compromises that reflect good negotiating practices but negatively effect usability. (Grudin (1986) gives an example in which developers working on the same application for two different workstations could not agree on whether to place a message line on the first or last line of the screen; they finally compromised by agreeing to always put it on line 25, which was the last line on one workstation, but would cause wraparound to the first line on the other workstation!)

Marketing and Business Goals, such as

10. Desire to maintain installed base by not innovating in ways that might create a retraining overhead for customers
11. Avoiding copyright violation lawsuits
12. Appealing (and thus selling) to customers or buyers, rather than providing real usability to actual end users

All these conflicting incentives and goals set up inhibitors and resistance to organizational changes that would better accommodate usability methods and goals.

Even when users interact with and even join development teams, the results may be less than productive, due to conflicting personal, group and social goals (Bond, 1992). Users who become integral members of development teams may suffer from the "hostage" effect, adopting the skills, ambitions, and values of the developers. Or, users are chosen to join the team precisely because they have technical skills and interests and thus don't represent the typical user well.

Dysfunctional group dynamics may also interfere with the ability of users—and developers—to contribute when they are too intimately involved with the design and development team. "Group think" may occur, where the group strives for consensus, tending to ignore conflicting or unsettling information. Members may fear alienation from the group, and thus fail to create conflict even when it would be productive. Users may simply be overwhelmed and intimidated by the technical nature of discussions, and keep quiet just to save face. Or, they may simply be unable to accurately recall aspects of their work activities when separated from them. And finally, the loudest, most persistent voice often wins out in group discussions, rather than the optimal design idea. Thus, even when attempts are made to involve users in interface design, other conflicting incentives may work against the effectiveness of their involvement.

Organizational Practices

Gould and Lewis (1985) point out four key principles for good user interface design that seem to be widely recognized by developers today. These are:

1. Early focus on users (direct contact between developers and actual end users).
2. Early and continual user testing (an empirical, rather than strictly theoretical, approach to design).
3. Iterative design (a repeating process of design, test, evaluate, redesign, retest, reevaluate, etc.).
4. Integrated design (parallel evolution of user interface, help system, training, and documentation under one management).

In spite of widespread *belief* in these principles among designers and developers, however, most development organizations still do not *apply* them. This seems to be because well-established practices, based in the historical roots of today's software development methodologies, present sources of resistance and set up inhibitors to change. These practices include:

- Limitation of contact between designers/developers and users
- Traditional emphasis on up-front, thorough design
- Traditional lack of efficient development tools
- Traditional focus of systems analysis
- Tendency to mimic the manual world

Limitation of Contact between Designers/Developers and Users. Typically, developers and users are isolated and "protected" from contact with one another, and customer contact is delegated to groups such as marketers, trainers, and field support. Even marketers are often restricted to contact with "customers" (buyers, user managers) rather than with actual end users. It is generally feared that developers will get bogged down by continual contact with users and fail to stick to project plans and schedules and that users will be "contaminated" with false expectations or that highly proprietary secrets of corporate strategy and new product design will be prematurely revealed if users have access to developers.

Also contributing to the limitation of contact between developers and users are (Grudin, 1991a):

1. Lack of motivation on the part of developers, who do not understand or empathize with workers with very different backgrounds and motivations.
2. Difficulty identifying the full range of potential users of technology-driven products under development in vendor companies.
3. Resistance by user group managers, who see—and want to protect—their role as user representatives or are reluctant to take time away from users' usual responsibilities.
4. Simple geographic distance between development and user groups.
5. Simple language and culture barriers between users and developers, which make smooth communication difficult.
6. Simple ignorance on the part of developers regarding how to systematically yet efficiently assess the needs of a large and diverse set of potential users.

Lack of contact between users and developers was not a liability in the days of developing noninteractive systems but clearly sets up a serious obstacle to Gould's and Lewis's first three principles of interface design (Poltrock and Grudin, 1992; Grudin, 1991a).

Traditional Emphasis on Up-front, Thorough Design. Traditionally, different aspects of a product—such as hardware, software, documentation, training, and marketing—have been the responsibility of separate organizational groups under separate management. Often, these groups are separated geographically, as well as organizationally. In order to co-ordinate the efforts of these separately managed and located groups, methodologies that emphasized complete and thorough design up front, frozen before development began, and communicated through formal specification documents, evolved. Again, such an analytical, logical, linear approach depending on communication by documentation—rather than an empirical approach dependent on informal, personal communication—was appropriate in the development of noninteractive systems. However, it clearly conflicts with Gould's and Lewis's principle of iterative design. Iterative design would require significant organizational and methodological changes in most development groups (Poltrock and Grudin, 1992).

Traditional Lack of Efficient Development Tools. Typical development methodologies evolved before the development of efficient prototyping and development tools. The lack of these tools made empirical, iterative design impractical. Even though such tools are now available, taking advantage of them would require radically altering existing methodologies (Poltrock and Grudin, 1992).

Traditional Focus of Systems Analysis. One of the sources of poor interface design is a focus on features and functions, rather than on overall user tasks. Traditional systems analysis encourages this focus. Lack of contact with real users is also responsible. In the office automation example, focusing on word processing functions and graphics functions independently would be an example of a typical systems analysis approach to system design. It fails to note that users don't build text or graphics; they build *documents.*

Tendency to Mimic the Manual World. Poor interface design is sometimes due to a simple-minded tendency to mimic the manual world. This made perfect sense back in the days when noninteractive systems were designed to replace simple number-crunching functions. However, in today's highly interactive systems, it often means that inefficiencies in the manual processes that computers are meant to automate are thus carried forward into the user interface. The power of the computer goes unexploited due to a simple lack of analysis and creative thought on the part of the designer. Thus, in the manual world, one might cut and paste illustrations drawn by a draftsperson into a document typed by a typist. This approach is mimicked in the office automation product.

Poltrock and Grudin (1992) sum up the traditional practices of software development organizations that present inhibitors to Gould's and Lewis's principles of good interface design, as follows:

> In summary, adopting widely recognized and accepted principles of interface design in a large project requires an organizational commitment. Interface designers and developers may recognize the value of these principles but lack the authority to recruit users or to plan for design iterations. Change will not be quick or easy. Training is required to maximize the benefit from access to populations of users. The development schedule must accommodate iterative cycles of design, prototyping, and testing with users, and the development organization must learn to tolerate the instability that results from iterative interface design. Careful prioritization and the use of concrete usability objectives and measures ... can prevent never-ending design iterations, in the same way that system performance and reliability are measured.

Organizational Structures

Traditional organizational structures within software development organizations can also inadvertently present obstacles to good user interface design practices.

Sometimes the design of an interface reflects the existing organization of the product development team assigned to build it (Grudin 1991a, 1991b.) In some cases, the development organization drives interface design decisions. For example, graphics and word processing capabilities may be separated into different applications rather than integrated, not so much because of technical implementation concerns, but because different organizational entities were already assigned responsibility for these different functions. Database inquiry capabilities of an application and on-line help systems may be implemented as separate, unintegrated functions in a whole application because separate development groups with specialized skills in these areas have traditionally designed and built these functions.

In other cases, the opposite happens: project teams are organized in a way that facilitates management of the project and division of labor. Then interfaces reflect this organization. For example, it may be easier to get additional programmers assigned to a project if their role can be mapped to a separate, distinct—rather than a smoothly integrated—feature or function.

In either case, it is always easier for specialized groups to work relatively independently than to coordinate with one another. Thus, ease of management and division of labor in implementation take precedence over ease of learning and ease of use in interface design.

Other aspects of organizational structures may present inhibitors to early and consistent user involvement in design (Grudin, 1991b). For instance, on development projects that are competitively bid on and contracted out, typically the development team is not identified, let alone involved, until long after users are identified, user requirements are specified, and design is complete. Design specs serve as the sole communication to developers, who are evaluated according to how faithfully they follow these specs. This inhibits any contact with users, including iterative design and testing, and motivates developers to conform blindly to specs rather than optimize an interface through usability techniques and methods.

In another type of development situation—vendor companies producing commercial software—potential users are never really completely known and identifiable during development. They also do not work within the same organization and may not be able to assess the potential utility of a new product, making it hard to recruit them into the design process.

In the type of organization where temporal and organizational distances between users and developers seem least likely to pose a problem—development groups internal to a business—organizational structure can still work against close collaboration between users and developers. Geographic, organizational, political, and cultural separation of the two groups may work against the type of smooth communication that could optimize meeting user needs and requirements through better user interfaces.

Positioning of the Usability Engineering Resource

There are well-documented reasons why it works well to have all usability engineers in a company or organization reporting into a centralized usability department (see, for example, Bias and Alford, 1989). Similarly, there are reports of successes "mainstreaming" or decentralizing usability engineers directly into first-line development departments (see, for example, Bias and Smith-Kerker, 1986). Just as one interface style does not succeed for all types of users, one organizational structure or another for usability engineers does not succeed in all corporate cultures. But, in any organization, either model for positioning the usability engineering resource—centralized or decentralized—can introduce inhibitors to effective usability engineering.

In the case of the centralized usability engineering organization, the biggest hurdle to overcome is the potential for an "us vs. them" attitude, which can inhibit the natural integration of usability engineering into the development process. This potential is increased when usability engineers cast themselves—or are cast as—simply the authors and enforcers of interface standards which designers and developers must then follow. When usability engineers are presented instead as valuable resources to designers and developers all during the design process, available to help them accomplish common goals, then the potential for this drawback of centralization is decreased.

Mainstreamed or decentralized usability engineers, who report directly into development project teams and are full-time team members, are less often regarded as outsiders and obstacles, but they face a different set of inhibiting factors. First, if the usability engineer has been too intimately involved with the design and development of a product, he or she may lose objectivity. He or she might begin negotiations for a more usable interface from a more compromised position, simply because of the intimate awareness of the development environment's constraints, or by falling victim to "group think."

A second problem might be referred to as "the care and feeding of the usability engineer." When usability engineers report directly to a development manager, rather than a usability manager, there is the likely possibility that the development manager will not understand how to evaluate the contribution of the usability engineer (it might be difficult to be the only person on the project team who generates zero lines of code). Similarly, there may be little support to help the usability engineer maintain and develop his or her expertise if the manager doesn't understand the field. And, it can be lonely to work in an organization without any professional peers. Too many highly trained and expert usability engineers have gradually been converted to developers because they did not have the support of a usability engineer as their manager and a group of usability engineers as their peers.

There are approaches to both centralization and decentralization of the usability engineering resource that can work. When usability engineers are centralized and have good interpersonal and team building skills and effective education about and marketing of the resource, they can overcome the negative potential of being viewed as outsiders. And, if usability engineers are decentralized, efforts can be made to form less formal organizational relationships with other usability engineers within and outside the company, both for professional support and to help avoid falling victim to "group think."

One hybrid approach to positioning usability specialists that has worked well in some organizations is to have user interface *designers* be full-time project team members, with support from usability engineers from a centralized usability department who perform *information gathering* and *testing and evaluation* services.

All organization structures have their potential drawbacks, but they can be overcome with proper attention and effort. The key is to choose an organizational positioning for the usability engineering resource that is compatible with the overall corporate culture in which it must operate and to then be aware of the inherent potential drawbacks of the chosen positioning, and to address them constructively before they become serious inhibitors to success.

Inhibitors to Change: Summary

The foregoing discussion of inhibitors to change, including prevalent myths and beliefs, well-established organizational incentives, practices, and structures, and organizational positioning of the usability engineering resource, presents an intimidating picture of the forces working against the individual usability specialist trying to effect organizational change to further the goal of usability. However, it is the very identification and recognition of these forces that will allow the aspiring change agent to plan an effective strategy for effecting change.

A user interface should be explicitly designed based on a clear analysis and understanding of the main tasks of the intended users. However, usability goals are not the only legitimate goals for development organizations, and sometimes conflicting forces such as marketing goals and technical constraints will lead to a less-than-optimal design. This is reasonable if the trade-offs are consciously considered and made. However, less-than-optimal designs from a user's point of view should never result due to a simple lack of information and consideration or irrelevant circumstances such as project team organization. Aspiring change agents can educate management regarding the historical forces that have shaped current development methodologies and the inappropriateness of these methodologies for developing interactive systems for today's users. They can also be on the alert for these influences in their organizations and combat them directly in the course of their interactions with developers.

Sooner or later, most development organizations will be motivated to make changes. The aspiring change agent must recognize these motivators as opportunities and take strategic advantage of them. We now turn to possible motivations for change and then to the factors for successful exploitation of them.

Motivations for Change

A variety of things seem to inspire a development organization's first attempts to integrate usability methods into their overall development process. These include:

- A powerful internal advocate
- A high-visibility disaster
- A perception of competition and market demand
- A desire to address general business goals
- A need for an objective means of resolving conflicts
- Education

These motivators are described below, with real case studies cited as examples. A summary follows.

A Powerful Internal Advocate

Sometimes a single individual plays the role of change agent. This individual may be at any management level, from a project leader who decides to hire a usability expert for his or her project team to a research and development (R&D) vice-president who decides to make usability a part of his or her organizational territory. In these cases, it is the vision of a single individual that motivates change, and it is that individual's raw organizational power that accomplishes change.

For example, Apple Computer's Steven Jobs was a powerful visionary who simply decided to make usability a key aspect of competitive edge in the personal computer market. He created a whole company dedicated to usability because that was his vision and he had the organizational power to implement his personal vision.

In another vendor company, a vice-president of R&D saw an opportunity to carve out some new organizational territory for himself, and he personally sponsored and managed the initiation and growth of what became a relatively large and powerful centralized usability engineering organization. The usability engineers in this group had very high-level support right from the outset, and this allowed them to effect change in the development process and have a significant impact on product design.

In yet another example, the product manager of an important, high-visibility, innovative product in a vendor company personally decided to hire a usability expert and cast that expert as the lead interface designer within the project team. This was unprecedented in the company, but the product manager had enough power to introduce and support this new role and expertise within his own project team.

In each of these three examples, the scope of influence and power of the individual was different: from a whole company, to an R&D division, to a single project team. But within his scope of influence, the individual—in none of the three cases a usability engineer himself—had the organizational power to hire and support a new type of expertise and alter the development methodology within his organization to incorporate and integrate input from that new job role.

A High-Visibility Disaster

In other cases, a clear, high-visibility disaster is an organization's first incentive. Perhaps a high-profile, very expensive development effort fails dramatically, and users clearly state that they reject a system because it is unusable. Or, a product fails in the marketplace, and customers point to its user interface as the reason for their rejection.

For example, one insurance company hired their first (external) usability consultant when a $3 million dollar application development effort failed dramatically. Users were employed by independent agencies and were thus discretionary users of the application. The application was intended to encourage and support the agents in selling this company's products as opposed to competitors' products. The agents simply refused to use the application, citing among other reasons an unlearnable, unusable interface. Such a dramatic disaster, which so clearly pointed to usability as the main issue, inspired this company to hire an outside usability consultant. Several projects with the consultant further inspired them to begin to build their own internal usability staff and a usability lab. The company is still evolving their development methodology to incorporate the skills, methods, and facilities of their usability staff and lab.

In another example, a small company developed a new software product to compete with some already-established products of its type. Part of their marketing strategy was to send their product unsolicited to prospective buyers, with a free trial offer. Customers were free to return the product but could pay for and keep it if they chose to after trying it out. The company assumed that the product was good enough to sell itself. The product consisted of the application on diskette, an on-line tutorial on diskette, and a set of hard-copy manuals. Each of these components was separately shrink-wrapped.

A disappointingly large number of products were returned. The marketing staff noted that, in most cases, the manuals had been taken out of the shrink-wrapping, but neither of the two diskettes had. Comments confirmed what these clues suggested—that the manuals were so unusable that prospective customers never even bothered to look at the software itself. They assumed that, if the manuals were difficult to use, the software would be as well. In this case, the product failed due to poor design of the documentation. Documentation has historically been a neglected aspect of user interface design, and this experience motivated this software vendor to hire an external usability expert to help them redesign their documentation.

A Perception of Competition and Market Demand

Sometimes, in the case of vendor companies, the marketplace clearly provides the motivation for change. Marketers hear a clear request from customers for improved usability and bring pressure to bear on development organizations. Or a company perceives that it is—or may be—losing market share and attributes this to competitive companies doing a better job of usability.

Apple Computer gets a lot of credit for introducing usability as an aspect of competitive edge in the marketplace. Prior to the first Macintosh computer, personal computer vendors were competing on such aspects as functionality, cost, and customer support. No vendors were spending resources on usability because they did not perceive it as a way to differentiate their products from their competitors' products. Apple consciously decided that their market niche would be usability. They successfully won a large part of the personal computer market from other vendors by competing primarily on this aspect. Now, as similar products (both hardware and software) proliferate and are not really differentiated on cost, functionality, or available support, usability has become a key aspect of competitive edge.

In another example, a division of one vendor of very specialized hardware and software products called in its first (external) usability consultant after reading an article in a users' magazine. The magazine had conducted a survey of the buyers and users of their type of product, asking them what was missing in current products and what they wanted to see in future products. Nearly one-third of the users' comments indicated that their main complaints with current products—and their desired features in future products—were related to various aspects of usability. This inspired this division to allocate funds and resources to focus on the user interface of their newest product line.

A Desire to Address General Business Goals

In the case of internal development organizations building systems for in-house users, a general motivation to address typical business problems such as low user productivity, high user training costs, and the desire to grow without increasing costs may focus on usability issues.

One company had a stated business goal of increasing their volume of customer service transactions by 10% without increasing customer service staff. It was recognized that better computer support for customer service reps might contribute to this goal, and so a usability consultant was hired to help redesign the user interface to a particular customer service application. This in turn led to an additional project to design a user interface style guide to govern the design of future applications.

A Need for an Objective Means of Resolving Conflicts

Sometimes the motivation to bring in a usability engineer, often on a consulting basis, arises out of a need for an objective, neutral means for resolving internal conflicts over design issues. Opposing parties agree to resolve a design issue by consulting an outside expert or through objective usability testing, but do not have the skills in-house or can agree only to abide by the findings of an outsider.

One product development team had too many basic, conflicting views on the design of a new product among the highest-ranking members of the project team. They could not resolve their differences and come to any agreement among themselves. The only thing they could agree upon was to hire an external (that is, a politically objective and unbiased) usability expert to come in and assess the alternatives through prototype testing and user surveys and to abide by the outsider's conclusions and recommendations. The combination of the outsider's lack of a political agenda and the objective data produced by the prototype testing and user surveys allowed everyone to accept the final conclusions of the consultant. In the process, the development organization was exposed to the special skills and methods of usability engineering and later recruited usability consultants on other projects right from the start.

Education

Finally, sometimes education, in the form of short presentations to management or seminars for developers, can begin the process of change. Many a project for usability consultants has been generated by offering workshops and seminars at conferences and through professional organizations. When managers and developers attend such seminars, they begin to realize that not everyone is a user interface design expert and that there really are structured methodologies and approaches available for engineering usability into products. They begin to comprehend that there is a lot they don't know and that there are experts out there who do know. What they learn about what they don't know is as important as what they can actually learn in such a short course. The realization that there really is a fairly mature and specialized field of expertise out there can provide the impetus for some change in the way that they conduct product development.

Motivations for Change: Summary

Unless one of the preceding motivators is present, trying to influence an organization to integrate usability methods into its development process is usually a thankless task. But when one of these motivators is present, an opportunity arises for professional usability engineers, either internal or external, to have an impact. Then, there seems to be a set of factors that influence the success or failure of these individuals in their role as change agents. Keys to success are discussed next.

Success Factors

Several strategies contribute to the usability specialist's success in playing the role of change agent in software development organizations. These include

- Establish credibility
- Communicate effectively
- Get "buy-in"
- Be an engineer, not an artist
- Produce well-defined work products
- Manage expectations
- Clarify value added
- Test whenever possible

These strategies or success factors are described, with case studies cited as examples in some cases. This is followed by a summary.

Establish Credibility

Usability specialists hoping to create new roles and methods in their organizations must move quickly to establish personal and professional credibility. Most likely, the engineers and managers that they work with will not be aware of their special skills and will see them as people with a different set of opinions who have been, for some unclear reason, assigned the job of interface design. They may be resentful that this job has been taken away from them and may be looking for confirmation of their skepticism. Therefore, it is critical that usability specialists choose projects that clearly demonstrate the special skills they bring to the team.

Conducting projects that require special skills, such as user profiling, task analysis, and usability testing, may be better choices for initial projects than, say, simply doing design or participating in design meetings. The former types of projects clearly demonstrate training, skills, techniques, and methods that are usually not within the repertoire of the average developer. Design projects, on the other hand, demonstrate little more than that the usability specialist has one more opinion to offer on design issues—something there is never any lack of among developers.

Many a usability engineer has discovered, after years of frustration trying—and failing—to have an impact simply by participating in design meetings, that conducting one usability test or one task analysis suddenly and dramatically established them as an important team member with useful and unique skills to offer. (Of course, it may be the case that there isn't the luxury of picking and choosing one's projects; one can't usually turn down a management-directed project just because it has a potential low return from a strategic point of view. In this situation, see the section on managing expectations that follows.)

It is equally important for the usability specialist to demonstrate knowledge of and appreciation for technical and organizational concerns. Part of establishing credibility is being able to speak credibly the language of one's organizational peers. It is a sad but true fact that developers usually reject any potential contributor who does not have at least some basic understanding of technology, and managers usually reject any potential contributor who does not demonstrate an understanding and appreciation of the realities of software development methodologies and the constraints of schedules, budgets, and other market pressures. While these skills are not necessarily *technically* required to be a good interface designer or tester, they may be *politically* and *socially* crucial to being accepted in an organization.

And, the usability specialist must have not only some rudimentary knowledge of technology and software engineering practices, but also be prepared to do a lot of listening and some strategic compromising and negotiating over usability goals.

Both technical and organizational/political skills will add credibility to the individual specialist. Specialized usability skills will also lend credibility to the profession.

Communicate Effectively

While the whole point of usability engineering is to communicate the nature of a product *to the user* more effectively, ironically, usability professionals are often guilty of poor communication of their design principles and ideas *to developers*. We need to be articulate and effective in our spoken presentations and in our written communications to the developers we are trying to influence; they are, in a sense, our users. We need to write "developer-friendly" user interface specification documents. We need to find even more effective ways than specs to communicate design standards. For example, a well-illustrated, oral presentation, may more effectively communicate design standards than any document would, and a prototype embodying design standards would be better yet. Best of all might be embedding design standards in development tools.

We need to offer well-designed classes to teach usability principles and methods and make effective presentations to communicate the importance and implications of our studies and tests. A usability engineer who cannot communicate design principles and study results to developers is like a user interface that does not communicate functionality to a user. (For a discussion of such usability engineer-to-designer communication concerns, see Gillan and Bias, 1992.)

One internal usability engineer spent a year and a half developing a user interface style guide for a family of products, producing a document several hundred pages long. Imagine her disappointment when, after distributing the final document, designers produced designs that bore no resemblance whatsoever to the standards! An oral presentation, videotaped for review, proved to be much more effective in influencing designs. And, note how effective Apple has been in controlling the designs of third-party Macintosh applications by embedding their interface standards in their development "tool kit."

If a style guide is the only vehicle for communicating a set of design standards, at least equal effort must be expended in designing the presentation of the design decisions as was expended in making the design decisions themselves. Too many a style guide, developed by many people over long periods of time, has suffered the fate of gathering dust on bookshelves, simply because the excellent design ideas it contained were not well organized and presented. Too many a usability study has failed to have an impact because of poor oral or written presentation of results and implications. We must all consider the interface between our profession, skills, and findings and the developers and products that we are trying to influence. Effective communication—not just good technical skills and design ideas—is absolutely essential to having an impact.

Get "Buy-In"

Usability engineers must work at casting themselves as team members rather than critics. They must work towards creating a process through which they can have an impact, and this involves getting other engineers in the development organization invested in their skills, methods, techniques, knowledge, and design ideas. Getting "buy-in" is crucial.

An external usability consultant failed dramatically several times at influencing product design by accepting the role of sole designer. She designed in the privacy of her own office, without interaction with developers, and presented a complete design as her work product. In spite of the fact that this is what she had been hired to do, her design ideas were completely ignored. Although she was paid for her time, she was disappointed at her failure to have an impact on products and convince her clients that they had gotten their money's worth. She has since developed a new strategy for working with clients on design projects, which has been very successful.

First, she simply refuses to accept the role of sole or even lead designer. Instead, she casts herself as manager, director, and consultant to an internal design team. She teaches design process and methods such as task analysis, user profiling, and style guide development to the design team, who then carry out these methods themselves under her direction and with her feedback. She runs design meetings but never attempts to impose a single design decision on the group. Instead, she facilitates discussion of design alternatives by focusing on advantages and disadvantages of design alternatives and always referring back to the results of user profiles and task analyses. She tries to get the design team to generate these advantages and disadvantages themselves but will bring her own knowledge and experience into the discussion when necessary. She tries to introduce a process of "egoless" design, in which the focus is on objective goals, principles, data, and analysis, rather than on conflicting opinions. In the end, she leaves the design team to make every design decision themselves, based on the objective and exhaustive analysis she has facilitated. The truth is, she has led them to each design decision. However, they experience the whole process as independent design decisions through logical information gathering and analysis, and in fact it is. This causes them to have a sense of ownership and investment in the final design decisions, and thus to champion them among others in the internal development organization who need to be convinced.

All this may sound somewhat inefficient and perhaps even manipulative, but the simple truth is that buy-in is necessary for developers to feel ownership of and be committed to a body of design ideas. A sense of ownership and commitment by developers is absolutely necessary when the usability engineer does not have any real organizational power to enforce design decisions. It is also true that the developers learn process, methods, techniques, and design principles much more effectively when they are involved in the design process in the way just described, and the usability engineer thus has a much broader impact—on a whole organization, rather than just on a product—when such a process is used.

Be an Engineer, Not an Artist

Software developers are engineers. They are trained to think and work in certain ways, and they relate to and work best with other engineers who think and work in similar ways. They view psychologists and artists as very different kinds of thinkers and workers and are often put off by the language and cultural differences of these professions.

To be successful working in an engineering environment, one must think and work like an engineer. This is not difficult to do for usability engineers whose background is in human factors or psychology. Several things help, including:

1. Logical reasoning from data and principles, rather than just arguing opinion and personal preference or experience (for example, presenting design principles in flow-chart form, rather than through prose discussion of determining factors).
2. Applying systematic, structured methodologies, rather than vague and ill-defined techniques (for example, usage studies rather than focus groups).
3. Focusing on concrete, objective measurable usability goals (e.g., time and error performance data), rather than on aesthetics or informal, anecdotal feedback from users.

And, the engineering-like approach of the usability specialist must be made clear and communicated well to the engineers. The more that usability methods and approaches seem familiar to the engineer, the more likely they are to be respected and accepted.

There are a number of usability techniques that, although valuable, smack less of engineering practices than others. For instance, interviewing, when skillfully applied, can yield invaluable results, as can intelligent and insightful interpretation of user introspection, and field studies in context rather than well-controlled laboratory experiments. However, these techniques may seem somewhat subjective—and thus suspect—to the engineer. It may be strategically important to *first* apply techniques such as classic experimental design, including time and error measures, until credibility and a secure role for usability engineering are well established, before introducing the other techniques to the usability engineering role.

Both psychology in general and human factors psychology in particular have evolved in this fashion. Traditional "scientific" methods (behaviorism, experimentalism) were introduced in these fields in order to establish credibility for the field amongst other "hard" sciences. Only more recently have other less-structured and less-controlled techniques (e.g., introspection, field observation) been introduced (or revived) and accepted. The individual usability engineer would do well take this lesson from history and apply it to his or her small world of developers who are still naive and skeptical regarding the value of applying psychology in an engineering environment.

Produce Well-Defined Work Products

It is easy to underrate the strategic importance of the *form* of usability input. Many usability professionals allow their role to be defined as just providing one more opinion in design meetings. It is difficult to provide detailed rationale for opinions during conversations in meetings, and developers cannot easily see why the opinion of a usability engineer has any more merit than anyone else's opinion. The specialized knowledge and skills of trained usability engineers usually are not communicated well in such a setting.

Usability engineers should certainly participate in design meetings, but, rather than just throw in one more set of opinions, they should use the meetings to identify opportunities for defining and conducting short information gathering, design, or testing projects aimed at answering questions being raised and debated in these meetings. They should highlight these projects—rather than their "expert advice"—as their primary role. This will cast them as experts with specialized skills who can be used as a resource in making design decisions, rather than as adversaries with differing opinions.

Projects should have a clearly defined scope, schedule, and deliverable, so that the usability engineer's contribution is clear, concrete, and readily identifiable. Projects should be as short as possible, so that results are timely enough to have an impact on a development project, and so that the association between design dilemmas and conflicts, and usability engineering solutions is clearly established.

For example, one usability engineer found that just participating as a regular member in design meetings made it hard to influence design decisions significantly. She identified a set of design issues regarding the design of the windowing capability of the product under development that were being heatedly debated by the design team, and she designed and conducted a short, simple task analysis project in which she interviewed a number of users of existing windowing interfaces to identify performance and preference determinants. She first designed and presented a project plan for her study to the design team, to clarify her role and get buy-in for her project and its results. Then, she carried out the plan and reported the results back to the team. The team was happy and relieved to have some relatively objective data on which to base their design decisions and began to view the usability engineer as a resource for resolving difficult design decisions. The relative objectivity of the study helped to foster this view of the usability engineer, whereas her opinions had seemed simply adversarial and unconvincing. This different approach to providing input was key in establishing her as a valued team member with specialized skills, and the key aspects of the approach were to engineer clear, simple projects that required specialized skills and produced clear, well-defined results.

Manage Expectations

One of the easiest mistakes to make as a usability engineer trying to gain respect and acceptance in a development organization is to feel that one must have all the answers. Credibility is seriously damaged when unrealistic expectations are encouraged. For example, it is important to make the limitations—as well as the value—of prototype testing clear. Developers led to believe that prototype testing is the answer to user interface design will inevitably feel disappointed and disillusioned with the field. Usability engineers must carefully point out that testing:

1. Identifies problems but does not solve them,
2. Focuses on ease of learning but not on ease of use (or vica versa),
3. Reflects on performance but not on preference and satisfaction (or vice versa),
4. Reflects only on the part of the system being tested, not on the whole system, and
5. Will not necessarily predict sales, etc.

Usability engineers should also make the limits of principles and guidelines clear. Developers should not be led to believe that there is a simple, "cookbook" approach to interface design, but should be educated on the heuristic, rule-of-thumb nature of principles and guidelines and the ultimate necessity of testing.

Never be afraid to admit what you don't know, haven't done, and aren't good at. Managers and developers can usually tell—or will eventually discover—that you are bluffing, and this will do great damage to your credibility. Someone who is confident enough to make disclaimers about their experience and skills enhances their credibility immeasurably. If, on one issue, you state that you have no idea which design alternative will be best, and on the next express complete confidence in one design alternative over another, people will have much more faith in the latter.

They will trust your strong opinions more if you are willing to admit when you don't have the knowledge to support a strong one.

If you have never worked on a particular type of application before, state clearly that you haven't, rather than being evasive. If you are not a graphic designer, do not pretend to be one. If you are completely unfamiliar with a particular technology platform, say so. If you've had minimal experience writing corporate style guides, don't try to inflate your experience. At the same time, express your complete confidence in your ability to make a significant contribution in spite of these "holes" in your experience. Point out that the development team already has experts in these various areas, but they are missing the special skills (background in cognition, skills in information gathering and experimental design, familiarity with the human factors literature, etc.) that you have. Or, that although you have only done one or two style guides before, this is much more experience than anyone else on their team has, and they won't find anyone with more—and more relevant—experience than you. Be candid about your experience and skills and express strong confidence in your ability to make a contribution.

The value of managing expectations cannot be understated. It is always better to accomplish more than you promised than less. And, it is always better to be up front about the limitations of the field and its knowledge base and methods, so that managers and developers appreciatively accept what you can contribute, rather than conclude that their disappointed expectations reflect on your personal professionalism.

Clarify Value Added

At least initially, it can be very useful to use the techniques outlined elsewhere in this book to cost-justify plans and efforts aimed at usability. It is not usually obvious to development engineers and managers what the potential payoff of usability engineering techniques might be, at least in the bottom-line sense. They will be reluctant to spend time, money, and resources for some vaguely defined benefit, especially in the heat of tight budgets and schedules. One must make a good business case to clarify the bottom-line value of adding usability tasks to the overall project plan.

It is also critical to choose initial projects that will quickly and dramatically demonstrate the value of usability engineering activities. For example, it may be wiser to start out by proposing a usability *testing* project, rather than a *design* effort, such as the development of a set of corporate user interface standards. The former will take a relatively brief amount of time, and the results are objective, concrete and usually quite dramatic and convincing. The latter will take a great deal of time, and the payoff will not be immediately obvious. In fact, it may never be obvious, if no objective data are ever gathered to evaluate its impact.

Choosing the right development project to get involved in is also important. If possible, initial usability efforts should be aimed at high-visibility, critical projects where, again, there will be maximum recognition and appreciation of the results of the usability techniques. Contributing to a project that not many people in the organization are aware of or invested in simply will not have the same impact, no matter how useful a contribution it might be to that project.

In general, it is important that usability experts hoping to change the development process of a large organization choose short-term usability projects with concrete, objective results and apply them to high-visibility, important development projects, in order for the projects to have the impact of organizational change, as well as product change.

For example, two frustrated, decentralized usability engineers in a very large R&D organization of a vendor company decided on their own to conduct a usability test of a software product that had already been announced and was close to release. They were aware that testing so late in the development cycle was hardly the optimal way to have an impact on the product, but they were more focused on having an impact on the organization and saw an opportunity. The product that they tested was part of a very important family of applications being released by the company and fell into the organizational and political domain of a powerful vice president.

The two usability engineers conducted the test more or less on their own time, without a formal mandate to do so, and managed to talk a few key vice-presidents of R&D into participating as test subjects. The product represented very simple functionality aimed at managers and other nontechnical professionals.

The data generated by the test were very dramatic. Simple tasks that would have been completed in a few minutes in the manual world took the average test subject over an hour, hundreds of keystrokes, and tens of errors to complete. Many subjects were simply unable to complete the task and gave up. And because a few vice-presidents (including the one responsible for the product) experienced this difficulty of learning and use first hand, several interesting things happened.

First, the release of the product was canceled. This is a very unusual event once a product has been announced. The product was called back for redesign and eventually released at a later time.

Second, one of the two usability engineers was named manager of a new usability organization, reporting to the vice-president who owned the product that was tested. Within a very short period of time, this group grew to include 14 usability specialists and became quite powerful and influential in the overall R&D organization. It wielded a significant influence on the design of many key products developed by the company over the next several years.

The reason that this one simple usability project had such a profound impact on the development organization was that it was short, produced dramatic results, was aimed at a key product, and caught the attention of some powerful, high-level decisions makers. This, of course, was the strategic intent of the usability engineers who conducted it.

In contrast, efforts to develop corporate standards that potentially could have had a profound positive impact on a development organization have often failed to do so because they were such long-term efforts, were not aimed at any one key development effort, produced no dramatic or even measurable results, and failed to capture the attention and support of high-level decision makers. Many a standard has simply gathered dust and had no impact at all, making the contribution of usability specialists even more suspect.

Test Whenever Possible

At least in initially introducing usability engineering skills and techniques into a development organization, data are always better than expert opinion. This is a political truth, not an objective truth. We are talking about effecting change in a development organization, not about objectively optimal methods in an apolitical, completely accepting environment. In reality, an expert opinion can often be a much more cost-effective technique than formal usability testing (see Chapter 11 in this book.) However, in getting a development organization on the usability bandwagon, there is usually no substitute for formal, objective usability testing. Data are dramatic, inarguable, and convincing. Use usability testing as a strategic political tool. It works.

Success Factors: Summary

In contrast to the success factors described, the factors that seem to lead to failure include the failure to:

- Find ways to establish credibility
- Communicate effectively
- Get "buy-in"
- Cast oneself as an engineer

- Define and produce clear work products by which the professional and the field can be evaluated
- Manage unrealistic expectations
- Clearly demonstrate value
- Provide objective data

The usability engineer who wishes to succeed in the role of change agent needs to first analyze and identify inhibitors to change and then to consider if the proper motivators are present in the organization. If none are present, the creative and ambitious professional can create one, for example, by educating appropriately powerful managers, making problems visible, or clarifying value added. A usability test on a high-visibility project that clearly demonstrates dramatic usability problems can be a powerful motivator. Until such a motivating force is present, most efforts, no matter how professional, will fail.

Once the motivator is present, then the usability specialist must take care to operate strategically and apply the success factors discussed previously. It is entirely possible to fail even in a receptive environment. Being a change agent requires political skills as well as technical skills, and choosing and conducting one's projects strategically is the key to moving a development organization in the direction of usability engineering and to establishing integrated roles for usability engineering and engineers.

References

Bias, R. G. and Alford, J. A. (1989). Factoring human factoring, in IBM. *Proceedings of the IEEE International Conference on Systems, Man and Cybernetics,* 1296–1300.

Bias, R. G. and Smith-Kerker, P. L. (1986). The mainstreamed human factors psychologist in the development of the IBM RT PC. *Proceedings of the IEEE International Conference on Systems, Man and Cybernetics,* 153–158.

Bond, C. J. (1992). Internal presentation, personal communication, Portland General Electric, Portland, Oregon.

Gillan, D. J. and Bias, R. G. (1992). The interface between human factors and design. *Proceedings of the Human Factors Society Annual Meeting,* 443–447.

Gould, J. D. and Lewis, C. H. (1985). Designing for usability—key principles and what designers think. *Communications of the ACM* **28,**(3), 300–311.

Grudin, J. (1986). Designing in the dark: Logics that compete with the user. *CHI '86 Proceedings,* 281–284.

Grudin, J. (1991a). Systematic sources of suboptimal interface design in large product development organizations. *Human–Computer Interaction* **6,** 147–196.

Grudin, J. (1991b). Interactive systems: Bridging the gap between developers and users. *Computer* (April), 59–69.

Mayhew, D. J. (1992). *Principles and Guidelines in Software User Interface Design.* Prentice-Hall, Englewood Cliffs, New Jersey.

Poltrock, S. E. and Grudin, J. (1992). Participant-observer studies of interface design and development.

Chapter 14

Summary: A Place at the Table

Randolph G. Bias

IBM Corporation
Austin, Texas

Deborah J. Mayhew

Deborah J. Mayhew & Associates
West Tisbury, Massachusetts

Imagine a book, published in the mid-1990s, entitled *Cost-Justifying Software Testing*, or one called *Cost-Justifying Systems Analysis*, or maybe *Cost-Justifying Management*. Now imagine a book titled *Cost-Justifying Usability*. You needn't imagine any of these books, but for quite different reasons. The volumes on software testing, systems analysis, and management seem unnecessary. And the one on usability is in your hands. But why did we believe that this book on cost-justifying usability needed to be realized, while the others didn't? We will try to answer that question in this chapter.

While we're imagining, consider the impudence of a user interface designer telling a programmer how to structure the underlying code. It rarely happens. Then why are programmers so quick to claim to be user interface experts? The answer is simple: All developers are also users. And so they have intuitions about what is usable. As a colleague of Norman's (1990) put it, "People, generally engineers or managers, tend to feel that they are humans; therefore, they can design something for other humans just as well as the trained interface expert" (p. 156).

It has often been claimed that good user interface design is just "common sense." This is an interesting statement. Given findings like Bailey's

Cost-Justifying Usability   **319**   Copyright © 1994 by Academic Press, Inc.
All rights of reproduction in any form reserved.
ISBN 0-12-095810-4

(1993) ". . . the human factors designers produced better designs than the programmer designers," (p. 204), what can it mean? That designers and developers *don't have* common sense? Or that we just need to remind them to *turn on* their common sense when designing user interfaces? If common sense is all it takes to design a usable product, how can we explain the decade's worth of microcomputer software, and three decades' worth of mainframe software, plus any number of other consumer products (such as programmable VCRs), that languish, unused, serving as silent pointers to the fallacy of these beliefs?

Some Historical Context

In the early 1700s, infanticide was an accepted practice in France. About 200 years ago, Thomas Jefferson and his peers, for all their strengths and acknowledged wisdom, owned and—by today's standards—mistreated slaves. Less than 100 years ago, women in the United States couldn't vote in public elections. What behaviors that are pro forma in the mid-1990s will be thought barbaric, or at least odd, in the 21st century?

It may not rank with treatment of the homeless or the lack of systemic child care, but allowing or expecting computer scientists and electrical engineers to design user interfaces for "end users" is already being recognized as inappropriate.

Usability is a maturing, rather than mature, discipline. And just like adolescents who are sometimes allowed to sit at the dining room table with the adults, and sometimes relegated to a card table in the kitchen with the "other children," usability engineering's place at the product development table is not yet firmly established and universally accepted.

In the olden days of computing (say, before the mouse), there was less need to worry specifically about usability. That was because, in large measure, the computer scientists and electrical engineers who were designing products *were* representative of their user populations; their intuitions *were*, therefore, relatively reliable. Furthermore, if their intuitions were wrong, and the interfaces they designed and developed were not easy to learn or use, then the captive and adaptive users would simply undergo eight weeks of training. And so products were differentiated in the marketplace based primarily on the value of their underlying function (more in a minute about "underlying function").

But with the inexorable ooze of technology into every nook of citizenship and the concomitant explosion of discretionary, untrained computer users, the tools and methods of usability engineering have become more and more essential to the development of usable products. Computer hardware and software developers are no longer developing products for other computer professionals. Norman (1990) characterizes the situation thusly: "Usable Design: The Next Competitive Frontier."

A look back at the historical context of software development methodologies may also point to the way of the future. In the 1970s, when formal, structured development methodologies were just emerging and evolving, programmers were surprised (and often dismayed and even offended) to find that development tasks that had previously been a part of their job—systems analysis, system architecture, testing—were being taken away and assigned to "specialists" in these areas. Furthermore, structured approaches to development, including specific tasks, milestones, and deliverables laid out in a specific time frame, and standards of various types to follow, were replacing an unstructured approach that left each developer to proceed in whatever way he or she chose. Many a programmer from that era of software engineering protested over what was viewed as a loss of control, too much management, and obstacles to creativity.

However, no one in the 1990s considers it revolutionary to have structured methodologies, standards, and several different kinds of specialists on the development team. In fact, no one even questions it.

Well, the usability engineer is just one more specialist, and the usability tasks that he or she carries out are just one more twist in an already structured methodology. Yes, developers are again bewailing the loss of part of (and an interesting and challenging part of) their traditional responsibilities, and the inhibiting nature of standards on creativity. However, as history has shown, it is simply a matter of time before these tasks become routine parts of formal development methodologies, and these specialists become just one more necessary and accepted type of expert on a development team. Change is always painful, but it also always happens, and everyone soon forgets that things were any different. Ten—or maybe only five—years from now, this book will hardly be necessary.

Justifying "Any" vs. "Which"

Cost justification comes in two flavors: justification of *any* investment, and justification of a certain *level* of investment. It is, unfortunately, often the case that *any* usability effort on a project must be justified; the cost-justification exercise is required to convince management to expend any resource at all on usability. In more enlightened environments, the worth of usability engineering is realized, and it becomes a question of *how much* resource to expend and how to apply that resource (i.e., what sort of usability engineering techniques, employed when and where, will prove most cost-effective?).

Usability engineering finds itself in this middle ground. Other disciplines are routinely employed in every computer development project. No one questions the value of etching characters on the keys of keyboards, rather than requiring the user to memorize which keys map to which characters. Less trivially, concern for machine performance is an accepted part of any software development effort; purchasers and users are known to expect, even demand, a certain speed of machine response time, depending on the task at hand. And so performance groups, with their performance-maximizing tools and methods, rarely have to justify their seat at the product development table. Of course, in any project with constrained resources (and it is hard to imagine any other kind), the performance professionals may have to justify the level of their support: Mightn't they realize nearly the same performance improvements with half as many test machines and two-thirds the head count?

Furthermore, there are other disciplines, areas, or practices out there on the product development horizon that are currently excluded, but one day might be considered an accepted component of product development. It is hard to imagine any cost-justification effort securing resources for "product acceptance psychological counseling" or "introductory online battery of learning style tests, to determine which user interface to display to the user." But maybe some day.

But usability is in that middle ground, between the routinely accepted performance engineers and the not-even-considered product acceptance counselors. Ten years ago, it was unusual for usability to be on equal footing with "product function" and "schedule" in the business decision equation. Ten years from now, this book will be unnecessary, except perhaps to help new usability professionals with their "level of usability" justification efforts. Today, usability engineers may be called on to justify the particular level of involvement that they expect for themselves, and they may be called on to justify their very existence on the project. Either way, they had best be prepared to do so.

Interdependent Investments

When accountants set about the task of deciding how to invest money, they identify a variety of possible investments, then rank-order them according to the criteria that the investor has established (e.g., growth, security). Then, again, according to another criterion (desire for diversification), the accountants make the top one or multiple investments.

It is not difficult to imagine a situation wherein the appropriate secondary or tertiary investment is important to support the projected gains of the primary investment. If we decide that we want to invest in a certain piece of real estate, it might behoove us to invest somewhat in certain neighboring ventures to keep the property value high. If your primary goal is to drive a really hot-looking car and so you are quite willing to invest in an expensive paint job, you would probably have to make some minimal investment in the engine and the tires as well (lest you be able only to *sit* in a really hot-looking car.)

And so it is with usability. Early mention was made of the term "underlying function," a catch phrase in the computer industry connoting the "real" stuff a program is supposed to do, not to be confused with the necessary user interface *to* that function. Well, "underlying" may mean "fundamental" and "supporting," but it also means "hidden": underlying function is the equivalent of *no* function if the user cannot figure out how to gain access to it. Even if producing the most usable product in the world is *not* the primary goal of a product manager, a certain investment in usability will probably be necessary, lest that product manager develop some fantastic, never-discovered or -used, underlying function (leaving the user sitting in a really hot program).

We've heard a product development team likened to a sports team. And to "play" on the development team, it is important for each individual to "try out" (i.e., demonstrate his or her value to the team.) Well, just because quarterbacks, running backs, and ends are, by and large, the only players who score points, doesn't mean you would want a team of only backs and ends. The other players must perform their tasks in order for the backs and ends to be able to score. In particular, defensive positions are important both to provide the opportunity for the backs and ends to score and to prevent the opposition from scoring.

Witness VCRs that nobody programs, or even sets the clock on, high-end video cameras on which all the powerful editing capabilities go unused, food processors that are used only to chops nuts, multifunction wristwatches that people use only to glance at the current time, sophisticated answering machines that people use only to play back messages in the order they arrived, phone systems on which people never master and use powerful functions like call transfer and conference calling, and all the software packages on which users never even discover 50% of the available functionality.

Our point is surely transparent: to appropriately justify the contribution of usability engineering to a product development effort, one must recognize, quantify, and communicate the broad and deep influences of usability on the rest of the development team's investment. The functionality of a software product won't "score" if the user interface doesn't give it the opportunity to and prevent competitive products from "scoring."

Why Wasn't This Book Written 15 Years Ago?

If usability engineering is destined to be an accepted part of product development, why is it taking so long? Put another way, given that the Human Factors Society (now the Human Factors and Ergonomics Society) is a quarter of a century old, why is it taking so long for usability engineering to achieve its place alongside the other accepted disciplines?

The examples proffered in the preceding chapters are, for the most part, at the same time conservative *and* robust; usability isn't "just barely worth it." It is becoming more and more clear that, at least in the realm of human-computer interfaces, usability engineering support is a "no brainer"—no longer a question of "if," but "how much?". "My experience . . . [has] proven to me beyond a shadow of a doubt that [usability] testing can *save* time, rather than cost time because I don't have to work on things that aren't broken" (Tognazzini, 1992, p. 89).

So if cost-benefit analyses consistently show such robust returns on the usability dollar, and usability techniques are proving "beyond a shadow of a doubt" their utility, why is progress so slow? We examined some of the reasons in Chapter 13. Other probable contributors to the delay in progress are:

• *Language:* Usability engineers and other developers don't speak the same language. And worse, they sometimes use the same words to mean different things (Gillan, Breedin, and Cooke, 1992). Grudin (1993) observes that even the phrase "user interface" is a "technology-centered term" (p. 112) and points to other language usage that insidiously keeps computer development in the realm of the computer scientist and the electrical engineer.

• *Operant conditioning:* Psychologists such as E. L. Thorndike and B. F. Skinner demonstrated that behaviors that are reinforced are likely to be repeated. Managers in the mid-1990s are people who exhibited certain behaviors (perhaps *not* expending resources on usability?) in times past and who got rewarded for them (i.e., were promoted.) The way to extinguish such learned behavior is to stop reinforcing it (as the marketplace is doing today, by not purchasing unusable products.)

• *Tradition:* Beyond the differing languages and the conditioning of managers, there is simply inertia: "We've always done it this way." That human factors professionals have begun couching their trade as "usability engineering" and adopting engineering methods has contributed to the growing acceptance by the rest of the engineering community. As we employ more of the cost-justification methods presented in this volume, methods allowing concrete comparisons with other engineering efforts, more acceptance will follow.

Follow-up: Marketing Usability

In Chapters 2 and 3, Mayhew and Mantei and Karat admonished us to be conservative in estimating benefits and liberal in estimating costs, so that in the interest of credibility our initial realized cost-benefit ratios would be better than the projected ratios. This is good advice. But we must also heed their later advice: "Report your cost-benefit and business case data to the appropriate audiences." And we would extend that to include the after-the-fact actuals, vis-a-vis the projected numbers. It will be up to usability professionals to *demonstrate* that investment in usability engineering does in fact pay dividends. And once a proven track record is established, usability engineers will never be shunted to the table in the kitchen again; their place at the product development table will always be set.

References

Bailey, G. (1993). Iterative methodology and designer training in human-computer interface design. *Proceedings, INTERCHI '93*, 198–205.

Gillan, D. J., Breedin, S. D., and Cooke, N. J. (1992). Network and multidimensional representations of the declarative knowledge of human-computer interface design experts. *International Journal of Man–Machine Studies* **36**, 587–615.

Grudin, J. (1993). Interface: An evolving concept. *Communications of the ACM* **36**, 110–119.

Norman, D. A. (1990). *The Design of Everyday Things.* Doubleday-Currency, New
    York.
Tognazzini, B. (1992), *Tog on Interface.* Addison-Wesley, Reading, Massachusetts.

Index